OM BABA

A MYSTICAL ODYSSEY

TOM HECKEL

Note for Librarians: A cataloguing record for this book is available from Library and Archives Canada at www.collectionscanada.ca/amicus/index-e.html
ISBN 1-4120-7290-5

Printed in Victoria, BC, Canada. Printed on paper with minimum 30% recycled fibre. Trafford's print shop runs on "green energy" from solar, wind and other environmentally-friendly power sources.

PUBLISHING™
Offices in Canada, USA, Ireland and UK
This book was published *on-demand* in cooperation with Trafford Publishing. On-demand publishing is a unique process and service of making a book available for retail sale to the public taking advantage of on-demand manufacturing and Internet marketing. On-demand publishing includes promotions, retail sales, manufacturing, order fulfilment, accounting and collecting royalties on behalf of the author.

Book sales for North America and international:
Trafford Publishing, 6E–2333 Government St.,
Victoria, BC v8t 4p4 CANADA
phone 250 383 6864 (toll-free 1 888 232 4444)
fax 250 383 6804; email to orders@trafford.com
Book sales in Europe:
Trafford Publishing (uk) Limited, 9 Park End Street, 2nd Floor
Oxford, UK ox1 1hh UNITED KINGDOM
phone 44 (0)1865 722 113 (local rate 0845 230 9601)
facsimile 44 (0)1865 722 868; info.uk@trafford.com
Order online at:
trafford.com/05-2185

10 9 8 7 6 5 4 3

DEDICATION

For all the masters, seen and unseen, who have
guided me through life's mysterious labyrinth.

And

For my wife, Luzclara, who has shown me
how to enjoy the process.

ACKNOWLEDGEMENTS

When a dyslexic mystic sits in front of a machine, whose superior intelligence is declared by beeping out threatening messages, and pecks out a manuscript, the first draft is usually a shambles and in need of considerably help to bring it to publishing form. I would like to thank my many friends who persevered through early drafts, giving me valuable reflections and encouragement all the way. Without their positive feedback this dream would not have become a reality. I would like to especially thank Rick Kline, the wittiest person I know, for his suggestions and faith in my efforts. John Seed for reading an early draft and spurring me on with his approval. Doug Ferguson for his ruthless editing and clear insights that allowed me to prune my thoughts to a manageable form and keep the essence of my story on track. To Eileen Dacre for reading several drafts and her fine work in putting the final touches on the manuscript after I could no longer face reading it again. To Lezak Shallat for the final editing (how many more words can we cut out) and proof reading. To my friend and mystic painter Humberto Tasso who created the original artwork that adorns the cover.

A deep appreciation to Claudio Naranjo, Juan Casassus, Antonio Pacheco, and all the people at Ediciones La Llave who first published this work in Spanish. It was the positive response to that edition which inspired me to pursue this first English edition. A heartfelt thanks to my wife, Luzclara, for her devotion and patience over the years as I foraged ahead with this project, often losing sight of other responsibilities and goals.

PROLOGUE

Drenched in salty sweat and panting harder with each forced step of my exhausted legs, I struggled through the lush foliage, climbing over fallen logs and parting thick broad-leafed ferns, hoping that this tortuous hike would soon end with a meal and a nap. Yet we keep right on climbing, with the trail becoming steeper all the time, and I struggled to keep up on the almost indiscernible path hoping that, if it was a monastery our Turkish farmer was leading us to, maybe the monks would have homemade beer. With what I thought was the last of my physical strength, I pushed back the heavy undergrowth and almost crawled to where the others were sitting on a fallen tree trunk lighting a cigarette.

"Oh! Now I get it," I muttered while staring transfixed at the ruins of an ancient stone structure, now hardly visible among the giant ferns and creeping vines. Its three floors clung to the contour of the hillside, commanding a panoramic view of the valley below, while giving the impression that it was an integral part of the mountain itself. Though abandoned for centuries, I began to feel some presence still there. *Why did I feel as if I knew this place?* The feeling was so strange that I tried to push it to the back of my mind and stared transfixed at the ancient structure now crumbling back to nature

Forgetting about my physical exhaustion, which had been my sole preoccupation for the last hour, I stood up on my shaky legs and scrambled up the hillside the last fifty yards to get a better look. After a hasty examination from outside, I entered cautiously and explored around what at one time must have been a magnificent structure housing many monks. As soon as I entered, something felt strangely familiar.

I moved cautiously around the mossy rubble, overgrown with creeping vines and broad-leafed ferns, alive with the fragrance of decaying earth and the soft trickle of water from a yet unknown source. There were the remains of a large hall on top, whose roof lay in a rotting heap of massive wooden beams, which must have been the main chapel. Another open area on the floor below contained the ruins of large clay ovens and a broad stone arch, still miraculously intact, leading into what must have been the dining room. On the lower floor were many cell-like rooms of coarse stone, all with one tiny window and low ceilings, which unmistakably had been the rooms of the monks. I was drawn to enter one of these damp cells about halfway down the narrow central hallway and decided to sit on a large, flat stone that had fallen through from the floor above.

I rested my tired back against the cold stonewall, and within minutes drifted off into what I felt was a kind of daydream. I saw myself dressed in a coarse brown robe with leather thongs on my feet. I could hear the sounds of many voices singing in the distance and even footsteps on the stone floor above me.

Then I felt myself floating around the monastery, which was not in ruins but complete with large wooden doors and shutters, candles glowing in brass candelabras, and elaborate tapestries hanging from immaculate white walls. Tracking the sound of voices, I entered the main chapel and joined many dark-robed monks joyously singing hymns of devotion. Light from tens of candles flickered amid wisps of fragrant smoke hanging over the great hall as voices joined in praise of God.

Suddenly I felt pulled toward a short, robbed figure near the back of the chapel and instantly I was that person. My voice, a rough tenor, vibrated out from my chest, joining in rich harmony with the other voices about me. Devotion filled me with the ecstatic feeling of unity as my spirit rose to commune with God.

I awoke with a jolt, taking several minutes to absorb my present reality. Strangely, I felt as if I had really been singing. This did not make me feel uncomfortable, but relaxed and peaceful. When I decided to leave, I took a narrow, unexplored stairway that I instinctively knew would lead me to an open terrace near where Todd and our guide were resting.

I found them and sat down, refusing a piece of fruit. The entire experience had left me with a sense of exhilaration, like discovering something new you could do and wanting to keep doing it over and over again.

"What was that you were singing in there anyway?" Todd asked, as the sound of rushing water and chirping birds carried me into their world.

CHAPTER 1

THE HASHISH TRAIL

What am I doing here, clinging to this sun-baked canvas, on top of a cargo truck in the middle of the desert? In that moment, wracked by intense abdominal cramps and my head pounding like the inside of a conga drum, I honestly did not know. I was convinced that this insane *quest,* or whatever madness one wanted to call it, was going to reveal the truth of reincarnation the hard way. With every passing mile, assaulted by piercing sand penetrating my eyes, ears, and nose, I became convinced that I had gone too far this time. I wasn't going to make it. I had to turn back to Europe now.

"God, Todd," I shouted over the howling wind on the afternoon of the third day of my torture by dysentery, "I have wrenching stomach cramps, my head is throbbing and I have to take a shit right now!"

"Just try to hold on, Tom. This is a great ride. We may get all the way to the border."

We had met on an island off the coast of Istanbul when I stumbled upon a tribe of spirit-struck hippies, draped in sandalwood beads and colorful cloth from India, living on a secluded beach. Most everyone was either coming from or going to India, which represented some kind of spiritual Mecca for them; a goal to achieve to create some kind of new perspective on life. Todd, a Californian in his late 20s, was coming directly from the Flower Power revolution of Haight Ashbury and he encouraged me to come along on the quest. Toward the end of August, we had started out along the mysterious Hashish Trail towards the hippie Mecca of India with about 500 dollars between us and only a miniature map of the world as our guide.

Our first night out, while heating beans in a can over an open fire and soaking them up with spongy white bread, Todd told me that he had joined the army at the age of 18 to get out of the house and away from the control of his father. While serving in Korea, he was caught one night crawling out into the demilitarized zone to trade cartons of cigarettes for opium and was discharged back into American society even more confused than when he enlisted. After drifting for a year, he eventually settled in San Francisco and became one of the *flower children*, searching for an alternative to war and materialism. He fascinated me with tales of the 'acid-expanded' reality of the most famous counterculture revolution of the 1960s.

He was now on some sort of quest to know his true self and spent most of the time talking in what seemed to me like cryptic metaphors about yoga, meditation, karma, reincarnation, and the illusive carrot of enlightenment dangling before his acid-inspired consciousness. He dazzled me with semi-coherent discourses about gurus, auras, charkas, liberation, and alternative dimensions of reality. Being a rational person myself, it seemed like too much LSD had fried his brain cells at the edges. For me, life was not a dance of orchestrated circumstances but a process of hard work and good luck.

During the Six Day War, we had been stranded in the mountains of northern Turkey while the Arabs and the Israelis fought their latest 'holy war' and had become even closer after my experience in a ruined monastery, which he insisted could have been a recall from a past lifetime. But now his overly philosophical perspective on life was beginning to get on my nerves. He just sat there with his head buried in his T-shirt, complacently, *following his destiny*, which, according to him, was something he could feel. Reincarnation was not just a belief for him but a certainty he felt from some mysterious place within; a truth more of memory than something he had learned.

"Bang on the god-damn cab, Todd! I'm going to shit right now! Get them to stop!" I screamed in desperation.

"Look around man. You can't get off here," he screamed back, trying to be heard over the howling wind. "There's nothing but sand for hundreds of miles. We'd die in a matter of hours."

"That's better odds than I give myself up here." I yelled back, not daring to look around for fear that the piercing sand would penetrate the shirt I had pulled up around my face.

He claimed to have had his dysentery initiation in Korea and assured me that my body would adjust with time; but for me time was running out fast. All the pounds of bread and cheese consumed in Europe over the last three months were oozing out of my flabby body by the rear door and just the thought of food sent shivers through my intestines.

"What was I doing here?" I mumbled to myself while drifting into a space of self-reflection. I recalled the candlelight mass for our stricken hero John F. Kennedy and the cloud of despair and sense of abandonment shrouding our spirits in lethargy and despondency as our candlelight procession moved silently about campus. Some cried while others screamed but we all knew that the system we were living in would never listen to our needs for self-expression and change.

Two years later, the warlord politicians forced the senseless conflict of Vietnam upon the uninformed public and our contained wrath erupted from the depths of our frustration. We took to the parks and streets and every US college campus to shout, 'NO! We don't want this! You can't make us fight your war! Stop it'!

I had wanted to study medicine but my high school guidance counselor said I wasn't intelligent enough so, at my father's bidding, I went for economics. What I ended up learning was that through global economic structures now being created, every person in the world will one day be converted into a consumer slave, enticed by subliminal advertising and slick devices of credit, to participate in a social-political destruction of our planet's non-renewable resources.

Every day it became more obvious that we were being coerced to participate in a conspiracy among governments of wealthy countries, who needed to maintain their standard of living by selling their surplus to poorer countries, even if that ruined the lives of those people, and financial institutions, which were afraid to admit that the system was bankrupt and hoped they could solve the problems by devising ways to finance debt with credit. They drove the huge multinational companies, who pillaged the Earth to line the pockets of a few, while fueling the self-destructive machine of capitalism. The world was bankrupt. But through credit and deficit spending they would drive the starving horse on until all the green pastures had been turned to dust.

Worst, when I decided not to apply to graduate school and continue in this game of mass deception, the army tried to grab me as my student deferment was about to expire. It was then that I told the recruiter, with as much scorn as possible, "I'm a conscientious objector and do not intend to take part in your little war games."

It was as if I had told him I was a communist and had just planted a bomb in the White House. His constant congenial smile turned to a scowl, his eyes reddened, and his fleshy neck began to swell around his permanent press shirt. *Bang!* His sweaty hands slammed forcibly on the oversized desk as he leaned forward and turned his battle-glazed eyes upon me saying, "If you want to live in this country, son, you're going to have to fight to defend her!"

Click! Something in my subconscious awoke that day. I had to leave. I could not really accept it as *my* country and be honest with myself about what I truly believed was right for the world.

"Bang on the cab, Todd, I'm going to vomit!" I screamed, having been jolted back to my present predicament by wrenching abdominal cramps like a hand of a giant squeezing my intestines. I had come to the point where I was going to vomit and shit and have an epileptic fit all at the same time. Then, like one of those miracles you forget to give thanks for enough, the truck ground to a halt in the middle of the desert.

I crawled down, stumbled to the side of the sticky asphalt road and down a sandy embankment, where I did everything but have an epileptic seizure, I think.

During a pause in the gripping cramps and squirts of liquid intestines from both ends, I fell onto the scorching sand and thought that maybe this was the end. Through the heat vapors rising from the dunes, I could see the distorted image of a man in a flowing gown and white turban mounted on a camel.

Was he calling me to the other world?

I tried to scream out but my throat was parched shut. There was no reality I could identify with. I panicked and began clutching frantically the small pouch hanging around my neck containing my passport and money as my last desperate link to a personal identity. Breathing heavily and hallucinating, I staggered up the bank and stumbled back towards the truck to find Todd, or my backpack, or something to assure me that I was who I thought I was.

I called a few feeble cries for my friend but heard nothing in reply. The only people I could see were standing around an old van stopped behind our truck, so I stumbled half-blindly in that direction, resisting the urge to vomit again. Three men were leaning over the motor of a pink Bedford van working on the engine, but I headed for the sound of voices at the rear.

"Is this your partner?" I heard a woman say from within as I reached the rear door.

"Looks like you're paying your dues to the ancient ones, brother" she said. "Get your head in out of the sun!"

I hardly understood her mystical references to my suffering as I fell into the shelter of the metal box to keep my brain from cooking. I wanted to ask for water but my swollen tongue was stuck to the roof of my mouth. I pointed desperately to my scorched mouth and made weak gestures of drinking.

"Here you can drink this," came a male voice with a strong British accent from further in the van. I drank eagerly of the tepid water and began to relax for the first time.

"Look at it as a purification instead of a punishment, brother." said the male voice.

"Try to swallow one of these," the woman suggested, handing me a white pill that seemed to glow against my dusty palm. I got it down on the first try and thanked her with a wave of my hand.

I could hear Todd's voice somewhere off in the distance explaining that we were on our way to India and all that we (he) hoped to find there. I opened my eyes sometime later, just as a tall, thin man with thinning blond hair and pointed beard on his angular face appeared at the back of the van saying, "We got it fixed, thanks to the driver of that truck. Let's get going before we all cook in this sun.

"Where did you guys come from?" he added, startled at seeing two dust-impregnated hippies with T-shirts on their heads, one of whom must have appeared half-dead. He glanced over the endless miles of sand, as if considering the possibility that we had just strolled by.

The woman explained that we were on our way to India, and a quick decision was taken — without consulting me of course — that we could ride with them for a day or so if we wanted. This sent Todd racing towards the truck to retrieve our packs while they rearranged the van around my felled body. Todd returned, tied our packs on the roof and we were off.

Our new hosts, Vic and Linda, had left London over a month ago and were traveling with their friend Mick, "in search of the deeper mysteries of life," whatever these might be. They planned to spend a year in Iran and Afghanistan, retracing the steps of someone called Gurdjieff and looking for a master to 'open the way' — to what, they never said.

"It's really happening out here. I can feel it everywhere," said Vic over his shoulder, while piloting the vintage van down the highway. "Even the Beatles have found an Indian guru and John Lennon says that meditation is higher than acid. Linda, show them that Time magazine."

She produced a tattered magazine and handed it back to us pointing to a certain article. There was a picture of an Indian man with long white hair and beard sitting cross-legged. The caption read, "Beatles Take a Guru." It mentioned that they had met Maharishi Mahesh Yogi in England and were planning to travel to India to study at his ashram.

Too exhausted to focus my eyes any longer, I fell back into a dysentery-induced trance, thinking that for some reason I was being pulled along the same path as these people who had inspired an entire generation. The painkiller Linda had given me began to take effect, and I fell into a deep sleep, finally allowing my first secret hopes of finding something that would help me know the greater meaning of life.

The merry Bedford glided along the highway for the next three days as Linda played a few Judy Collins and Donovan tunes on an old guitar and we all sang along. She had given me a couple of pills to stop the dysentery so I was able to enjoy myself for the first time in many days. An atmosphere of excitement and anticipation grew among us as Vic spun a continuous yarn of mystery and intrigue, telling stories of Gurdjieff crossing this desert using stilts to avoid the sand storms and about the mystical sects of the Dervishes and Sufis. They talked about the new Beatles' album "Sergeant Pepper's Lonely Hearts Club Band" — news for Todd and me — and of Mick Jagger going to India to find his master.

Our prophets and masters were the musicians and poets, who opened us to new vision and taught us to question it all because 'you can't buy love'. We shared this common influence that conditioned our beliefs and attitudes about life. While growing up in the shadow of the atomic bomb, we had turned to these lyrical voices to guide us in our search for an alternative expression of life's meaning. We resented that our fathers before us had created weapons of mass destruction and poisoned our natural environment to the extent that soon might threaten all life on the planet. In the name of progress, their dream of peace through wealth, they were denying our right to a future.

Three days later, after leaving our new friends to pursue their quest in Iran, we hitched a ride on a truck crawling along at an agonizingly slow pace in the blistering sun for almost six hours before reaching the border with Afghanistan. The border guards, noticing 'irregularities' in our visas, told us that we would have to return to Teheran "to consult the proper authorities". This sent Todd into a fury, banging his fist on the table and screaming profanities, which I hoped they couldn't understand. His outburst only caused them to hold more securely to their machine guns — a universal symbol of who's got the power — and motioned for us to get out of there.

"They can't do this to me. There is nothing wrong with the stamps in our passports. They're just taking it out on us because the United States supported Israel in the war," he said, once we were outside.

"I'm not going to take their shit, man. I know that kind of smart-ass. Just wants to mess with our heads."

"Now Todd, remember the yogis. No anger," I said, half-trying to calm him down and half-getting back at him for all the high and mighty philosophy he'd been indoctrinating me with for the last two weeks.

"That's right man, no anger," he said, calming his voice. "Don't put your passport away," he insisted in a hushed tone as we were putting on our packs outside the building. "We're going to walk right out of here and turn left and head for Afghanistan. No one is going to even notice. I'll show'em a trick or two."

"Control yourself, Svengali, you're not going to...." He cut me off mid-sentence by turning and starting to walk.

"Follow me and look the guard at the gate straight in the eyes. Don't look down as if anything is wrong, got it?" he commanded in a super cool manner. "Make sure he sees your passport and expect the best."

Todd walked out of the building, smiling politely to the poker-faced guards, and turned toward the Afghanistan border. Breaking a sweat inside my tight Levis, I followed, afraid that he was going to get us killed. The guard at the gate stood up as we approached but Todd just waved his passport, as if telling him, 'It's all right. Just sit down', and we kept right on walking into the desert sun.

By this time, I was shaking in my sandals and dysentery was knocking hard on my back door but I didn't dare stop. My mind was running every worst-case scenario and I wanted to scream at Todd to stop, but I didn't. It was as if I was in a spell and resisted all temptation to break it. Fear had definitely altered my consciousness.

By the time we reached the Afghanistan checkpoint, the spell was fading and the fear of getting caught without an exit stamp in our passports began to invade my mind. I repeated to myself, *we're not going to get caught,* and followed Todd. We walked past two laid-back border guards resting in the shade of a scrubby palm-tree, who motioned us into the building where we presented our passports to a glazed-eyed official in a disheveled uniform, installed behind a wooden desk too big for the room. After noting the required names and numbers in his large ledger, he inspected our passports, turning them every which way to read the stamps. My heart sunk and I struggled to stay cool while trying not to wet my pants.

Making little sense of anything he saw, he looked up at us and smiled through his dropping mustache, then banged his rubber stamp onto our passports while saying in heavily accented English, "Welcome to Afghanistan." I almost cried with relief.

"How did you do that, Todd?" I asked once outside and walking away.

"Do what?"

"You know, just walk out of the border checkpoint. I mean how did you know we wouldn't get caught?"

"In The Haight, we used to play games with the cops while on LSD. Walk by without them seeing us. We could even make them turn the other way. We did it by sending loving thoughts to them, which they had no defense against. I re-tripped on the same energy the moment you said 'no anger' and just knew we could do it.

"It's all in the mind!" he said, turning to walk on. "You think, therefore you are."

We pulled into the Afghani town of Herat in the late afternoon and treated ourselves to our first night sleeping on the roof of a hotel since leaving Istanbul three weeks earlier. After a meal of soup and bread, battling the flies for every mouthful, we went into the cool evening air to walk around town.

"We're doing great," commented Todd, as I opened a fresh pack of smokes and offered him one. "With luck, we'll reach Kabul within a week and that'll put us halfway," he said, studying our miniature map of the world and measuring the distance with his thumbnail.

"Where did you get the cigarettes? Lift them?" he asked, referring to my chronic shoplifting habit.

"Not good for your karma," he admonished. "Better be careful out here. These people carry guns and knives and I have a feeling they intend to use them on thieves like you. If you don't want to spend the rest of this life dead, you'd better stop it."

"That's crazy." I laughed at his weird humor while helping myself to a smoke.

"Depends on what one considers life to be," he intoned. Since my experience in the monastery and Todd's dazzling display of mind power at the border, I was more disposed to listen to him, but he sure pushed my buttons at times.

We could hear music drifting across the soundscape of the city, as we penetrated into a maze of dusty streets lined with shops closing for the night. At an intersection of lanes, a young boy came up to us gesturing as if he was playing music. When we nodded yes, he took my hand and led us through a narrow alleyway to a lively teahouse.

We stood at entrance looking in at men in great turbans sitting on carpeted platforms smoking from tall water pipes. A man waved for us to come in and, after a greeting which entailed hugging, kissing, and shaking hands, he led us up a rickety ladder to where the music was coming from.

We found ourselves under a canopied rooftop with a cool evening breeze blowing through the patchwork walls of woven palm branches and faded cloth. About twenty men lounged on Persian rugs listening to music, drinking tea and smoking tobacco from brass water pipes. Our presence caused some concern until one of the musicians made a sign, indicating that everything was all right. Tea arrived from downstairs as we settled across from the trio of musicians playing a lively tune — on a lute-like instrument, deep-based clay drum, and a reed flute.

We sat in a circle and, as we were finishing our tea, a young boy entered from behind a curtain carrying an elaborate brass pot spewing a thick cloud of sweet-smelling smoke. He made a few passes around the room, filling it with an exotic aroma, then disappeared behind the curtain. The music accelerated to frenzy, the flute squealing like a banshee, and then stopped. The boy reappeared, this time carrying an ornate brass and copper water pipe, which he placed ceremoniously on the carpet in the middle of the room. Behind, two boys respectfully guided an old man, whose bent stature, long white beard and furrowed face hinted at a century of life. Squatting on his haunches in the center of the room, his body assumed a firm natural appearance, and his sunken eyes screened the room in silent greeting to all. I could not say that he really saw us but slight facial movements signaled his awareness of our presence. I sat motionless, absorbed by his profound presence.

He was joined in the center by several older men who prepared the water pipe, putting glowing charcoal in the ornate bowl and placing a large black ball on the coals before closing the lid and turning its long curved stem toward the ancient one.

First, he motioned with his hands, saluting in the direction of the setting sun. Then, bowing his head slightly while chanting something to himself in a barely audible voice, he took hold of the stem and placed it to his lips. Inhaling and exhaling rapidly, he filled the room with swirling clouds of smoke before taking a final deep breath and resting back on his heels.

The pipe was then passed around the room, first to the elders, before working its way around to the rest. When it came to me, I followed what I observed to be the standard procedure of two or three long inhalations, retaining the last one. The smoke was hot and I could sense the potent hashish quality in it. I leaned against the wall, closed my eyes and exhaled out all the tension and fear I had accumulated over the last month. My attention wandered to the sounds of the room and the town beyond as I drifted to a space of no concern.

Suddenly it did not matter that I was half way around the world from the safety and security of my father's checkbook or my mother's love. It didn't matter that I had studied hard to earn a degree only to head off on a mysterious quest that I only half-believed in. My awareness had shifted. It might have been madness, but I felt that I was doing the right thing. The rest of life would have to wait. A new sensation was growing within me and I wanted to nourish it by going with the flow.

Sometime later, the music resumed with a slow, eerie tone that carried me further to a place where rationality held no power over thought. I drifted on the wings of my imagination to a magical valley where people lived only to experience today, not planning always for tomorrow. There, human relationships were based upon what it felt like in the heart to be with someone, not how much money they had or which god they believed in.

The music stopped and Todd nudged me to wakefulness. The old man was squatting in front of me, making slight gestures with his wrinkled hands and mumbling something that sent a young man running downstairs. For a moment I looked into his dark eyes, shining like pools of wisdom, and sensed a deep compassion and trust. I relaxed my customary defensive guard and opened in an attitude of non-resistance.

The messenger quickly returned with a shy girl whose bare feet, just visible beneath her black dress, edged closer to the old man as she covered her face with a faded blue garment. The room came to silence as the 'Wise One' leaned forward and rasped out in strained pronouncement something he wanted me to hear.

The young girl leaned closer to me and said in slow deliberate English, "You have the mark of Allah on your face. He is calling you."

CHAPTER 2
KABUL

We left Herat the next morning on an overloaded cargo truck in the direction of Kabul. My violent attacks of dysentery resumed and on the evening of the fifth day I plunged into oral hell behind a restaurant, where, among piles of human excrement and the stench of urine, I vomited time and again as billions of flies swarmed at my face, entangled in my soiled beard, and tried to fight their way into my mouth and eyes. I was growing desperate and wanted to go home.

On the morning of the next day, after a spectacular sunrise ascent from the desert plains to the foothills of the Hindu Kush Mountains, our truck, spewing smoke and with one of the rear tires audibly unraveling, limped into Kabul. Todd, acting as guide and carrying my pack, led us through the maze of narrow, dusty streets to the Noor Hotel, where I curled up in a corner of the garden and slept.

During the first week my health improved considerably on a diet of bread, tea and fruit. By the fourth day, I had hitched my belt in a notch and was feeling just about normal, under the circumstances. Todd, down to his last 20 dollars, tried hard to sell his camera, but the economy of Afghanistan, with the average wage less than 100 dollars a year, produced no buyers for expensive consumer goods. It seemed that almost everyone in the hotel was waiting for money to be sent from friends or relatives at home so they could continue on to India or return to Europe.

I rarely ventured out of the hotel, mostly resting and talking to anyone who wandered by. That included John Brown, an American who had flipped-out in India and been deposited here by some Dutchmen over a month ago. Barefoot, with tattered orange cloth wrapped about his emaciated body, he walked about the garden staring off into space and carrying on a monologue with himself.

"I am The Christ. I have come to show you the way. The time will come when the sky will be aflame with the wrath of God! Turn not to others to save you in the hour of awakening but trust all to The Christ in your heart. I am The Way! I have come to save you!" came the booming voice of John as he wandered by us on his afternoon rounds of the garden.

"What do you mean by 'the sky will be aflame with the wrath of God', John?" I called out.

My question got through to the few brain cells still on duty and he drifted our way.

"Do you believe I am The Christ, man?"

"Of course. You know that," I replied, beginning our conversation in the usual way. He would not talk to you if you didn't first accept him as the Christ. He could not relate to the material world, but sometimes he said things that seemed to come from some other dimension of knowing and I often probed him to see if there were still a few synapses firing.

"The world is full of hate and you came here to love. You blew it! And now God will send his fiery messenger to give *life* another chance.

"When the heavens rain down fire upon you sinners and the sun no longer rises and sets as it does today, all will fall to their knees and pray to be saved!

"I am The Christ!" he boomed out. "I have come to save the world!"

"Hey John, when is all this going to happen?" I asked to see if he could go into more detail.

"The signs will appear in the heavens. But will you be able to perceive them?" he replied in a hushed tone.

"I am The Christ. Believe in me and I will show you the way," he added, staring blankly into space and walking off.

"The guy gives me the spooks," commented Todd. "There were lots of them in the Haight. At some point they get stuck in some private illusion that becomes their reality and they can't get back to identification with the material world. Why do they always think they are the Christ? Was he that far out?"

"I don't know, Todd," I replied, seriously, "But it freaks me to think that there is a point after which you lose it and they come and take you away. I wonder how close to that point I was? Or am right now?"

"Don't think about that," Todd reassured me. "You're tough. You're not going to end up like that. He was probably off the edge before coming out here."

At the end of the first week, I started to venture out and explore Kabul. The city offered little to do except wander through the market and watch the aggressive looking tribes people from the surrounding hills hankering down in front of dusty stalls buying and selling a range of goods that all looked like they belonged in an antique store. Kabul presented striking contrasts; a city caught in

12

traditional ways unchanged for centuries yet beset by the encroaching values of the Western societies beginning to influence its people and its customs. Russian cars and trucks jostled for the right of way alongside donkey carts and camels. Hooded shapes of women crept along in the shadows while their Westernized contemporaries strolled about in high heels and makeup. The men were proud and moved about with the attitude of warriors, quick to anger and often visibly armed with knives and guns. They defended a tradition that was eroding away with each new shipment of Goodwill clothing and old beauty magazines.

One morning an US embassy jeep came to pick up John. Many of us escorted him to the hotel door and waved good-bye. Someone had given him a wrinkled white shirt, which he wore over his tattered orange cloth. He paused before getting in the jeep to say, "Don't wait until it is too late. Accept The Christ in your hearts, now! God has a plan!"

I learned from John that the *quest* could have a sad ending. Yet slowly, without my taking notice, I was being convinced that I must go on, as if this entire adventure had been my idea and I must complete my mission.

After a month of living in this hippie haven, Todd wrote a friend in the States for some money to be wired ahead to the American Express office in New Delhi and we decided to move on with the money I still had. We boarded an overloaded bus, with only a hint of tread on any of the tires, and headed out through the Khyber Pass to Pakistan. The road, an engineering miracle of its time, was endless miles of hairpin switchbacks descending into a dry canyon whose sheer rock faces formed a natural frontier between two worlds. Here the British made their famous stand only to lose in the end to the natural drive of humanity to choose its own destiny. Crossing this frontier in search of my own freedom felt symbolic.

Nothing could have prepared us for the sea of people, moving like a stampede of ants along the main road, which swept over us as we entered the Pakistani town of Peshawar. *If the flies outnumber the people, we're in trouble,* I thought as the bus came to a sudden halt and its passengers scrambled madly out the door to keep from being trapped inside by the wave of people flowing in and about the bus. Todd, a foot taller than most, managed to catch our packs as they were thrown from the top of the bus and we fought our way up a nearby street towards a sign indicating: Hotel.

The next morning we fought our way through the multitudes to the bus station and bought a ticket on the next bus going east. The station was packed with men in baggy cotton clothing and coiled turbans, all squatting in small groups around water pipes smoking their morning tobacco. There were many fierce looking tribesmen from the northern hills armed with old single-shot, breech-loading rifles, and criss-crossed leather ammunition belts. We had been told in Kabul that they belonged to the private armies of the hashish barons who occupied the high, fertile valleys to the north and were a law unto themselves. Locked in bloody feuds with rival clans that lasted for generations, they walked about with a cautious eye, ready for battle.

After hours spent watching the endless stream of people moving about in some unapparent coordination, we boarded a bus adorned with every conceivable religious bric-a-brac, cramming ourselves into wooden seats at the rear, hoping the bus was finally ready to leave. There we sat for another half an hour, stifled by the heat and humidity. As merchants continued to load more cargo on top, an old man walked to the rear of the bus and squatted down on the dirty floor followed by a boy carrying a water pipe. Then every available inch of space in the narrow isle was filled with people who had not bought seats but paid less to fill in the empty space however they could.

Just as it looked as if we were about to leave, shots rang out from behind the bus and everyone, as if on cue, fell to the floor, placing their arms over their heads or fingers in their ears. Todd, who had been looking out the window at that moment, screamed and pushed me down just as more cannon-like bursts sent glass flying into the bus. There among the pile of frightened bodies and screaming children, I turned to see the old man, whose face showed no signs of fear, reaching for the stem of his water pipe and taking a slow draw on the rich black tobacco.

In that moment, his eyes told me something about life that I could not have learned reading a thousand books: It is all happening in the moment.

CHAPTER 3

INDIA

Ten days later, after surviving a train robbery and a bus accident, we crossed the border from Pakistan into India and caught a train to New Delhi where we camped out on the roof of a cheap hotel in the old section of town. Having made the crossing without feeling sick, I was feeling a new sense of excitement, but Todd was low on energy and complained of not feeling good. I had paid all of the expenses since Kabul so now neither of us had enough money to do anything but wait for the requested funds. By the second week, Todd was ill and spent most of the time lying in the shade on the roof while I wandered through the city. Having gotten over the initial shock of multitudes of people, striking poverty, and teams of deformed beggars, I was fascinated by the sheer survival instinct of the people. On the streets by day, vendors offering everything from fancy silks to curbside dentistry filled every inch of space, leaving only a narrow strip for people to pass. The crowds never stopped coming and the country of over five hundred million people made one thing clear from the start — everything happens in a crowd.

The people were clean, wearing loose-fitting white cotton clothing wrapped about them in some ingenious fashion. The women were strikingly beautiful in their colorful saris draped about their tallish, thin bodies and many wore a dot of colored paint on their foreheads, adding to their intrigue.

Rather than feel frightened by the magnitude of it all, I wanted to know more about the customs and spent hours sitting on a corner just observing people in their routines and movements. At an intersection near our hotel, a lean man sat on a burlap sack waiting for someone to come hobbling along with their torn rubber sandal in their hand. He promptly stitched it back together with salvaged fibers and pieces of leather and sent them happily striding on their way. Just behind him sat a barber who shaved peoples' faces and entire heads with a straight razor, trimmed mustaches and gave head massages. Even further back from the throng of people was another man who sat before a sample of teeth and array of pliers waiting for someone with an inflamed tooth to come by. I never saw him pull any teeth but a few people did stop by and he peered into their mouth with convincing authority.

I began to feel more comfortable each day, as if it were all familiar in some distant way. I was caught up in a fascination of contrasts and contradictions to my ordinary reality — not that the last month had been ordinary. I felt from watching the multitudes of different types of people all coexisting along side of each other that India could accept anyone regardless of what their trip was, but one had to accept India the way she was.

Todd's money arrived within the month, but before we could resume our journey, blood tests confirmed our suspicions that he had hepatitis and could not go on. I learned that the quest could come to an end for physical health reasons as well.

I saw him off on an embassy-sponsored ticket to the US — after surrendering his passport, of course. He gave me his Austrian backpack and over two hundred dollars in Indian currency saying, "Don't give up, Tom. You're tough."

Early the next morning I made my way to the train station and, after waiting an hour to buy a third class ticket, walked along the packed station platform looking for a square foot of space to put down my pack. People everywhere were squatting on piles of baggage as others moved about selling food from large baskets balanced deftly upon their heads. I had decided to go to Agra, the home of the Taj Mahal, and work my way toward Katmandu.

What size train could take this load? I wondered as an ancient steam locomotive rumbled up the track like a hissing monster, triggering mob-like activity on the platform. Everyone hoisted their bundles and began to run after the train before it even came to a stop. Stunned by the charge, I retreated to one side watching baggage being stuffed through windows and doors. Suddenly I realized that the train would be full in another few minutes and I would never get on.

I ran frantically along the platform looking for my car and bumped into a porter wearing a red turban. He looked at my ticket, grabbed my pack and indicated that I should follow him. Every car we passed appeared to be over-full and people continued to stuff the smaller bundles and children through the windows. Just as I was about to give up, he jumped down from the platform, crawled between cars to the other side of the train and moved rapidly towards the rear. Realizing that he had my pack, I jumped down, slipped between the cars and raced after him. He stopped a ways down the train and I caught up to him. Pointing to an open window, he indicated for me to climb up and crawl through the window and he would pass me my pack. Having come this far and not wanting to spend another night in Delhi, I scrambled up the side of the car and slid head first through the tiny window into a pile of bodies. After much commotion of people pushing and shoving to defend their territory, my feet found the floor. I turned to the window to see the porter, who had climbed up after me, holding my pack out of my reach and saying *baksheesh*, the common word for a bribe.

I realized in a moment he had me. A clever trick or maybe one doesn't have to be clever to trick a fool. I protested, screaming in English, 'Police' and 'American Embassy', two words I detested, but he just hung on holding the pack slightly out of my reach and repeating *baksheesh*. The train lurched a bit, as if it might be ready to leave, so I hastily pulled a ten rupee note from the bag tucked inside my shirt and began waving it at him, insisting he hand me my pack first. Our eyes met as we cautiously tested each other's confidence. Finally, he allowed me to hook my arm around one of the pack straps while he reached in the window with his free hand and took the note. Then, shaking my hand as if it had all been just good-natured fun, he jumped to the ground and did a little bow before running off. Feeling ripped off, I squirmed around to face the inside of the car and looked out over a hoard of people, packed shoulder to shoulder, squatting on top of their baggage while others continued to crowd the doors and windows trying to get in. Not the smoothest of entrances into the mysterious India, but I had made it.

The train departed an hour later and the ensuing eight-hour trip was a human close encounter that made me feel like an animal riding along to an unknown destiny. I was in a car used only by the poorest people and my presence was as much a shock for them as their sub-human traveling conditions were for me. Sitting there atop my pack, jammed in shoulder to shoulder, with the smell of human vapors hanging in the stale air, I couldn't believe this was normal and acceptable for them. Only by hanging out the open window for most of the journey could I control my claustrophobic panic. My values, my sense of order and cleanliness and, above all, my compulsive need for privacy were under great stress. It was becoming uncomfortably obvious that none of these intellectual identities were going to survive the rigorous contrasts of India.

I spent that night absorbed in the presence of the Taj Mahal floating in the light of the full moon, as if suspended by a mysterious force. The distorted reflection shimmering in the surrounding pools of water enhanced the sensation that the Taj Mahal was in some way alive. Once inside, this feeling was reinforced by the perfection of the acoustics that sent the slightest whisper reverberating throughout the main hall, giving the impression that the thousands of religious figures intricately carved on the marble walls were laughing and singing. I sat inside for a long time sensing some special feeling of lightness and hearing harmonic overtones of the slightest whisper of any visitor. I had the strange sensation that its structure was acting as a mystic energy collector. It made me feel at peace.

I arose early the next morning and walked towards the outskirts of town having decided, after my experience in the train, to try hitchhiking.

After walking for hours among the ox carts, rickshaws, bicycles, and the endless flow of people and animals, it was clear that no truck would stop, fearing to be mobbed by the multitudes crowding the way. I walked all day in the shade of the tree-lined road, taking long rests alongside the flowing irrigation ditches. I ate fruit and drank tea in the tiny teashops that were spaced along the way. Whenever I stopped, a crowd would quickly gather, everyone eager to try out their rudimentary English. I used these times to practice my Hindi from my little phrase book. When the crowd reached a certain intensity, which never took more that a half an hour, I would put my pack on my back and hurry off as if I had some place to get to.

Towards the end of the day I was rescued from a pack of children shouting, "What is your name?" by a wealthy Indian merchant in a private car who took me to his house for the night saying that it was his duty and honor to serve a foreigner traveling in his country. Over dinner we talked of the differences between our countries and of the special needs of his country, which claimed its roots before our recorded history.

When he asked me why I had come to India, I surprised myself by talking about yoga and a search for inner peace. He presented me with a copy of the *Bhagavad Gita*, the teachings of Lord Krishna, printed in Sanskrit, Hindi and English, saying:

"The wisdom of this book will prepare you for the path of yoga, if this is to be your destiny. That is a great mission and one to be taken seriously," he continued, straightening his spine to demonstrate the importance of what he was saying.

"There are many who say they are yogis but the real ones are tucked away somewhere in the jungles and mountains where few people ever go. If one is serious, one must prepare one's physical body through the right diet and exercises, to promote calmness of mind and freedom from negative thoughts, until the time is right for your master to appear. You should consider a vegetarian diet for one year and pay careful attention to the effects of this diet on the quality of your thoughts."

"How does one notice the quality of his thoughts?" I asked,

"Arise early, take a bath to awaken your body and mind, and go sit in a quiet place and ask yourself, "What am I thinking?" Then watch the flow of your thoughts, as you would view a movie, with an interested detachment. That is all. If you're successful in this practice, someone will come along to guide you further.

"We have a saying here in India. 'When the student is ready the master will appear'. Start your quest by looking within yourself, that is where it will lead you in the end."

CHAPTER 4

VARANASI

In the morning, my benefactor took me to a friend and asked him to get me a ride on a truck. We parted the best of friends with him saying, "From here you should go to Varanarse, the greatest of our holy cities. There you will learn more about our religion and customs and meet some of our holy men."

I rode all day on top of a truck thinking about our conversation and taking in the scenery from a first class seat. The road, which was only slightly wider than one lane and crowded with people, bicycles, ox carts and animals, passed through flat farmland ribboned with broad irrigation ditches. Ingenious human and animal-powered pumps, scoops and water wheels were in full activity, as were teams of oxen pulling wooden plows. Scores of men, women and children worked with crude hand implements.

Occasionally, we would pass within a few feet of overhanging limbs and riders on top would flatten out on the canvas tarp and cling to the ropes as branches lightly brushed us. Exciting moments occurred when another overloaded truck, rocking from side to side, approached from the opposite direction. Both vehicles charged at each other, lights flashing and horns blasting, yielding half of the road at the last possible second. It was obviously a matter of pride who turned first and they seemed to take great pleasure in the game.

We stopped often for food and rest and I began to understand the scene of hitchhiking in India. One had to meet a driver and ask for a ride when the vehicle was stopped at one of the many out-door truck stops, which were mainly hemp-strung cots placed about in the shade of giant, spreading trees. Once they were rolling down the road, the trucks stopped for no one, fearing, I'm sure, to be mobbed by the multitude that lined every inch of road from New Delhi to Calcutta.

The owner-drivers were mostly bearded Sikhs from the northern province of Punjab, who, unlike their Hindu countrymen, ate meat, drank alcohol, and were quick tempered. They were industrious, working hard to better their material lives and taking great pride in their religion and what they called 'their country' — Punjab. They were the backbone of industry and commerce and, without them the country would come to a stop or at least be thrown into greater confusion than existed already.

When I climbed down from the truck before dawn the next morning, the driver shook my hand and said, "Varanarse."

I thanked him and began to wander the dark streets. Secluded in every sheltered nook, bodies huddled together beneath tattered cloths moving now and again against the chilled morning air. The early risers were already up and about, gleaning every scrap of paper, cardboard or anything else recyclable with the cows, dogs, chickens, and goats foraging alongside them, devouring anything edible, including the cardboard.

Soon the street sweepers appeared — women with rustic brooms fashioned out of palm branches and men with large goatskins filled with water. They cleaned the gutters in preparation for the day's activities. By the time the shadows of dawn had dispersed, the streets had been swept and washed clean and vendors of all kinds were arriving to stake out their spots.

Before long, I arrived at a lively street followed by a pack of beggars who had attached themselves to me after I had given one of them too large a coin. I had become used to them, and, after my talk last night about the origins of Hindu customs, I tried to understand the necessity of beggars and the caste system in a new light. My host believed that the caste system was necessary to give everyone their proper place within a society of five hundred million people. It presented an opportunity for everyone to serve each other. I stopped looking at beggars as poor and helpless and related to them more as a necessary part of Indian society; a living opportunity for people to worship God by helping those in greater need than themselves. But I still gave them my loose change out of guilt and pity.

"Ha eera hay!" came a piercing scream from one side of the road. I turned to see an old, barefoot woman with a faded white tunic draped about her extremely thin body, rushing towards me and waving her arms at the parade of beggars. At the sight of this charging crone, they retreated immediately, crouching back in fearful respect.

"Man man coming! Me, Mataji tea taking!" she called out in a high-pitched, commanding voice, while taking me by the arm and leading me off through the crowd toward a row of tea stalls on the opposite side of the street.

"Man man tea taking? Sitting down," she went on in her polished pigeon English, pointing to a place on a wooden bench that corresponded to one of the curbside tea stands. I sat down, somewhat stunned by her appearance and assured manner. I observed her intensely as she directed the owner of the teashop, perched upon his platform above the street, to serve us tea, hers receiving an extra portion of sugar. She made a slight motion of her head and eyes and the person sitting next to me moved to another spot on the bench so she could sit down.

She was old, but how old was impossible to discern. Her face and hands were wrinkled with age. Long, flaking fingernails sprouted from her thin leathery fingers. Her gray, brittle hair hung down to her waist in matted ropelets, which she tossed about with quick movements of her head, creating a dynamic presence like a mop in full motion. Her shallow eyes were cloudy and slightly glazed, yet steady in their gaze. Her remaining teeth were stained red from chewing betel nut paste. Her movements, however, were quick and agile like those of a much younger woman and she carried herself with a practiced air of dignity and authority, holding her spine and head erect and moving like she was on stage. I was fascinated.

We went through the usual formalities of establishing where I was from and where I was going while a continuous stream of people flowed by in both directions.

"Big man coming! Me, Mataji LSD taking. Big brain having," she said, holding her hands out around her to indicate the size of her head, revealing her haggard teeth through a blissful smile. "You man, LSD taking?"

I half-voiced yes, referring to my two acid experiences in university, but I really couldn't understand what she was talking about. Not the LSD I knew. Where would she get such a thing way out here?

"Big man coming...." she went on repeating the same basic phrases. Then, bursting into laughter and slapping my knee, she leapt to her feet and spread her arms saying, "Many peoples LSD taking! Big brain having!" She screamed with laughter and spun around in a circle as if she was re-tripping right there in the street.

"All peoples LSD taking!" she shouted to the beggars across the street, then laughed herself into a deep coughing fit that calmed her down. By this time, I was beginning to think we were thinking of the same thing.

"LSD big medicine. Me Mataji big big brain having. You, man, LSD having?" she said, pointing to my pack while wiping tears from her eyes with the corner of her faded tunic.

"No. No having," I replied, holding my hands in the air and putting a sad expression on my face.

We talked in this way for sometime about how long I had been in India and where I was going, with her frequently returning to the subject of LSD and eyeing my backpack suspiciously. By now, beggars sat lining either side of the street and streams of people were passing by tossing them small coins and handfuls of rice. I forgot about Mataji and became enthralled by the scene before me. Even for India, it was mind-blowing. Where were all the people coming from?

We sat for over an hour with Mataji coming and going from time to time until she returned saying, "Me Mataji, houseboat going. Man man coming."

From the accompanying motions of her arms I deduced that she wanted me to go along with her. I didn't know why, but I liked her and thought I would just follow along and see what she was up to. I paid for the tea, and we went out into the stream of people and worked our way along in the direction of the greatest flow.

I had to struggle to keep up with her as she bobbed and weaved through the dense crowd until we finally came to a wide stone stairway, which descended towards a river.

What unfolded before my eyes caused me to shudder with amazement. Thousands of people lined every inch of the river bank, each performing some ritualistic bathing procedure — chanting, ringing bells, saying prayers with hands joined high in the air and all shouting, "Gangaji!" They were lined up five and ten deep in places, waiting to get near the water, with more coming all the time.

Deformed lepers and maimed beggars were packed in along both sides of the brick walkway, screaming and banging on tin pots and thrusting their rotted limbs forward to get the attention of the returning pilgrims tossing small coins and grains of rice to them.

I panicked, not even knowing if I was allowed to be there, and froze in place, reluctant to enter the thickening crowd. The deafening noise and the intense vibration of thousands of people packed in one upon the other was making me feel short of breath and dizzy. I tried to retreat to less chaotic grounds.

"Man coming! Houseboat going!" came the now familiar cry of Mataji, as she took hold of my arm, pulled me through the suffocating crowd and along the sandy riverbank to where the throngs had thinned out. Releasing my arm and motioning for me to follow, she zipped up a narrow board and on to an old wooden houseboat tied to the shore with a long rope. Once on board, she pushed open the doors and entered, shouting *"Bum bum boli Gungaji qi ja!"*

The discordant cry of many voices answered her, *"bum boli,* Mataji"

She moved quickly across the low-ceilinged space and disappeared through a small door at the far end and I stood facing another bizarre scene. A candle illumined one corner where an altar had been set with many colorful pictures of Indian saints, prayer beads, and burning sticks of incense. Fragrant plumes of incense blended with the shafts of golden sunlight filtering through the louvered shutters, creating a purple haze. As my eyes adjusted to this new reality, I could make out the shapes of three western hippies, all with long hair falling below their shoulders and naked except for a strip of loincloth. They were sitting cross-legged on separate mats, heads bowed slightly in my direction and saying *"Namaste"*

I felt uncomfortably warm in my Levis and T-shirt but managed a confident *"Namaste"* back and set my pack on the floor.

"Leave your sandals outside. You're in India man," came a voice with a heavy German accent, speaking perfect hip English.

Now overheating with embarrassment, I deposited my sandals outside and reentered, taking a seat on one of the benches that ran along both sides of the cabin.

"Hi, which direction you coming from?" asked a blond Englishman sitting on the floor nearest me.

"Kabul vía Delhi. But I left over a month ago," I added to keep the conversation going.

"That's real slow now. What'cha been doing, walk'n'?" teased the German man. "Did ya meet an Englishman named Gerald in Kabul? He was headed that way about a month ago."

"Yea, we met in the Noor and had some great conversations about India. You all must be the ones he talked about living in Varanarse."

I learned that Jasper, a tall, thin Englishman with his body toasted almost black from the Indian sun, had been here more than two years, looking for a master to initiate him into the secrets of yoga. Hans, the German, had been on the road for the last five years and had come to India a year ago. A musician, he played like an angel on a silver flute and had a humorous perspective on life.

"That guru stuff isn't for me," he said. "Most of them don't know any more than you or I and they want to run your life for you."

"No sex! Can you imagine that? I think they're all hung up on sex. Maybe it's too powerful for them."

Mataji reappeared followed by a thin, dark-haired man dressed in a bright yellow cloth wrapped about his waist, his long black hair tied back with a silk scarf of many colors.

"Hi, I'm John," he said looking in my direction. "Mataji says you just got in from Delhi."

"He met Gerald in Kabul and was with Edward in Istanbul about three months ago," commented Jasper before I could even answer.

We talked about the friends we had in common and John told me his story. Having left Australia to escape booze, he had been living in Varanarse for almost five years, first studying music then yoga with local teachers but still looking for *his* master. He must have been in his early thirties but his deeply lined face and hazy green eyes revealed that they had been a hard thirty years.

"John," interrupted Mataji, "Man man LSD having?"

"She wants to know if you have any acid, man?" asked John, shaking his head and smiling at her.

"I already told her I didn't. How does she know about acid, anyway?" I replied, now more curious than ever.

"Some doctor from the United States came through here the other day and turned the whole town on to acid. He went up and down that street out there passing hits to beggars as he strolled by. She took we don't know how many and hasn't stopped talking about it since," answered Jasper.

"Who was this guy? Anyone know him?" I asked, sorry to have missed that one. "There was some American in Kabul turning lots of people on to acid when I was there. Was he traveling in a nice looking Land Rover?"

"Never saw any Land Rover, but he had lots of LSD. He turned thousands of people on. You should've seen the beggars giving their old rags away to one another and dancing in the gutters. Mataji says some people who hadn't walked in years stood up and walked that day. I can't say, but we had a blast," said Jasper.

"By late afternoon, there was such a scene of mob ecstasy that the bigwigs from the famous temples came to see what was going on. That evening, as everyone was coming down, some important Swami, who must've had a great trip, called a big feast and served food to all the street people. After the feast, he talked about the return of the sacred *soma* and the awakening of humanity to the light. We chanted for hours and cries of "LSD qi ja!" could be heard among the happy voices."

"Did any of you get a trip?" I asked, unable to imagine hundreds of people tripping in the streets.

"We all did, of course. Mataji came to get us. There were hundreds of crippled people dancing, laughing, and hugging each other. The pilgrims returning from their sacred bath at the river passed by unnoticed with no one interested in their coins and grains of rice that day. I don't think anyone is going to forget that day for a long time," mused John, as if remembering his own personal trip.

"Man man hashish smoking? Me Mataji going. Hashish bringing. One rupee man man giving Mataji," she said rapidly.

"What does she want now, John?" I asked, feeling she wanted to buy or sell hashish.

"Just give her a rupee if you have one and she will bring some hash in the evening," he replied. "It is part of the scene here."

"You mean she deals hash in the streets?"

"No way, man!" replied Jasper, finding my question humorous. "She'll get the hash free from someone in exchange for a favor. She just wants the rupee to move about today. Someone gives her one each day under the same pretext. You're new, so it's your turn. Some of the time she does come up with the hash, but don't ever give her more than one rupee. She would just get into some kind of trouble if she has too much money," he concluded, tipping his thumb and fist toward his mouth to indicate her fondness for alcohol as well as hashish.

I happily gave her one rupee. She had more than earned it entertaining me for the morning. John and the others invited me to stay on the houseboat with them — one rupee a night to be paid to the boatman before sunset — and I settled in, feeling immediately comfortable with the whole scene.

CHAPTER 5

MATAJI'S TRIBE

During the next week, I spent my time exploring Varanarse and becoming more street-wise with the help of Mataji. Morning sessions with her at the teashop introduced me to the world of people who live and die in the gutters of the holy city.

John told me that Mataji had been a powerful sorceress at the burning *ghat* where they cremate the dead, and was still considered a powerful witch by her contemporaries in the street. She had moved over to the bathing *ghat* where I had met her after a dispute with a Kali Baba who had forced her off her seat at the sacred fire.

She now took care of an extensive network of tribes and extended families; all of them street people who stole and begged throughout the city by day, ate in communal kitchens in the evenings, and slept huddled together like piles of rags in sheltered spots at night.

All morning long people would come to the teashop to ask her for favors, the nature of which I was never quite sure. She would act as a judge in disputes, designating who had the right to sit and beg where and solving problems in the communal kitchens. A street healer, she dispensed medicines tied in the ends of her tunic to her homeless patients: a charcoal-opium mixture for stomach problems and white powder for headaches.

I learned of the alternative economics of the street people — a system of favors. If you owed a favor to someone and they asked you for something, you were obligated, within the best of your abilities, to fulfill it. If someone asked you for a favor and you could respond with help, you were saving for a rainy day. No money needed.

The Ganges River, considered the most sacred river in India, was the focus of Varanarse and pilgrims from all over the country come to bathe in her holy waters. They consider it a blessing and purification of the soul to be submerged in her muddy waters. Many people came to Varanarse to die, believing they would achieve instant liberation from the cycles of life and death.

At the place where our houseboat was tied up, the river was almost a half a mile wide, chocolate brown in color, and anything but inviting to bathe in. John had assured me that a team of scientists had tested the river water last year and found it, against all rational deduction, to be uncontaminated. Still, I wasn't sure if the people were praying for the purification of their soul or to survive the bath. With great trepidation, I began to splash some muddy water on myself each morning.

The traditional Hindu rite of death was through cremation and the lower banks of the sacred Ganges was an extensive burning grounds where dead bodies, dressed in their best for the occasion, laid upon flaming piles of wood at the water's edge. The smell of burning flesh trailed on rising plumes of black smoke while the crying and wailing of mourners blended with the screeching of ugly vultures waiting to descend upon any charred flesh left unprotected.

"They don't cut down their forest for paper to wipe their ass but to burn the empty shells of their dead," observed Jasper.

"Someone get up on top and push that body out of here!" called John from the inner room one evening, as a putrid odor overpowered the sweet smell of our temple incense.

I scrambled up top with Hans to see what he was talking about. Looking down at the back of the boat I saw the charred remains of a human body, swollen white and bobbing up and down in the strong back-eddy.

Hans brought a long pole, obviously around for this purpose, and, with some difficulty, we pushed it back into the main current sending it down river.

I sat staring at it floating in the soft orange glow of sunset. Death was pressing in all around, forcing me to accept its fatal presence. That morning, while walking in one of the crowded alleyways of the old bazaar, a man fell over dead in front of me. I even tripped on his foot as he was falling. I stood watching as two people rolled him face up onto the cloth he was wearing and left him right there, staring up at me. People passing by began to toss coins and flowers onto his stiffening body and someone stuck some burning sticks of incense in his hand.

When I passed by on my way back an hour later, he was still there gathering coins and flowers. I asked a shop-owner why they didn't take him away. "When there is enough money to buy the firewood to burn him as accords his caste, someone will carry him off. Maybe in the morning," he replied nonchalantly.

"*Bum Bum boli, Gungaji!*" came the salute of Mataji as she scooted up the ramp. "Me Mataji hashish bringing. All man mans coming! Shivaji coming.

Bum! bum! boli!" she burst into her hacking laugh and disappeared below, leaving me to my reflection.

In the week I had been living on the houseboat, dramatic changes in the way I viewed life had taken place. Not only death but also the stark reality of the everyday struggle of living in the streets prompted me to question, not just basic necessities, but even, why we are here on this planet. In *Bhagavad Gita* I read:

> For all things born in truth must die,
> and out of death, in truth, comes life.
> Face to face with what must be,
> cease thou from sorrow. (2:27)[1]

I went below, took my customary seat on the rounded bench, and looked out the window at the pink cloud-ribbons wrapping the western sky. Mataji had finished her preparations of the *chillum*, a funnel shaped clay pipe, and was chanting and rocking gently on her haunches. Her voice gained intensity as Jasper and John joined in the chant to Lord Shiva, patron saint of hashish. The rest of us hummed along in unison. Hans lit several sticks of incense from the candle burning on the altar and began filling the room with a thick, sweet fragrance as Jasper, now chanting full on, struck a match and held it up to the sky. Mataji concluded with a tremendous shout *"Bum! Bum! Boli! Shivaji!!!"* and began a series of deep inhalations until the hashish-tobacco mixture glowed red. She passed it to Jasper who did the same and we were off on another sunset in Varanarse.

I took a long slow pull on the sacred pipe, enjoying its relaxing effect. After each of us had *talked to Shivaji* as Mataji called it, we resumed chanting until we each drifted off into our own inner place.

I became absorbed in the cloud-shapes of crimson dragons dancing on the horizon, and let my body relax back against the wall. A light breeze moved across the river and carried my attention off to the distant rumbling of a train crossing a bridge over the river. At first it was definitely the sound of the train, but the more I concentrated it seemed to change into the call of animals and then the high-pitched ringing of bells. I felt a little jerk in my body and milliseconds later I was seeing the train below me on the bridge. I jerked again and opened my eyes. Jasper and Mataji were laughing through a haze of incense smoke. I closed my eyes, and the sound of the train called me again.

'BE CAREFUL, TOM! You do not want to lose control. Don't give in to the sound of the train,' came an insistent inner voice.

I suddenly knew that this insistent voice had guided me most of my life and I had never even noticed it before.

---

[1] All quotes from *The Bhagavad Gita*: Penguin Classics edition, Juan Mascaro, Penguin Books, Middlesex, England. 1962.

I opened my eyes again. Nothing had changed but an absurd thought invaded my mind, *Keep it together! For what? Nothing can be crazier than what you see before you; an old crone laughing and hacking while a bunch of spirit-struck hippies look on and ponder the deeper meaning of it all.*

I closed my eyes thinking to myself, *If I've come this far there's nothing to hold on to. I don't care what you say, voice...*

With a little jerk like I was falling asleep, I was floating above the train again. A silver glow called my attention to another reality. Hesitating, my mind looked back in the direction of the houseboat and instantly I was viewing Jasper, Mataji, and the others as if I was floating above them.

I looked to my corner and there I was! But how could I be there, sitting with my knees drawn up to my chest looking out the window? For a split second I questioned the reality of it all and, jerk, I was back in my body looking at the last dancing dragon decomposing into my imagination.

The experience lasted maybe half a minute but it occupied my mind for many days. I was sure of the vision of Mataji and the others and of seeing myself looking out the window, but what really happened became more vague, slowly slipping into an uncertain reality as if I had dreamed it. I began to remember other childhood experiences of looking down at my body and the sensation of floating, but they, too, had quickly become like dreams. Had the mind tricked me all along into accepting them as unreal, unimportant, or imaginary?

My routine changed as I began to rise early and bathe in the river, keeping a watch out for dead bodies. Somehow, I was closer to the river, as if I attributed my out-of-body experience to its influence rather than the hashish I had smoked. I tried to watch my thoughts in the morning but they were usually fixed on a warm cup of tea and some fruit for breakfast, so most times I gave up quickly in favor of joining Mataji at the tea shop. I tried, under all conditions, to repeat the experience, but nothing out-of-the-ordinary ever happened, so after a few days I gave up. There was something special about my attitude that night of not caring, aided by a momentary shift in awareness and a feeling of detachment, which made me reject my habitual voice of caution and self-control. The voice had always been there but now I was listening to another part of myself. But what or who, I couldn't imagine.

"Hi, Tom!" cried Jasper from the shore as I sat writing in my journal on the roof of the houseboat. "Eddy is in. Come on, I want you to meet this guy"

"No one really knows where he's from. Armenia, I think, " he informed me as we walked along the sandy shore toward another houseboat. "He says he's *free*. Nothing more to do in life. Some people think he's enlightened. Maybe he is, who knows?"

"What's his name?" I asked as we reached the narrow plank leading up to the boat.

"Everyone calls him 'eight-fingered Eddy.' You will see why in a minute."

We called out from shore and the soft reply of voices lured us up the ramp and into the houseboat. There were eight people, many of them young women, sitting about the main room reading, writing, and talking to one another. In the center of the room, sitting Zen fashion with his legs tucked underneath him, was a thin, clean-shaven man in his early forties, with a well-trimmed moustache and short, neatly combed hair. Not your standard guru type.

"Hi, man, what's happening?" he greeted us in perfect hippie slang, while motioning to come in and join them.

"Hi, Eddy. How was your trip to Nepal?" asked Jasper, taking a seat on the floor. "I see the women still follow you wherever you go. When are you going to give us your secret?" he joked.

"About the same as last year, you know. For me nothing is different," he replied in a distant voice, ignoring the reference to the five beautiful women draped about the place. "I spent most of the time sitting in The Blue Tibetan restaurant talking to people about being free. Once you reach this level, you just want others to get there also." After a short silence, during which time I noticed that he had only three fingers on one hand, he added, "Lot more people this year. The energy is building now. Soon we all will be free."

I listened intensely as he talked to Jasper about his trip to Katmandu and his plans to return to Goa for the winter. I became restless, uneasy with his references to himself as having reached some level of consciousness different or better than the rest of us, until I impulsively blurted out a question.

"What do you mean by 'being free', Eddy?"

"I'm no longer attached to anything. I have no history, no past, just the present moment," he replied before going into a long explanation about being the son of Armenian immigrants and growing up in the United States. He said that after many years of being involved in the scene of drugs and sex and trying to get free that way, he woke up one morning and the whole world was different. He didn't care anymore what others thought of him and didn't have anything to prove to himself or to others.

"I was free to see life as an impersonal adventure; not centered around me but something that was happening to me. No big deal you know, man."

"But do you believe in God or meditate or anything like that?" I asked, amazed by his totally nonchalant approach to enlightenment.

"No man, I dance. That's all," he replied with a smile, then closed his eyes and began to move his hands and arms from his sitting position as if he were dancing to inner music. Soon he was making gibberish sounds to himself as the movements of his arms accelerated into rapid circular motions, and he was off. The young women, noticing that Eddy had taken off into his *dance*, slowly joined him in their own way until the room was filled with people waving their arms and moving their bodies to the imaginary music.

I sat motionless, wanting to laugh but not daring to. On an impulse, motivated more by wanting to impress some of the women who were by now becoming quite sensual in their gyrations, I stood up, closed my eyes and began to move my arms and hips to the phantom beat.

Nothing unusual happened, except that I let go of my usual self-consciousness and allowed myself to look and feel ridiculous.

Eddy hung around for a week with his road show of beautiful women and imaginary dances and we all thoroughly enjoyed it. I would join them every evening, usually beginning by questioning Eddy on his self-proclaimed state of *freedom* but gravitating more towards talking and dancing with the women as the evening wore on

One night while walking back to the boat, I wandered into a side alley and stopped to buy a cigarette and a package of incense. As I turned to walk away, I noticed that I had slipped two packages of incense in my hand. It was a habitual trick, but I instinctively started to move faster towards the main street, when a commanding voice went off inside my mind:

"Put it back, Tom. Now is the opportunity to change your life forever!"

I turned around quickly to see if the shopkeeper was after me. No, he was busy with something else. In a second slowed by creeping expectation, I decided, *yeah, why not.* I handed the stolen package back to the shopkeeper and started walking toward the main street.

Three steps and Bang! I became transfixed in front of a small stone shrine and a powerful energy began sucking the balls of my feet into the earth. An idol in the shrine with many arms began to slowly move, as if dancing. My awareness began to fold in on me like a balloon loosing air and the entire world about me rapidly lost form and solid consistency. A force swelled up in the lower part of by body and moved upward in blissful undulations, neutralizing any resistance by its peaceful, transcendent presence, until a mass of dark negativity mushroomed out of the crown of my head.

Then, a spiraling energy field of golden light pierced the top of my head and flowed like nectar throughout my body, penetrating every cell of my being. I existed as an energy field sustained in consciousness, between time and eternity; the physical body was an idea rooted within my rational mind; a reference point of thought within an infinite sea of identity.

Light, brilliant white light flooded in upon my awareness and bathed me in its all-pervading presence until I was no more separated from the oneness that was light. Beyond thoughts and words, personality and individuality, I no longer existed as separate from the All.

Some undeterminable time later, my eyes popped opened and, superimposed on a fluid reality, the stone idol danced before me and luminous human energy fields of different colors and intensities floated by. Everything was connected by a luminescent vapor, within which all forms seemed to be suspended and out of which all was in a constant state of creation.

I wanted to call out in joy, "WE ARE ALL ONE!" — the only realization that had any importance at that time — but all rational functioning was beyond me. There had been no time to resist or even to surrender unto it; it had called me, not to ask me to pay attention, but to tell me, "*My time had come*"

I closed my eyes and became an eternally expansive mass of light and sound.

PART TWO

THE AWAKENING

IN A MOMENT THE SOUL REMEMBERS
AND LIFE IS TRANSFORMED FOREVER

CHAPTER 6

KATMANDU

Blissed-out, crazy, I wandered the streets most of the night seeing people as luminescent bubbles of energy, connected by radiant fibers of light. Overwhelmed by the presence of love and unity all about me, I shouted, "I love you! We are all one! We are all love!" I tossed away all my pocket money, hugging the deformed, glowing creatures that swarmed around to pick it up.

"I love you! We are all one. We are God! WE ARE GOD!!

A voice, like that of a mother to a newborn child, caught my awareness at the height of the euphoric bliss and directed me to a hill overlooking the river. There I sat absorbed in the feeling of perfect peace and harmony, holding only to the single thought, "we are all one". As the first graying of the starry sky began to announce the coming of a new day, Divine Mother whispered to me again: *"You are awakened to a greater sensitivity of your human potential. Pick up your things and go to the train station. You will be leaving now."*

"Hey, you there! That monkey is eating your food!"
"Yea."
"Why don't you stop him?"
"We are all one."
"What did you say?"
"We are all God! So what if the monkey eats the food. It's all the same!"
"Hey man, you on some drugs? You tripping?"
"No, we are all one! Get it?"
"Why are you here?"
"I don't know why I'm here. Do you?"
"Sure man. I do... I think I do... what are you talking about?"

34

"I mean the Earth. This planet. Do you know why you are on this planet?"

The man walked back to a woman waiting nearby and they stood talking and looking in my direction from time to time. This had been my first verbal exchange and it seemed to pull me closer to material reality. The monkey had taken the food out of my hand while I stared off into space. I had been aware of its movements but made no attempt to stop him. I was at a train station in India. I had my pack and sleeping bag, I had brought food, and I could talk. But everything was different.

"Hey, you all right? Need some help? My name is Richard and this is Leslie. We're from California. Where are you from?"

I looked up from my mind tripping to see the same bearded man and a young woman standing nearby eyeing me with such a genuine expression of concern on their faces that I burst into uncontrolled laughter. Why this response, I don't know. I felt fine, better than ever in my life.

"Look man," he continued in an emphatic tone, placing his hands on his hips and staring at me intensely, "I've been watching you for over an hour now ever since you handed that vendor ten rupees for a half a rupee of food and walked away without caring about your change".

"If it is all one, does God Exist?" he demanded, changing his tactic.

"How do I...?" Caught in mid-sentence, I started to feel the same energy, with less intensity than last night, filling my head with light and, closing my eyes..."*If you believe It does then It does, if you do not believe, then It does not.*"

I heard myself answer without really listening to what I was saying. It was a strange yet pleasant feeling, leaving me almost floating as I sat there on the ground.

"If I believe and It does exist, what form will It have or how should I look for Him?"

"*God is like water that takes the form of whatever vessel you pour It into. Your beliefs are your vessel. They determine the form that God will take for you.*

"*Seek with your heart not with your mind. Let love be your guide.*"

I opened my eyes to a suspended silence and allowed myself to return to the here and now.

"What did you say your name was?"

"Tom." I replied.

"We're on our way to Katmandu. What about you?"

"Me too."

Richard and Leslie must have been sent by God — my belief — because in those initial hours of reentry into solid form I needed someone to pull me back; to remind me of practical necessities like food, money, and the physical body, and to help me regain my identification with life in general. Richard, in his early thirties, with long curly brown hair and short cropped beard, was a psychologist who had become disillusioned with his work and was taking a year off to explore life in a different way. Leslie, his girl friend of two years, was slender with dark blond hair and striking big brown eyes. She was into computers and worked for the government of California. They had to fly to New Delhi from Israel, not being able to go overland because of Israeli stamps in their passports. They were not your stereotypical trail wanderers, being well dressed in new jeans and hardly worn tennis shoes, carrying straight-looking matching backpacks.

They were both interested in what had happened to me — Richard from intellectual curiosity and Leslie from a motherly concern. They took care of me like a child — exactly how I was feeling at that time — guiding me to the border of Nepal and haggling with the driver of a truck to take us over the mountains to Katmandu. By noon the following day, we were lumbering down the asphalt strip atop an ancient truck heading towards the snow-capped peaks of the Himalayas.

We rode all afternoon, climbing over mountain passes and descending into fertile valleys, whose terraced hillsides, alive with vibrant fall colors, looked like a gigantic patchwork quilt draped over the landscape. The few people we passed on the road were short, stocky and dressed in the drab grays and browns typical of the peasants I had encountered in Turkey and Afghanistan. Both men and women carried baskets of potatoes and corn on their backs while traversing the steep slopes barefoot. The mountains that surrounded the isolated valleys were stark, depleted of native trees, and intensively eroded.

We stopped for the night at a teashop. After a meal of soup and peasant bread, we arranged our bedding on the floor of a loft for the night. I went for a short walk in the crisp night air to take in the Himalayan sky. Forty-eight hours had passed since my mysterious awakening. My euphoric bliss had not yet become a dream. At any moment people could become glowing orbs and the etheric mist could engulf me in its embrace of unity; and I would be gone from the confines of time and space.

"May I join you, Tom?" came the voice of Richard from behind me.

"Sure. We're traveling together, partner." I felt close to him, as if he was taking over for Todd in my life and was going to help me along on this razor's edge of madness.

"Remember the other day on the train platform when I asked you that question about God? How did you come up with that answer?"

"Look, I don't know but don't take it too seriously."

"Can I ask you another question?"

"Sure Richard, go ahead."

"Was the entire universe created with a 'big bang'?"

Again, a sensation of energy rising in my body drew my attention to my head, which began to fill with light, and I shut my eyes as if getting ready to concentrate.

"There is no event in the universe that happens only once!
"Your universe is the result of a slow and deliberate expansion and contraction of potential — creation upon creation. All that exists has been created within and sustained by the movement of this potential.

"Does an acorn become a mighty oak with a bang or does it grow slowly, expanding into its majestic form?"

A suspended silence passed, during which time my awareness remained absorbed in light and peace until Richard asked, "Well then what started the first movement? I mean, why did it all come into being?"

"Contained within perfection was the potential to manifest itself; the first and ultimate creative act. That this perfection may come to be, an impulse, like your inspired thought, moved out in search of full expression."

"Then why does life appear to be destroying itself?"

"Creation and destruction are really the two polarities of change. Change is the manifestation of movement and movement is the essence of your universe!"

After a pre-dawn start in the chilly air, we rode most of the morning winding our way through high mountain passes where a few ancient, wind-stunted rhododendrons and oaks survived on the rocky hillsides. During the final descent into the expansive central valley, I reflected on the person who started out from Istanbul four months ago. I could hardly remember what I was like, what I had thought about, or why I had decided to come all this way.

Katmandu was as if frozen in the Middle Ages. The narrow dirt streets were lined with two-story, pagoda-style wooden houses with ornately carved balconies and tiny wooden-shuttered windows without glass. There were almost no motor vehicles but the streets were crowded with pack animals and people carrying tremendous loads balanced on the ends of bamboo poles. Open trenches, serving as drainage for the houses, carried murky water off toward the river. Pigs and flies swarmed around piles of human excrement in every vacant lot or patch of grass. Everything warned of lurking disease.

After we had settled into the low-ceilinged room on the second floor of a group house, my usual outgoing, adventurous spirit gave way to a more contemplative, introspective mood. The first week went by in a blur, sitting on my crude straw mattress and staring out the glass-less window, but seeing nothing. I was not sad or lonely, but in peace. I did not need to fill my daily life with the customary quest for adventure or stimulation.

I started to rise early and wander down by the river to sit and watch the endless stream of thoughts flow through my mind. The cold air had a stimulating effect on me and often an hour or more drifted by without awareness of the outside world.

People flocked to the river in the misty morning to take their ritual bath and say prayers at the nearby temples. I liked the atmosphere, yet the chilled mountain air was anything but inviting for a dip in the river. I preferred to sit wrapped in my sleeping bag and observe both the inner and outer worlds go by.

When Richard and Leslie went out to eat, I usually went along too. Our favorite restaurant was The Blue Tibetan, which was the ultimate in good, cheap food, and lively conversation of an international flavor, all engulfed in a cloud of hashish smoke brought to you by the waiter. The long finger of Uncle Sam had not yet reached this Himalayan outpost and the King preferred to sell hashish through his government stores rather than give the profits to the illicit dealers who broker in crime. Here one could spend hours talking and listening to music being played over an ancient hi-fi system. This was the end of the trail and many lingered for months in the haze of indecision as to where to go next. We were all a long way from anywhere and it took a great motivating force, most often the expiration of one's six-month visa, to move us toward the next adventure.

I usually left after dinner, preferring the company of my own inner space to the lively, hash-induced entertainment of the smoke-filled restaurant. One night at the end of my first week, I met Leo, a Dutchman who spoke many languages and wore a child-like grin plastered on his hairy face. He was a broad-shouldered man in his mid-twenties with a black, bushy beard and a drooping moustache. His dark eyes, barely visible in the hazy light of the restaurant, were shrouded in bushy eyebrows and his hair hung down in ringlets to his shoulders. He had been traveling for over two years and said he had seen me in Kabul in the Noor Hotel when Todd and I were held up there. He expressed some concern over what he called 'my spaced-out head' and was interested in what had happened to me.

That night, Leo and I were walking back to the house and stopped to buy some candy. I noticed that the shopkeeper had given me extra change, and, in a split moment of decision to be honest — much like the night at the incense shop — I returned the extra amount. When I started to leave the shop, another burst of energy and light filled my body causing me to stand motionless in the doorway.

"Hey Tom! What is the matter? You feeling sick?" Leo called out, shaking my arm slightly as if to bring me back into the world. "Come on, let's get back to the house. You don't look too good."

I mumbled something, more to indicate that I had heard him than to communicate. He took me by the arm and guided me back to the house.

"What happened back there at the shop?" asked Leo, after we were settled in our room. "You sure were far out there. As if you were there but not really there. Just like that John Brown guy in Kabul."

"What are you talking about?" interrupted Richard, who had returned home before us from the restaurant. "Did it happen again, Tom?"

"Happen again? He just had some space-out at a little shop on the way home," replied Leo perplexed.

"Was it the same as in Varanarse?" inquired Richard, taking a seat on the straw-filled mattress beside me.

"Not exactly the same. I didn't go so far out. Leo was with me and his talking kept me fixed on what was happening around me," I replied, still not feeling grounded in my body.

"What's all this about, Tom?" inquired Leo, beginning to sense that there was more to my little space-out than he had considered. "Have you been sick? Is that why you're so quiet these days?"

I told to Leo what had happened that night in Varanarse and how this second act of honesty had prompted a similar experience of lesser intensity.

"And what about the way you can answer metaphysical questions. That says that something more is happening than just being stoned out," injected Richard in his usual enthusiastic manner.

"That question and answer stuff is Richard's thing. I don't see it as important."

"You don't!" interrupted Richard, forcefully. "But I do. Anyone can be stoned out of their head and claim they have seen God. Insane asylums are full of them. But how that experience has altered their consciousness in some concrete, positive way, to me, is of great interest.

"Come on let's try another question? You want to?"

"OK go ahead if you want, but this is your idea. I'm not saying I can answer anything."

After a short silence, Richard asked, "If it all began with an impulse of perfection to manifest itself and not a chaotic big bang, how was life created out of this movement? How did the ONE divide to become the many?"

The sensation of losing touch with every day reality, my head filling with light, and a deep sense of relaxation began immediately. Rather than concentrate on the meaning of the question, I just waited for the answer to come. Slowly, patterns and impressions within etheric space molded themselves into rational thought and words, deliberately arranged in a precise way by some organizing intelligence, gently flowed forth.

"Out of the state of no motion, the seed state of perfection, where total harmony creates the illusion of stillness, came the impulse, like a tonal inspiration splashing into a void of potential, to create itself. Thus began the first movement of the creative process.

"When the first stage of expansion unto maximum potential was achieved, there came a pause before the enfolding, or returning of the flow began. This movement continued on past its original point of inception until an equal and opposite point of contraction was reached, thus completing the first cycle of creation. A unifying field of consciousness was created out of this first, and all subsequent movement

of creative potential, and thus was born the substance that sustains all life and out of which all life is manifest.

"This original movement — the breath of God — once set in motion by the primary impulse, continued in ever spiraling cycles of expansion and contraction, sustaining the field of consciousness and giving rise to the potential for life. This universal creative process repeated itself seven times until consciousness had permeated infinity and the structure upon which life was to be created was completed.

"The ONE did not divide into the many like a simple one cell amoeba divides and becomes two. The ONE expanded and, through this timeless process, fueled by the intention to manifest perfection, the seven primary movements arose and all creative appearance subsequently came to be. That is why God exists in all things yet all things exist not in God"

"Is there a pattern or form to the universe or is it based upon random chaos as it appears to our rational minds?" probed Richard.

"To know the form of the universe, one must perceive it through primary patterns of movement and the effects of their interrelatedness, one to the other. Energy arises out of the interactions of two fields of movements or patterns of change.

"If constant flow toward equilibrium can be considered a form, then the universe could be said to have a form."

Total silence pervaded the room as I felt awareness returning to my body. I breathed deeply and slowly opened my eyes to see flickering patterns of candlelight dancing upon the ceiling, welcoming me back to the world of time and form. Leslie had joined the session and now stared in amazement.

"Why are you staring at me like that, Leslie? Did you understand what was said?"

"No, not a word," she answered in a hesitant way, "but, while you were talking, I had a strange feeling that I was in the presence of an ancient being or maybe an ancient source of wisdom. For me, what was said was not important. The feeling of where it came from is still vibrating within me."

CHAPTER 7

Two Crazies

An exceptional energy began to build as we moved into the first week of December. Word had moved out along the trail that a special gathering was to take place in Katmandu for Christmas and the town began to fill up with travelers from all over the world. Evenings in the Blue Tibetan took on a unique flavor as the people with spiritual-metaphysical interests gathered in one corner to pursue long conversations about meditation, gurus, and the never-ending discussion of enlightenment. I mostly listened to others discuss their search for someone to show them the way to "break out of the illusion and be free" and stories of all the well-known gurus and their magical powers. The Beatles led us again, this time into full scale 'guru mania', and everyone had both ears open for the mention of some new miracle worker of enlightenment.

As the weeks passed, my life in the Himalayan kingdom molded itself into some form of routine, helping me to slowly return to greater awareness of material reality. I spent my mornings by the river in contemplation and practicing the game of 'thought watching'. Richard, Leo, and I had reached an agreement that we would meet in a quiet tea shop two or three mornings a week, when I was in the mood, to explore the mysterious phenomenon of 'questions and answers'. My afternoons were spent either wandering about town watching the movements of people and contemplating the elaborate temples or taking long walks in the surrounding countryside.

One day, after one of these wanderings watching the peasants tend their water buffaloes and harvest corn and potatoes, I stopped at The Monkey Temple. It was situated on a low hill half an hour outside of the city. This had become a favorite place for me and I would often make the short walk in the evenings to watch the sunset and be with myself without the noise and excitement of the city. I enjoyed watching the monkeys frolicking in the giant spreading limbs of the ancient trees that surrounded the temple grounds and the many people who came there each day to place flowers or burn incense at one of the many shrines.

Like most of the temples of Nepal, the complex contained an array of both Buddhists and Hindu shrines with the most ancient constructed out of wood and stone in a pagoda style typical of Tibet or China. Their exterior walls were adorned with a multitude of ornately hand-carved figures of gods and goddesses in various acts of meditation or worship. Since my 'bliss-out' in Varanarse, I had begun placing flowers and fruit at the local shrines two or three times a day. More and more, prayers were within my thoughts and a rising spirit of devotion filled me with glimpses of a greater unity with which I was ONE.

I fed the remainder of the fruit I was carrying to the monkeys and tripped out on the freedom and fun they seemed to be having leaping about in the higher limbs playing tag. I took my customary seat on a grassy hill facing the distant mountain range covered in eternal snow. The sun was low on the majestic peaks and cast long shadows of the peasants working in the terraced fields below me. The crescent moon, three days into its journey towards fullness, hung surreal-istically in the graying sky, reminding me of another month gone by. I sat for sometime reflecting on what was happening to me while waiting for another Himalayan sunset to appear on nature's screen.

On a physical level, except for recurring bouts of dysentery, I felt great. I had been following a vegetarian diet now for about two months and felt more peaceful and had plenty of energy.

Other than my newly discovered relationship with God and the blissful unfolding of the spiritual reality of life, nothing really mattered anymore. I now spent most of my time alone or remained silent, staring into nothingness, when around people. I was not unhappy or lonely, but something inside of me was signaling a dramatic shift in my being.

This whole thing of the questions and answers began to intrigue me. How could I answer a question about God? I had never considered myself particu-larly sharp when it came to abstract theories or metaphysical concepts. Yet in the last month, I felt brilliant, able to understand the most intricate spiritual discussions, even to the point of picking out the fallacy in reasoning and logic at times.

It was like the experience I was having on the physical level of being tall. Of medium height, five foot nine inches to be exact, one of my childhood wishes was to be taller. The Nepalese are short, five foot being about the average height, and since coming to Nepal I was experiencing what it was like to be tall. I would bump my head on doorways, could touch the ceiling in almost any room without standing on my toes and when I walked in the streets, I towered over the crowds. My entire relationship to who I was, on both physical and psychological levels, had been altered through a strange set of events. I felt like a child searching for my identity within a strange new world.

The stillness of the moment was interrupted by a familiar voice, "Tom, may I join you?"

"Sure Richard. But remember, no questions. Only in the teashop."

"Where's Leslie?" I asked, after he had taken a seat on the ground. "I hope you didn't leave her alone with all those French mountain climbers in town." We were close, at times like brothers, and I liked to put our relationship on the light side whenever possible.

"No, she's over there feeding the monkeys. She says they understand her. I'm just happy she's having fun."

"Maybe they can. Who knows?" I replied. "Maybe 'the Doctor' gave them a hit of acid and they now speak the language of love." I joked about the mysterious Dr. LSD who had also passed through Katmandu just before our arrival, leaving a wake of acid-inspired hippies talking about his LSD bash at the city's swankiest hotel.

"Hey Tom, what are you always staring at?" asked Richard, always turning things toward a more serious note. "I've been watching you look out into space, as if you're seeing something but there's nothing there."

"Maybe there is, but we don't know how to see it." I replied, leading him on in his game of questions and answers. "What if I told you I'm seeing space?"

"Well I could say you're crazy but that's too logical a conclusion," he joked. "Are you really seeing something?" he asked with such sincerity that I had to laugh.

"If you don't want me to think you're loony, tell me what you're seeing," he insisted after I had calmed down.

"I might not be seeing anything or I might be seeing everything. I'm not really sure."

"Now you do sound loco," he chuckled to himself. "What do you mean?"

"Ever since that night of my first *mystical experience*, as you refer to it, the world has not always been a solid, three-dimensional phenomenon. I saw, among other things, that we all exist in some imperceptible energy field and we — I mean our physical bodies — are surrounded by, or suspended, in this field. I can't say what this reality is but it seems like an emanation of a life force.

"If I relax in a certain way and try not to focus my eyes on anything but just gaze without any real purpose, at times, I can perceive this energy field. It appears like a mist of charged movement with no recognizable pattern, just filling space; molecules densely packed yet vibrating at some high frequency, like electric plasma. It seems that when my rational mind can accept that there is some form in invisible space, I can enter further into it."

I paused to think about what I was saying because this was the first time I had tried to put into words what was happening to me.

"You know when you have a hallucination on LSD," I continued, using a common experience we had never talked about but I was sure he could relate to, "that wispy image, real or imaginary, appears, or is created within this energetic mist. Maybe it is projected there from within our own minds or it may have its origin within the mist itself. I don't know. But this mist is alive, always in movement, ever-changing but always the same."

"I still don't understand. How do you make it appear?"

"I don't make it appear at all. It doesn't happen when I'm trying to see it. First you have to relax your vision and half-gaze at the beauty of nature all around you. Don't try to see with your understanding. Try to feel what you perceive. Then relax and focus on the space between two objects.

"Look over there," I said pointing to a tree about a hundred feet away, "and stare at it for awhile.

"Then, without moving your head," I continued after a short silence, "focus on something closer to you like that wilted dandelion in front of us. Slowly go back and forth between the flower and the tree a few times until you have these two points of focus established in your mind."

After we had experimented with that for a while, I said, "Let your vision come to rest half-way between these two points. Relax there and don't try to see anything. Be open and receptive, that's all"

We sat in silence for a few minutes while we both played with our vision in this way.

"Go back to the tree, then to the flower a few times rather than try to make it happen," I commented to keep the game going.

After a few more minutes of experimenting, Richard broke our silence saying, "I don't know. I thought I saw a speck of light and even a slight wavy pattern but it could be just my imagination."

"It feels to me like I'm reaching out with my imagination and bringing into focus another reality that is beyond my rational mind," I commented, trying to guide him through my own experiences. "As if my imagination is a bridge to other realities.

"When it first started happening, I couldn't believe in it like I can believe that you're sitting here next to me. It was more like fantasy. It's somehow connected to thought, as if what I can perceive is determined by what I'm thinking, or more specifically, by what I believe. When we alter our beliefs we alter our reality!"

At this point I became a little frustrated because I knew that I was not making much sense yet it was so clear for me. Why couldn't I communicate it to him?

"What is it, Tom, that you're actually seeing," inquired Richard, having become frustrated in his own attempts.

"Well, at some point in the process," I began, "my entire vision, or means of perception shifts its focus and the solid, three-dimensional world becomes a hazy blur superimposed upon a backdrop of fluid light. Things of the material world lose their predominate features of solidity and the energies that emanate from them pulsate forth into reality.

"Now, for instance, I'm not seeing that tree as a solid, three-dimensional object of definable form and consistency, but as a translucent energy field of a green-gold vapor which extends for twenty feet or more beyond the physical boundaries of the tree itself. If I relax even more in the process of perception, the entire mass of energy appears as an imposing spirit; alive, vibrant, dancing with the joy of life.

"Even crazier, that spirit might, at times, talk to me and tell me of the sacred reality of all life," I concluded, shaking my head at myself for believing such a thing could be true.

"Don't tell anyone," I said, smiling and looking him in the eyes, "I think I'm crazy but it doesn't matter to me any more. The world about me and the prospects of life have become interesting for the first time since I was a young child."

"Now, Richard," came the voice of Leslie from behind us, "don't pester him with your questions any more. You're not going to solve the mysteries of the universe in one day."

"Tell us," I asked her after she had crouched down next to Richard, "what the monkeys said to you today. They often tell me things too but I don't let Richard know because he believes only humans can think," I joked with her.

"Well," she began, showing obvious signs of displeasure at Richard for revealing her little secret, "if you want to know, they said that 'humans are not very intelligent. They come here all day long asking for things, when desiring too many things is already the cause of their suffering."

Neither one of us said a word. Compared to what we had been discussing, that was real wisdom. What difference did it make if there were a hundred other worlds. We were, for the most part, confined to this one, so why not figure out how to be happy here. Why were we so anxious to forget this one and move on to the next?

I reached over and hugged her, something I was not accustomed to doing, and said, "Thank you for bringing us back to reality. The monkeys can talk and so can the trees if we learn how to listen but never have they said anything so wise to me. They must trust you a lot."

Her large brown eyes glistened with emotion as crimson cloud patterns danced off in the distance, signaling the end of the sun's journey for this day. The peasants, carrying their baskets loaded with potatoes and driving their animals before them, moved along the narrow foot trails returning to the shelter of their mud houses for the night. The bells of the temple rang out in a sudden burst of celebration, calling the end of God's day and giving thanks for the many blessings. *Life is truly a blessing,* I reflected, *we need to learn to see it that way rather than try to make it conform to our desires.*

"Come on, you two mystics," came the voice of Leslie breaking in upon my daydreaming, "I'm cold and hungry. Let's get going back to town. Maybe a good meal will bring you both back down to earth."

As we entered the door of the Blue Tibetan later, we were greeted by the noise of the crowd and the voices of Country Joe and the Fish crackling-out over the tired hi-fi, synthesizing the American cynicism:

> And it's a one, two, three,
> What are we fighting four?
> Don't ask me, I don't give a damn.
> Next stop is Vietnam.
> And it's a five, six, seven,
> Open up the pearly gates.
> Well there aint no time to wonder why
> Whoopee! We're all gonna die!

Did I really feel like that or did they want me to believe that I did? The U.S. and its reality seemed far away to me now.

As I was searching for three seats together, my eyes fell upon a beautiful young women sitting off in one corner and we locked in an intense gaze for several moments. There was a special radiance about her, as if a light was focused behind her, and her big green eyes held fixed to my gaze. For just an instant, everything else in the place faded into the background and I felt a bridge of light forming between our hearts.

We quickly found a table and ordered a meal, while our prophet, Mick Jagger, shouted out his message through dilapidate speakers to the frustrated youth of the world: *I can't get no satisfaction!*

I turned several times to look at her and she was still staring in our direction with the same radiant, spaced-out look on her face. At some point after our meal had arrived, I looked as she was leaving the restaurant in the company of two tall Frenchmen who looked as if they had traveled the trail the hard way. She turned one last time, as if to say, *I recognize you,* and was gone.

A few nights later, I went to the restaurant alone. The same pretty young woman was sitting in the corner and we immediately embraced each other with our eyes. I had forgotten all about her and our encounter the other night. As I stood there mesmerized by her stare, lines of energy and light seemed to form between us and I walked, without thinking, directly toward her. I sat down opposite her at one of the long communal tables and fell into the beauty and depth of her magnificent green eyes. We said nothing, acknowledging each other instead with a slight bow of the head and an innocent smile.

Something strange was happening; some connection or reminder was surfacing from within me. Time passed and our energies merged into oneness without fear or desire. My heart first strained, as if under stress of expansion, then, with a great sigh accompanied by a rush of energy, I let go into a flow of love between us. Everything else in the room faded and a radiant glow appeared around her. In that moment, I knew that she knew what I knew; we saw through the same awakened eyes and knew within our hearts that we were one with the All.

We sat transfixed in our state of unity until the same man of the other night came up to her and said something, while motioning towards the door and indicating that she should follow. Almost as if the whole experience was a dream, I found myself sitting there alone in the restaurant staring intensely at an empty chair. I wasn't sad or disappointed. The euphoria of the moment stayed with me and I felt encased in a soft glow of peace as Simon and Garfunkle consoled a wounded heart with their eulogy of American feelings:

I am a rock, I am an island.
A rock feels no pain and an island never cries.

I left the restaurant without eating and walked aimlessly around town giving my pocket money to the beggars and watching the evening routine of street merchants packing up their portable enterprises and heading home. After hours of wandering, I returned to the house, lit a candle next to my mattress on the floor, and crawled into my sleeping bag. Some time ago, I had moved my mattress to a tiny space formed by the slope of the roof at the head of the stairs and hung an old blanket up over the opening so I had a semi-private space about the size of a closet but with a tiny window that looked out toward the river. I tried to write in my journal but nothing flowed so I put out the candle and stared out the window at the half-moon as she hung swelling in the dark sky.

A short time later, the blanket moved and I looked up from my daydream to see her standing in the doorway with the moonlight reflecting in her eyes. She was not alone, as the French boy entered from the other side of the curtain and keeled down next to me.

"You both crazies," he said in broken English, making the universal motion of circling his finger at his temple. "She stay with you. Two crazies!"

He left as quickly as he had come and we were alone. She sat at one end of the bed and we melted into each other's eyes as if no time had elapsed between the restaurant and the room. I thought of saying something or holding her hand but these impulses resolved themselves into non-action; just being was enough.

My heart opened, this time without the slightest resistance, and a golden light formed a bubble about us as we merged once again into unity. A long span of time passed looking into each other's eyes before I realized that we were talking to each other within our minds.

You can see like I can see and the world will never be the same, she said within my mind.

We are all one, I said by thought to her.

*Not all can see what we can see. Yes, we are all one,*she gently placed her thought within my mind.

Two crazies, I thought and we both laughed.

We passed an eternal moment of love and acceptance and the room filled with a sense of peace and bliss as we physically joined in an embrace. There was no passion or excitement, just surging waves of bliss uniting us in love to all. It was as if I was holding another part of myself, reunited at last after countless ages of separation.

All of a sudden my body began to shake as thoughts of wanting always to be with her and that she might not be there in the morning clouded in on my mind. The peace turned to fear and I began to hold her tighter until her thoughts penetrated my mind saying, *It is not me nor is it you. It is the essence of the star out of which we have been born; the origin of our souls uniting us as one.*

I felt Truth and did not care to understand more. The peace returned as abruptly as it had gone and I let go, as never before in my life, into a total acceptance of the moment. The ebb and flow of our breathing joined us in perfect harmony as endless waves of bliss bathed us in eternal oneness. I existed no more apart from the moment.

At some point, without breaking our physical contact, we lay down, pulled the sleeping bag over us, and drifted off together to the space where all souls are one.

CHAPTER 8

Mad Hadder's Party

I awoke at dawn to find us in the same embrace, apparently neither having as much as rolled over during the night. I felt the rhythm of her breathing blending with my own but the intensity of the energy passing between us had subsided, without diminishing the feeling of peace and love. It had been a magical night. Something had been resolved within me. I felt so light and free, as if my fear of loneliness had gone forever and a search for something had come to an end.

I slipped out of bed, my movements causing only a slight change in her breathing, and I heard within my head, *We are one,* as if to acknowledge my departure.

Sleep, I shall return, I thought to her and, half in a trance, I started off toward the river.

It was a foggy, damp morning and the few people up and about were wrapped in thick blankets to ward off the chilled air. Following habit or routine, I crossed the river and walked along the deserted fields until I found a secluded place to do my morning necessity before returning to the river to splash some icy water on my face and brush my teeth. I sat in my favorite spot under a stunted tree near the temple waiting for the sun to burn off the morning mist and bring the clarity of a new day to my mind. I closed my eyes and watched the array of thoughts dance upon the screen of my consciousness. Of course, this morning an entirely new theme was being played.

Whenever I looked back on my life over the last four or five months, I could perceive how a carefully orchestrated set of circumstances seemed to be pushing me beyond my threshold of reality and transforming me into an insane mystic. What last night had to do with it all I could not imagine, but it definitely had the same mysterious vibration, like my meetings with Todd, Vic and Linda, Richard and Leslie, and many other influences that had crossed my path. Maybe life was always like that and I was only just beginning to pay attention to it.

At times I could see how I had been transformed through these encounters from an atheist to a believer in the reality of an All Pervading Presence. But where was it all leading me? I didn't even like asking the question. Just to consider why, sent an eerie chill through my body. I feared I would be no more. Somehow, the more detached I became from everything, the less I cared if life, as I now knew it, continued or not. My nagging fear of insanity no longer had the power to force me to 'hold it all together'.

Tearing myself away from my own mind tripping, I went to the teashop to find Leo, the master of many languages, and ask him to help me discover who this 'angel of madness' was. Explaining the circumstances of last night, I asked him if he could help me find the Frenchman who brought her to my room.

"Sure man, but would you answer one of those questions for me first? It's early. None of that crew is going to be up yet anyway."

""What is it you want to know?" I asked, settling in to my customary seat.

"I always wanted to be an artist. I mean, I'm a good painter but my father says that's not a real profession and it has no value to society. What do artists of all kinds contribute to society and the evolution of humanity?"

I straightened my back, closed my eyes, and let go into feeling the answer arising from within me until words began to come out in a slow and deliberate way.

"Artists are really the impetus for all scientific, technological, and philosophical discoveries upon which the evolution of society is based. By penetrating into fields of original thought and inspiration, they guide an entire civilization by keeping the bridge of imagination open for others to follow. Through their efforts to awaken within themselves creative inspiration, they make it available to everyone.

"All consciousness is one consciousness. You cannot have a creative inspiration that does not send an impulse rippling out through the infinite sea of consciousness, affecting the awareness of all humanity. All artists are following the inspiration of the masters who have gone before them, deepening their insights and expanding their creative influence on humanity.

"You mean that I'm being inspired by Rembrandt?"

"You are being inspired by the impressions that his creative genius left upon consciousness. That is all of Rembrandt that is left. As Rembrandt he exists no more in your world or any other world. That which has been, has become through being, that which it will be."

"Are you saying that the concept of reincarnation is not true?" asked Richard, surprised.

"Truth is all relative to one's state of awareness. Reincarnation, as it is conceived

of from within the Earthly domain, has a degree of relative truth. Your reasoning processes are limited, however, by your acceptance of your individuality; that you exist independent of the whole. Therefore, your concept of reincarnation involves the belief that you have been on the earth before.

"That you exist in relationship to impressions that have been created through interaction with Earth plane consciousness, other than in your present lifetime, would be a closer approximation of the truth.

"When it rains, a drop of water falls to the earth. It filters through the ground into the river, which flows into the ocean. The sun heats the ocean and the water rises in the form of vapors, which form clouds that will eventually bring another raindrop to the earth.

"Has that raindrop been there before, or has water in the form of a rain drop been there before? That depends upon whether the identification is as a separate drop of rain or as water itself."

"OK Tom, or whoever it is that's talking to us, you tell it like everything is in perfect harmony but I don't see that any perfection is being created on this planet. Looks to me like the development of civilization is bringing us closer to our end," commented Leo.

"Perfection can only be perceived in relationship to greater patterns or cycles that are occurring within life's flow. When a flower has shared its beauty and fragrance with life and begins to wilt and form its seeds, is it not following its perfection?

"Within states of human awareness, perfection is the acceptance of what is."

"You mean that there's no evil, no reason to stop the destruction of the planet and its peoples?" jumped in Richard at the first pause in the dialogue.

"Ignorance confuses choice! The results of decisions created out of disharmony are what you call evil. Good and evil are interpretations of the consequences of one's actions, not really forces in opposition.

"One should be careful not to contribute, through action nor thought, to any destructive process. Do not concentrate on what you are against but work for what you believe will create unity and harmony on your planet. That is where the hope of all humanity lies; not only in stopping the destruction but in creating positive alternatives through your help and your hope."

"How can positive changes arise out of your deteriorating civilization when God is imagined as something that created life to tempt you with it, seeks to judge and punish you rather than assist and guide you, and causes you to suffer rather than enjoy the creative abundance of life. Rather than criticize and rebel against what you correctly perceive as ignorance, you could try to formulate a more positive image of your Creator and how you, as a part of creation, can contribute positively to the on-going creative process."

I was beginning to enjoy this morning ritual.

After our morning session, I accompanied Leo to a house on the far side of town to find out what he could about my new houseguest.

"I don't know how you got yourself into this one." he began, after returning from inside the house.

"Come on Leo," I said, impatiently interrupting him, " you're sounding just like my father. She came to my room I told you. What's up anyway?"

"Well, the French guy said that he took her to your room because she's crazy just like you and you seem to be the only person who can relate to her. But there is more," he continued, looking serious. "No one knows how long she's been around Katmandu. She has no passport or anything for that matter and, what's worse, the French embassy is looking for her to send her home.

"He said that she's been in their room for about a month now. She's flipped out, Tom. It's best for her to be sent home. He said that she doesn't talk but understands French. I could try to talk to her if you want," he suggested sympathetically.

"No Leo. We understand each other just fine," I answered, in a detached way. "Did he say what her name is?"

"She answers to the name of Bridget, but no one really knows what her name is."

"Thanks Leo. That's all I wanted to know," I replied.

Leo and I walked back to the house and talked along the way.

"What is it with this girl, Tom? Since we met over a month ago, I've never seen you get emotionally involved about anything."

"It's not her, as a person, that has me turning around like this. It's that I can understand her. Do you get it, my friend? To me, she's not crazy! Am I going to be the next one to be shipped back to the nut house?"

"You shouldn't think about that, Tom. You have it together. You're taking care of yourself. You have money and can make decisions for yourself. It's different," insisted Leo, patting me on the back to make me feel better.

The next two days were blissful as well as demanding. Bridget had a special brand of craziness and would watch people for hours, like a soft kitten from the corner of the room, observing the things they were most attached to — Leslie's hair brush, Leo's colored pencils, and clothes, shoes, and books of anyone coveting them. When they left the room, she'd steal that very thing. She wasn't interested in the things, most of the time throwing them out the window or hiding them somewhere in the house. I was sure she was trying to teach them a great lesson about attachment, but when I tried to point this out to the others, I became as crazy as her. Of course, two crazies.

Most of our time together was spent in the same force field of blissful unity that we could enter into just by relaxing and looking into each other's eyes. At times we would touch in tenderness, which triggered a kind of remembrance, as if we felt our common origin. The energy never moved to passion or lust but transcended this earthly reaction and by-passed attachment and possession. We just were. No rules. No form. Two crazies in a mad world.

Returning from the river on the morning of the third day, I saw a jeep with diplomatic plates parked near the house and knew inside my heart that they had come to take her away. I raced to the house to meet her coming out the front door in the company of a proper-looking lady, shouting loudly at her in French. She pulled her arm free in an unusual show of aggression and embraced me. Our hearts said in a flash what our minds might never know in a lifetime, *love is eternal*. We drew apart and stood engulfed in each other's eyes, oblivious to the material surroundings while sharing our last moment of eternity together.

Her eyes began to fill with tears and her lips quivered as she strained to pronounce the only words she ever said to me, "No let them take you. They make you forget."

The days intensified after Bridget was taken away as I spent most of my time sitting on my mattress staring off into nothingness, questioning my own sanity, or rather my attachment to it, which waged battle with the forces of 'you have to hold it together'. 'Not really caring' seemed to win consistently.

I began to feel a surge of creativity and carried a notebook with me and, for the first time in my life, started to make simple drawings of the snow-capped Himalayas and the local peasants pasturing their water buffaloes. Poetry of nature, God, and the universe flowed freely from within me, expressing in word-pictures the sensations of oneness with all life I was living. I welcomed this new self-expression and the sense of peace and creativity it brought to me. At the same time, I became more withdrawn socially, talking little, mostly staring off into the emerging reality, beyond self-importance or personal identity.

Leo and Richard stayed close during this time, asking me to come along when they went out and accepting my spaced-out condition. As we walked through the crowded market one cloudy afternoon, an old Land Rover pickup, loaded with cargo and eight or ten longhaired hippies, rolled up. Sitting on top of the cab was a burnt-out, old-growth hippie with gray hair and beard, wearing a faded black leather jacket with a 'Road Devils' emblem on the back, shouting out to any one who would listen.

"OK, Everyone! I want ya ta listen to me! I got somethin' I'm gonna tell ya'll," came a booming voice in gutter English. "Ma name's Lee Hadder, and ma friends call me Da Mad Hadder," he continued, laughing at his own joke while waving a big, three-paper joint in one hand and stroking his disheveled beard with the other,

"I've come here ta start ma own country! Ya'll can be part of dis here country and dere gonna be no laws! None a dem rules and things dhat dem *authorities* can get'cha with. Whadaya think of dat?"

He went on puffing on the joint and talking louder, as Americans do when they think people can't understand them. I stared hard at him trying to figure this one out. What was this ex-biker from Los Angeles doing in Katmandu? .

"I'm a gonna start me own country and we'll be free at last"

I couldn't help wondering what Eight-Finger Eddy would think of the Mad Hadder's version of freedom, while Richard, in his own practical way, shouted out, "And who's going to pay for it?"

"I got ten grand, man, and I'm puttin' it all into tents, stoves, blankets, tools and stuff like dat. With dis, we can get'er started and den build some build-ings, maybe even our own airport so we don't have ta go through dat customs stuff no more. Ya know what I mean?" he emphasized his point by waving the smoking joint in front of his face.

He explained in his over-emphatic way that he had gotten it all together, even bribed an official to get permission to set up camp on a piece of land out in the mountains east of here. He had a little mimeographed map indicating how to get there by bus and said, as he was banging overly hard on the roof to tell the driver to get going, "Dis is da ultimate trip, man. Don't none a ya'll go and miss it now. It's da Mad Hadder's tea party."

With just a few days before Christmas, Leo decided to go for it and took me along. We took a local bus to a small village and walked a short distance to the Mad Hadder's village, which consisted of three canvas wall-tents and a makeshift lean-to on a large plateau that commanded a spectacular view of the distant Himalayan range and Mt. Everest as her crowning jewel. As we approached, people I had seen around Katmandu came out to welcome us to Camp Wonderland.

The founder and king himself, dressed in '60s hippie attire of overalls, denim shirt and gray-striped engineers cap, hustled over to shake our hands saying, "Gonna hav'ta stamp ya passports with da official entrance stamp but I got'er in da tent over dare. We're gonna do it later. Don't ya forget now. We're real proper here," he concluded, breaking into a deep belly laugh, which ended in a hacking cough, causing tears to roll down his whiskered cheeks.

"No visas and it don't cost ya a thing," he went on, vivaciously.

"Thanks, Lee," I said, " I'm starting my own world and you can come free anytime you want."

"Now dat sounds far out, man," he replied, scratching his head as if trying to envision another world. "And where'ya gonna do a thing like dat?

"Oh, the world is already there! I'm just trying to figure out how we all can get into it," I answered, half-seriously.

"Dat's real groovy, man. Stay with it," he said, still scratching his head while inviting us to a hot cup of tea.

Some 50 men and women were hanging about the tents or taking in the rays of afternoon sun on a nearby rock out-cropping. In the evening, we gathered in a great circle on the plateau — I counted sixty-five — and held hands, sharing inspired thoughts and prayers as the spirit moved us. We stood in silence for sometime, each in their own world of personal reflection, until, like a whisper at first, we began to hum *Amazing Grace* and sway back and forth. At one moment, an Italian woman broke out in a loud voice and we all, in our language and intonation, joined in what must have been my first inspired Christmas carol with chaotic harmony but perfect spirit. I knew in a flash why singing had been a central part of spiritual expression in all religions; the union of oneness it created among the group was unmistakable. We had one thing bonding us on a deep level of human awareness; it was a mad, mad world out there and we enjoyed the company of those who shared the same worldview.

Slowly we all gravitated towards the tents, the mood having been set for the night. Dinner was a long communal affair as plates with hot food circulated around the tents and we each took two or three mouthfuls and passed them on to the next person. When the two large pots were empty, fresh fruit and sweet cakes were passed about in the same manner. By this time, we were packed in almost one on top of the other and the act of sharing in this way created a special intimacy among us all, giving rise to much spontaneous hugging, laughing and singing. We felt close, looking each other in the eyes while passing the food about and enjoying the differences that made us all unique, while feeling the love that made us all the same.

All through the night we sang and improvised music on drums, guitars, banjoes, flutes, and pots and pans. During one of the lulls in the festivities, our Italian choir mistress started another round of song, until we all joined in a harmonious blend of vocal inspiration that transported us to a space of total unity. I became enraptured in the overtones of our harmony and floated upon a cloud of sound until I imagined that we were all vibrating in unison to the universal music of our hearts; the music of love.

Christmas 1967; no stockings hung by the chimney with care, just lots of love and joy for all to share.

Leo and I hung in at the hippie camp until after New Years then said good-bye to its "citizens" and caught the bus to Katmandu. It was a cloudy day but bright sunlight would occasionally break through, lighting up the terraced fields below us as if the director was bringing a movie set to life. As the bus groaned and growled down the steep grade to the valley below, we talked about the strange phenomenon of questions and answers and where this information could be coming from.

"It is like my new interest in writing and drawing," I said. "I never tried to draw anything before in my life and poetry never appeared in *Popular Mechanics*, yet now these things just naturally come out of me, as if I have become a different person. There must be many different levels within us or maybe we are many different beings living out a lifetime through one body. Or we are one being living many lifetimes simultaneously."

"Now, that sounds far out, Tom," commented Leo, " but I wouldn't be surprised at anything after what you said about God being a human choice the other day"

"I am, for the first time in by life, convinced that God, or some organizing intelligence exists." I said. "But I think that human beings have attributed too many human qualities to It. It may be some kind of impersonal energy field that holds it all together. I think we are trying too hard to make God in our own image and make It responsible for everything, even our love life and bank account."

"You said once that you saw God. What did He..."

*Clank! Bang!*A loud noise suddenly reverberated throughout the bus as the sound of the straining motor, backing off down the hill, stopped and we began to accelerate. I looked out the window to see the scenery whizzing by and realized that we were out of control. The drive shaft, now pounding and clanking underneath us, had given way under the weight of the bus. Without the help of the transmission it was doubtful whether the driver could stop this runaway rocket with just the brakes.

Terrifying screams and the stench of the burning break linings filled the bus as the driver, in his own focused panic, did what he could to get it under control. The screaming intensified, like a scary ride at an amusement park. Mothers tucked their children under their skirts while other people began frantically prying at windows in an effort to get out. Some shouted out in desperate prayer to any god who might be listening, perhaps the sanest reaction of all. I looked at Leo. His mouth was frozen open in a silent scream, and his knuckles were turning white as he gripped the seat, preparing for what was now the inevitable — the crash.

A voice from within grabbed my awareness and instructed me, *You are not going to die. Brace yourself.*

Suddenly I was aware that time had warped and I was in two realities simultaneously. The landscape was still racing by out the window and the horror within the bus was in crescendo, but my perception was speeded up to the point that everything seemed to be happening in slow motion. I thought about trying to jump out the window but the terraced fields zipping by a hundred feet below told me 'no'. I glanced towards the back of the bus to see if I could jump out the rear door but others were already frantically kicking and pulling desperately trying to get it open. I remember feeling my body tensing and my stomach filling with the sensation of fear. Yet another part of me was calmly looking for a solution to the situation, as if choosing what I wanted to buy at the supermarket.

A few seconds later, the bus veered into a drainage ditch, scraped along the soft bank until it crashed into a large boulder and came to a stop. There was no applause for the safe landing, but the screaming subsided and people began to push and shove to get out the door and onto solid ground. Leo and I had been sitting near the center of the bus and were among the last to climb down into the expansion of the chaos that had started inside. Only one person appeared to have been injured by flying glass. Many of the peasants were still crying or praying, frozen in the attitude with which they had reacted in the moment. The driver was being attacked with insults and threats by those who felt they had to blame someone instead of being thankful for being alive.

I jumped onto the roof and grabbed our packs from the mad scramble that had begun, tossing them down to Leo. We slipped out of the confusion and sat on our packs looking at the crushed bus, thankful that the driver had run it into the inside of the road instead of off the precipice. The nearest field was a hundred feet below.

"Shit, man, we made it alive!" exclaimed Leo, just now getting his breath. "God was sure there, man. I could feel It all around me!

"During those few minutes," continued Leo, his eyes now alive with a new brilliance, "I wasn't me. I was everything that was going on. I think I surrendered caring, just for a split second, and I felt connected to everybody else."

"Yeah, I know what you mean, Leo," I said, just now realizing the mystical nature of the accident we had just survived.

After we had calmed our nerves with a cigarette, I said, "This thing isn't going anywhere for a long time. Let's walk. It'll do us more good than hanging around here."

CHAPTER 9

ORACLE

$\mathbf{B}$ack in Katmandu, Leo and I resettled on straw mats in the common room of our old house with Richard and Leslie. A changing of the guard occurred as many visas of the old crew expired and they moved on to other retreats in Bali and Goa or back to Europe.

Morning exchanges in the teashop continued two or three times a week as Richard and Leo, joined by Leslie and others at times, asked questions and received astonishing wisdom, which I was beginning to tune into myself. I found that I could focus my attention on listening, and be participating in the experience on two levels at the same time. Richard was convinced that some ancient master was using me to deliver messages and that my voice had an East Indian accent. Leo, noticeably changed after his 'feeling of God' as he called it, saw Asian faces superimposed upon mine as the messages came through, perceiving many different entities according to the question asked.

I reestablished my morning ritual of going off to the fields to answer Nature's call, splashing my face with icy water, and sitting beneath a tree to watch my thoughts float by in my continued attempts at meditation. These sessions were taking on a definite form and consistency as I could now perceive thought-loops of specific themes repeating over and over as my mind struggled to retain dominance over the moments of inner peace arising out of the absence of thought. I made no attempt to stop the mind. Its persistence and dominance were eroding however with each session, as if it was relinquishing its hold on my identity as I became more aware of its presence.

After my thought-watching practice, I would stop by the teashop for a cup of tea and figure eight doughnuts and, if I was in the mood, answer metaphysical questions, carefully formulated by Richard.

Questions like, "Does time exist as part of all creation?"

Time is the field of awareness within which change or movement takes place. It exists as a concept, created within the minds of humanity, to measure experiences, which take place within their fields of perception. It is not an element of any reality. Within dualistic perception, time arises as a temporary relationship to a specific awareness. Time measures space."

"What is the relationship between karma, destiny and free will?"

"Karma is that which sustains the balance within the universe. It is neither a punishment nor a limitation but rather that which outlines the path, or designates the direction that each soul will follow during its journey on the planet Earth. It is governed by impressions, created by intense emotional experiences, fixed to the soul through the process of attraction or affinity; a type of cosmic magnetism.

"Destiny is the path that each soul has chosen to best achieve its purpose for returning to the physical plane of reality; that which karma defines as the most efficient way through the maze of life. It is the course of action and expression that will allow the soul to achieve its maximum potential.

"Free will is the higher-mind capacity to guide thought, through intention, necessary and essential for every soul to become the source of its perfection. This allows each soul to select its experiences from the infinite potential within each lifetime. Unique to the human condition, it is the means by which the soul guides itself within its karma to achieve its destiny."

"Did humanity evolve out of a primitive animal, the ape?"

"Your present theory of evolution is based upon a linear development of life with survival as its motivating force. An expanded understanding would encompass the perspective of the planet Earth as a fertile jewel of the universe, which has been seeded and grafted with life for millions of years. And life as a cooperative interaction of all seven of the vibrational frequencies of consciousness — mineral, protoplast, plant, animal, human, angel, and archangels — each aiding and guiding the development of all the others.

"The essence of evolution should be seen as an exchange, or cooperation between these basic levels of existence not a struggle or competitive challenge. Creation is an interaction of different frequencies of consciousness constantly exchanging energy within these primary levels of existence according to density, with each level contributing to the creation and existence of the others. These exchanges act to stabilize the existence of the whole; a kind of vibrational homeostasis.

"The development of the physical strength and dexterity of the ape has created evolutionary patterns that have benefited humanity in these areas while the advancement of logic and reason on the part of humanity has influenced the development of the ape, aiding in its adaptation and survival potential."

"What is the difference between man and the ape then?"

"They both can procreate but the ape cannot make the act sacred. For that, an expanded frequency of mind is required."

Leo pursued a more personal line of questioning such as, "What is faith?"

"The experience of the potential to do all things through a coordination of will and intention."

"What is the best type of meditation?"

"The one that you believe in and practice each day. The potential of any discipline originates in the intention and motivation of each individual, not in its form or origin."

Leslie usually preferred to stay in bed until the sun had burnt off the haze, letting the men solve the mystery of creation. But when she did participate, she contributed a more intuitive, inspirational direction with questions like, "What is love and how do we participate in it?"

"Love is the force that binds all things together and makes them one; the harmony within the polarity of creation. It may be called the essential nature of all existence.

"The development of attitudes of devotion, reverence, gratitude, and acceptance of all people and situations opens the doors of the heart to let the experience of love permeate your entire being."

"Do angels exist and, if so, what is their relationship to us here on the Earth?"

"Angels, as one of the seven original waves of creation, exist within the consciousness frequency of compassion and joy, as opposed to yours of desire and fear.

"These two levels of reality are not independent from one another but rather inter-penetrating frequencies of consciousness; two parts of a greater whole. From an expanded perspective, angels are your divine potential but, because you are steeped in duality, the only way you can relate to an angel is as something other than yourself. In reality, there is no distance of time or space between you and the realm of angels, there is only a difference of awareness; where your attention is. Angels are the level of guidance most accessible to your own consciousness but you must learn to reach out to them because they cannot enter your thought viruses of desire and fear. To contact the angels one should become like a child and relate to the finer substance of angelic reality through your imagination."

I arrived at the teashop early one morning and, after my morning tea and donuts, agreed to another session of questions and answers headed by Richard on the effect and nature of karma. He began by asking, "Most interpretations of karma call it the law of cause and effect, but you're calling it an outline of one's destiny created by *impressions* attached to the soul by some kind of attraction. Please help me to reconcile these apparent differences"

"Imagine that all souls are adrift in a sea of consciousness and surrounded by an energetic field, whose polarity is determined by impressions, or emotional charges. Cause and effect are interpretations based primarily on the theory of linear movement of evolution and the individuality of the soul. These same concepts of cause and effect, when perceived from an expanded perspective, will

appear as attraction and deflection; the process out of which arises the movement and direction of evolution.

"A soul moves into relationship with another entity because of attraction and exchanges a charge of energy according to the impressions most active in each. Out of this exchange, an impulse of deflection arises, which sends the soul drifting off towards its next encounter. Sometimes pairs and groups of souls are formed according to the compatibility of their impressions and they drift together, attracting and deflecting, until an alteration of their polarity — their karmic charge — is effected through repeated exchanges within this process of karma.

"This drift, which takes place within a multidimensional sphere, is not random nor linear but derives its form out of each attraction and its direction from the intensity of each exchange. Karma is not fixed but is variable according to one's reaction to each exchange and the willingness to flow with each deflection.

"Is there a greater purpose in it all or is it just a process set in motion without beginning or end?" he went on, trying to understand with his mind what his heart already knew.

"From within the present conditions of human evolution, the purpose would be to enhance awareness, through the results of each exchange, of the essential unity of all life; to release the unbalanced emotional charges of doubt and fear and to awaken higher vibrational potentials of compassion and unity."

"Is there no God or higher intelligence involved in the process? Is it just chemical and electric as you're stating?"

"The harmonious functioning of the whole may be related to as an overseeing intelligence but to think that this presence is in any way responsible for the attraction and reflection process would be incorrect. Perfection is contained within the whole. It does not require an outside force to create that perfection nor to determine the interactions of each individual part.

"By relating to this perfection in accordance with one's beliefs, it is possible to influence the nature of the exchanges and create positive patterns of drift within the process. That effect has given rise to your concepts of prayer and devotion."

"You are drifting but not without some means of control. Your intentions are your rudder and your will is your sail. With these you may guide your soul as it drifts within the infinite sea of consciousness."

I slowly opened my eyes and became re-accustomed to the smells and sounds of the busy teashop. Richard conferred with Leo over the last information received, while I stepped outside and found a convenient place to relieve myself. Shafts of golden sunlight were breaking up the morning mist hanging in the muddy alleyways and I began to think of my notebook and the possibility of making some drawings in the countryside.

"OK, Tom," said Richard, after I rejoined them, "I have another one for you. Ready?"

"Just a few more," I replied. "I want to go outside of town. It's going to be a beautiful day."

I closed my eyes as Richard began to ask something about thought, but my attention wasn't on his words. For sometime now I'd been aware that he was asking these questions to see if I could answer them and I was obliging by showing him that the answers would just pour out from some universal source of wisdom. In that moment, I realized that playing the game in this way was influencing the effect of what was being said and a wave of genuine concern for Richard broke upon the shores of my consciousness. With an intense feeling of compassion, I prayed to the universe guiding this entire process: *Please let this be the last question he ever has to ask. Let him know from within himself.*

Time distorted and my awareness split into several different realities all occupying the same time-space perspective. Within my physical body a rush of energy surged forth, first accumulating at the base of my spine then releasing in an upward thrust, causing my spine to straighten and my head to fill with golden light. At the same time, I could hear my voice grinding on in a meta-physical monologue about the effects of thought on the molecular consistency of the physical body, as well as the typical sounds from within the tea shop and outside in the street.

I was overcome by the feeling that I was merging with everything. In a flash, I was inside of Richard and could feel the way he was receiving each word, how he was formulating his reaction, and even that he had to go to the bathroom soon. I kept fluctuating between these three realities until suddenly, I became the words themselves and could feel the specific origin of inspiration for each word and their intended affect upon the people listening. Understanding became the *effect created by the intention* inspiring each word, not something inherent in the meaning of the word itself.

I began to glimpse the origin of all thought and suddenly, like a neon sign lighting up within me, I saw the message: *Beyond this point you no longer exist.* I can't say that I made a conscious decision to go beyond, but felt more pulled along by a force going that way. One last thought formulated within my mind: *Then, who am I?*

At that point, all reality shattered and the only recognizable consistency was light. It was not that I became light but more like I stopped being something else, arranged for me out of my thoughts and beliefs, and I let myself be light.

CHAPTER 10

MONKEY TEMPLE BLISS

I can't say how much time passed in this state. I was later to find out from Leo that I lit up like a sphere of light and lost consciousness for almost half an hour, creating quite a disturbance in the tea shop and causing the owner to close for awhile because of people crowding in at the open windows.

When I first reentered the awareness of my physical body, I heard the voices of Richard and Leo speaking softly to me: "Tom can you hear me? Are you all right?"

One of them was rubbing me gently on the back of my head. I opened my eyes but all I could see was light. The teashop was empty except for two luminescent forms in the customary places of the owner and his wife.

"We have to get out of here, Tom," came the gentle, yet urgent voice of Leo. "You've been like this for sometime now and the owner wants to reopen. Can you walk?"

I could feel them lifting me, one on each side, and guiding me towards the rear door of the shop, thanking the owner as we passed. Once out in the sunlight, I felt a new burst of energy filling me with bliss and transporting me out of my physical body again. We came around to the front of the teashop where a few people were still peeking through the closed shutters and, with Leo and Richard on either side of me, we moved along the crowded street. Everything was aglow with life, pulsating and vibrating; nothing was solid. A fine mist of white light connected everything. People, once again, became luminous energy fields radiating brilliant spectrums of light and their faces became universal images of love, causing great waves of compassion to sweep over me. I was immersed in the realization of total unity and began to shout, "We are all one!"

Overcome by a wave of bliss, I freed myself from the gentle assistance of my two friends and began throwing my passport and all the money I had in my inner pouch into the air and spontaneously trying to embrace everyone who raced to pick it up. I shouted at the top of my lungs, "I love you all'! I am the Christ!"

I was blissed-out, crazy, and insane, but it didn't matter any more. I had passed some threshold of personal importance. There was no reason to hold anything together, to maintain a constant grip on it all through my rationality and determination. From that continued effort, I was free.

The psychedelic reality that was bombarding my awareness began to overpower me as I found myself standing in the middle of a crowd of people crying, laughing, and shouting all at the same time. There was no solid consistency to the people, the buildings, or even the ground itself. I experienced no heaviness of my body. The only reality was an energy field of fluctuating emanations that was uniting everything together, sustaining and supporting all life.

The people reacted with caution and fear and most ran when I tried to hug them, or shouted at me to get away. One old lady, however, began to cry with me and we embraced, communicating our love without words.

I found myself being guided down the street once again by Richard and Leo, who must have rescued me from my euphoric madness and were trying to convince me to go back to the house so as not to create any more disturbance. I must have been experiencing lapses in contact with the material plane because the next thing I remembered was crossing the river alone and starting out along the path leading to the Monkey Temple.

Without the intensity and stimulation of all the people in the city, the waves of transcendent bliss and hallucinogenic perception began to diminish. I became aware of my feet for the first time lightly flitting along the dirt path, more like floating than walking. Every person who passed by sent a surge of emotion racing through me as I shouted, "I love you," and kept on walking, past peasants working the fields, children herding water buffaloes, and people stacking clay bricks to dry in the sun. Many times I had walked this path but never before was everything so alive, glowing with a radiance and pulsation of a unifying life force.

Time remained totally distorted. I felt like I was walking fast yet all the activity around me appeared to be moving in slow motion and my voice was like a record being played on a slower speed. As I turned my head, the images before me seemed to blur, as if changing slowly from one to another, and all sounds blended together in to a harmonious overtone without individual pitch or intensity.

The half-hour walk passed as if it was minutes and I came to stop in front of the main shrine of the temple. I closed my eyes and instantly reentered the mystical world of bliss and unity. My body vibrated with the force of life racing up my spine, transforming me into a luminous sphere of consciousness. Once again, I existed not.

After some indeterminable length of time, the energy subsided, like a fire that had consumed its fuel, and I reentered physical awareness. My eyes opened, my head bent forward and I kissed the feet of the idol saying, "We are all one. I love you."

*Clang! Clang! Clang!*rang the small bell hanging to one side of the shrine as I yanked the cord three times. I turned to see Richard and Leo standing some ways behind me looking a little apprehensive as to whether I was in control, which I definitely was not. As if taking one step to cover the distance of five, I leapt towards them and flung my arms around their glowing forms as tears of love and joy overwhelmed me.

"I love you! Thank you for making it possible!"

"Hey Tom, what's happening to you? You all right?" they both seemed to ask simultaneously. "You're acting kind of flipped out. Can we help you?" continued Richard, in such a concerned voice that I went into spasms of laughter that must have confirmed their fears: *he's lost it.*

Still laughing, I floated towards my favorite tree on a small mound off to one side of the temple and began to shout, "I have found God. It's marvelous, beautiful, perfect... It's all one."

I moved around in the bliss of my insanity seeing small etheric spirits dancing within the inter-penetrating dimensions of material reality, hearing the trees say, *we are one too*, and perceiving time and space as merging into one continuous field of unity. The overriding sensation was that nothing mattered. Everything I had thought was important became part of a grand illusion that had unraveled to reveal another truth of who I was and what life was all about.

Leo, Richard, and several other people, who must have been attracted by my antics, moved cautiously toward me.

"Tom, can I talk with you? No more questions, I just want to help you if I can," came the now timid voice of Richard, who had come closer than the rest but was still several feet away, observing me with frightened concern. "What is happening to you?"

"I am in it, Richard," I replied exuberantly, "and so are you but you don't know it yet!"

"In what?" asked Richard coming closer?

I could no longer see the expression on his face because it had become one swirling mass of energy but I could sense he was worried.

"The energetic mist I was telling you about one day under this very tree," I said. "I'm in it! It's all around us, supporting us and giving life to us all. Richard, if only you could see the world the way I'm seeing it right now — liquid, irides-cent forms floating in an electrified mist of bright light.

"That guy John Brown was one of the sanest people I've ever met," I went on in a semi-coherent way. "He was right. He *is* Christ, and so am I, and so are you.

"The Christ is our human potential. We are all Christ, man!" I shouted as loud as I could.

"How did this happen to you, Tom?" asked Richard, having understood my reference to our previous conversation. "What did you do to make that happen?"

"You did it, man! You and all those questions pushed me to the realization that I wasn't trying to help you but rather trying to show you how much I knew. Compassion for you and *your own freedom* opened the mystical doors of perception," I said, laughing hysterically again.

"My self-importance was preventing me from being one with you and everything else," I continued, after calming down a bit.

"Then what is that mist?" he asked.

"I still don't know. It is that out of which awareness arises but it is not awareness. Your presence doesn't end where your skin meets the air but there is an energy field radiating in all directions. This energy merges into the mist, connecting you to every other living thing. It's as if you're not really walking on the ground — that's only a material sensation. You're really somehow suspended in this mist, which doesn't stop where the ground begins but inter-penetrates all material substance as well.

"Your body is just energy condensed into form through thought, sustained and supported by the energy field that surrounds you. Your mind is just a process, nurtured through emotional stimulation, to allow you to interact with this material reality."

"You mean I'm only thought in the end, just like Descartes said?" he asked, beginning to probe deeper into this mystery.

"No! That's not it. Thought is a definition of consciousness used by the individual mind to maintain the illusion that you are your physical body, separate and distinct from everything that surrounds you. Mind is a process within consciousness. Consciousness is infinite and therefore the potential of mind is also infinite, when disconnected from the illusion of individuality.

"It might be closer to say that you are love since that is the feeling that arises from being united with all, but that, too, is only a word. You are what you're capable of being aware of at any given moment. That is never fixed but is some kind of probability depending upon intention and personal vision."

After a period of silence, Richard continued, "You know, Tom, sometimes you make perfect sense, you're brilliant, but right now everything you're saying is only confusing me. What is life all about any way?

"Don't take it so seriously, Richard, it is just a game of cosmic bumper cars," I said, breaking into uncontrolled laughter at my comic perception of the moment. "Don't resist it. You will miss all the fun."

"Now that is the craziest thing you've said yet, man. Explain yourself, if you can."

"All life is taking place in an infinite sea of possibilities, which must have something to do with this mist I am perceiving. And we just drift around bumping into others involved in it with us.

"Desire and fear arise out of identification with your individuality and they create the unbalanced polarity of the energy field around your soul. Without them, compassion and unity would be your primary identification and all exchanges would result in peace and harmony among the whole."

"But isn't there something basic to it all. If it isn't thought or form is it light and love?" asked someone whose voice I didn't recognize.

"Light and love are the physical and emotional emanations of the whole but what it is cannot really be reduced to any one concept. Trying to reduce or define it dissolves the wholeness and distorts its reality.

"There is a movement, as if the entire existence is breathing; expanding and contracting at many different rates all at the same time. This movement is sustaining the mist out of which awareness arises. It is breathing all of us! Pay attention!"

"Are you saying that God is a fog, and that we go around bumping into each other in It?" came another unknown voice. "Man, you're crazy! You lost your marbles, that's all."

"You can't know what you are beyond your beliefs by hanging on to your sanity out of fear and insecurity. Having the courage to experience insanity, that is a real challenge," I shouted in laughter while spinning around with my arms held out to the blue sky. "And perhaps the only way to know the *you* that exists beyond your fears.

"God is not the mist, nor light or love. God is the *way* we love!

"It is not even correct to say that God created your universe because creation and creator can never be divided; the whole cannot exist without the sum of its parts. Because you're limited in awareness by concepts of your individuality, you struggle to contain God within these restrictions. You want God to be responsible, not only for the creation of your world, but for everything that takes place within it as well. You want It to be definable as love and light or to be feared as someone looking in the bedroom window, but It is none of this. It is the unity out of which all diversity has come, but It is not the diversity itself.

"God is a great mystery which can only exist as the unknown. Step outside of your rationality! Learn to interact with It as a *sacred mystery*, using breath and intention to guide you into Its' reality of light and love. Then vision of the sacred can begin."

All were silent. Either what I said had touched them in some special way, or they didn't understand a word of it and resigned themselves that I was just the next hippie to flip out along the hashish trail. I sat down with my back against the tree, closed my eyes, and relaxed into the peace of my own inner world.

When I opened my eyes again, it was already afternoon and the sun was beginning to cast long shadows on the fields below. I felt the presence of someone next to me. Thinking it was Richard, I turned to say, 'no more questions', and saw the face of an old *sadhu*, a Hindu holy man, dressed in simple white cloth, carrying a walking stick and a brass begging bowl with a thick wool blanket draped over one shoulder. His long gray hair was tied in a bun on top of his head and his forehead was streaked with bright orange paint.

"*Om namo narayana*," he greeted me, bowing his head slightly in my direction.

"Om" I replied respectfully. Thinking that he might be able to understand me, I started to say something but he put his finger to his lips indicating that I should be silent. He then motioned to a woman and a young girl standing some distance away and they approached and stood next to him.

"This is Shiva Baba from India and he would like to talk with you. May he?" asked the woman speaking elegant English.

Without saying a thing, I bowed in his direction and he began talking slowly in his own language.

"You have been blessed with the vision of *Shiva*," she translated for him. "*Shakti* (spirit energy) has awakened in you to transform you into a being of light. That will be a quest in itself.

"I'm not the one who can teach you of her ways," he went on. "You will need one who has known her as you have.

"She is the force that animates all life; that out of which *will* arises. When she calls, surrender in reply to her bidding. Let not fear or disbelief block the door to immortality.

"She is all and everywhere, and will lead you on a journey through her web of mystery and delight you in her ways of bliss. In those times when doubt draws near and fear knocks upon the doors of your heart, remember: You will never be where breath is not. Let it guide you in the quest to know your eternal self."

CHAPTER 11

RETURN TO INDIA

I walked back to town around noon the following day, having spent the night with Shiva Baba, wrapped in a borrowed blanket beneath the same tree. By now, much of the euphoric rush of energy had dissipated and the first callings of hunger and sleep guided me slowly along the path. The overwhelming feeling of love and unity still dominated my consciousness but, rather than grab people passing by and shout, 'I love you', my heart reached out in a silent OM. I was eternally united to the All. That certainty would never again leave me.

The next two weeks passed in a fog of not caring, spending most of the time sitting on my mat absorbed in my private vision of totality. At any moment a rush of energy would fill me with light and transport me to other time-space dimensions beyond body and mind. The material world had lost its stability. Life was a dance being acted out upon the stage of cosmic mind and I was observer and participant at the same time.

The strangest of all occurrences was the inconsistency of time. The past and the future both bombarded my flowering imagination with images of what had been and what would be, causing monumental confusion in my present-time awareness. I would go into the streets and live the same images I had experienced an hour or day ago in inner vision sitting on my bed. The cosmic joke of it all would cause me to break into fits of laughter and cry out in the streets about God and love and oneness. There was no fixed time reference I could hold on to. Past and future were both somehow contained in the present and no longer confined themselves to linear, sequential unfolding but warped and distorted into a hodgepodge of unrelated events.

It became a great effort to think in a rational way and relate to physical realities. I ate little, preferring fruit, peanuts, and yogurt to anything cooked, and ventured out into the sensual bombardment of the teeming city only to visit certain temples to pray and give thanks for the feeling of oneness.

Leo, Richard, and Leslie remained close but they all made it clear that I had flipped-out and it would be impossible for me to survive out here in this condition. One of them had recovered my passport and fifty dollars of the money from the mad scramble in the street caused by my euphoric generosity but they refused to return these to me until I could 'get it together'. Leo, overcome by some brotherly responsibility, offered to take me back to Europe in a month.

"No thanks, man," I said one morning while we were hanging out around the room. "Everything considered, I'll take my chances out here. Death seems to be the only thing certain about life. I can't see living trying to avoid it."

"Shit, man, if you go tossing your money around and yelling about being the Christ, you'll be 'John Browned' right out of here!" he shouted back, having had enough with me. "Do you remember that crazy freak? Would you like to end up like him? Well you're not far from it right now!"

A month or even a week ago, that threat would have caused instant panic but now I just laughed back at him. I now believed that John Brown had been right — *we came here to be united in love and we're living a reality of hate and separation.* But my laughter was a private joke. No one else was experiencing it.

"You know, you're really insane, man! I've seen you light up, like some fire is consuming you from within. And you get this blissed-out look on your face, your body shakes as if getting ready to explode, and you go off somewhere else," he emphasized, twirling his hand about in the air. "And this question and answer stuff's interesting but it's racing your motor beyond your limits. Don't crash, Tom!"

That night, I overheard the three of them saying that a straight-looking man had been in the restaurant asking about the American who had thrown his passport away and was wandering around town totally spaced-out.

"As soon as his money runs out, they will be here repatriate him and that will be the end of it," said Richard in a disheartened way. "He's not crazy you know, Leo," he went on, "just not able to relate to the world around him.

"In the good old USA they would give him drugs and electric shock to blast him out of it."

"I offered to take him to Europe with me," replied Leo, "but he said he'd rather die in the street than go back. And I'm afraid that's exactly what will happen if he stays out here."

I lay there pretending to be asleep, listening to them write me off as just another spaced-out freak. My warrior spirit rose up in determination to avoid both repatriation and the nut house. The image of Shiva Baba and how he lived with almost nothing, perusing only his contact with God, gave me courage to believe that survival depended on something more than money.

I woke up the next morning having made my decision to return to India and take my fate as it might unfold. I sold my backpack and sleeping bag the same day and bought a simple shoulder bag and a thin wool blanket. That night I announced to my friends that tomorrow I was off to India.

"Tom, you can't make it out there," they counseled. "You've lost it. Why don't you let them ship you home and get some help?"

"That kind of help I don't need. They'll just try to make me forget all *this*," I said emphatically, waving my arms about me, (not that they could relate to what *this* was).

"What are you going to do there, Tom?" asked Richard, as if he was quizzing me.

"I don't know," I replied. "Something's happening to me, which you have helped me to see as a mystical awakening. I don't ever want to forget this feeling of oneness. We are God, Richard!"

"You may well be right," he replied. "I used to see people in the hospitals flipped-out, but not violent, and wondered to myself what would happen if they were told to go out in the world and live it the way they see it."

"Richard, the only path for me at this moment is the quest to know my eternal self. If you're really concerned for me, help me get out of the city," I half pleaded. "Give me back my passport and money and let me try it. John Brown never had a chance to live his version of reality. Either did Bridget. I want to try. I can't go back now."

An arrow of compassion pierced their hearts in that moment and they agreed, saying, "It's your life after all. I guess I wouldn't want my father to stop me from doing what I wanted to do," added Leo, "but I don't see that you have much chance to avoid repatriation in the end."

"We'll see."

I climbed into an ancient truck before dawn the next morning and hid myself among the cargo while my friends paid $25 to the driver to sneak me past the checkpoint and take me back over the mystical Himalayas to the Indian border. I crossed the border the next morning and began walking toward Varanarse and the Dancing Shiva shrine, secretly hoping that the world would never return to its former coherency. The kaleidoscope reality that danced before my perception changed the world of time and form into one fluid expression that held neither consistency nor meaning for me anymore. All people still glowed with the luminescence of the life force, which formed an etheric radiance about their bodies, causing emotions of unity and bliss to swell up within me. I loved everybody and they, in turn, blessed me and welcomed me in every way to wander as a pilgrim in their land and take food and shelter in their temples at night.

I wandered aimlessly along tree-lined roads teeming with multitudes, through village after village of crowded markets ablaze with color and soaked in the blare of transistor radios, and through over-cultivated fields ringed with muddy irrigation ditches. I forgot that life was supposed to have a purpose and that I was supposed to care about anything. Was existence really dependent on effort?

My blissful reality made it hard for me to communicate with the many people who stopped me each day to ask me why I was in India wandering like one of their holy men. Since my last flip-out at the Monkey Temple, I had been constantly repeating to myself and aloud the sacred sound OM. Since no one in India shook hands but joined their hands together with a slight bow saying *Namaste,* (your soul and my soul are one) I began to bow and answer OM to all questions. Any references to my beliefs about God were answered with OM while placing my hands together over my heart. To some people this indicated that I was a mystic — to others I was insane — but it served the purpose of avoiding long verbal exchanges. Only when I felt a sincere connection with the person asking the question would I go into any detail about what was happening to me; not that I really knew what was happening.

I arrived in Varanarse several weeks later, having gone *native.* Along the way I had traded my jeans and shirt for two pieces of white cotton cloth which I wrapped about me Shiva Baba fashion, and was walking barefoot, having had my sandals stolen the first night out. I had noticed how Shiva Baba's arrangements of cloth could serve as a wrap, or *lungi* in the day, a light cover for sleeping at night, and could be wrapped about the head for protection from the sun. In addition to being cooler, the light wrap was easier to wash in the river and dried in minutes in the hot sun. Since everyone bathed and washed their clothing everyday, I felt more in harmony with the ways of the people, as well as lighter and cleaner. I decided to forget about another pair of sandals, not wanting to be molested by someone trying to steal them again. Except for the money I had left and my passport, which hung under my left arm in a small pouch and somehow now represented my sanity and security, I had only the cloth I was wearing, my yellow Shiva scarf wrapped around my head, a notebook, the *Bhagavad Gita,* and my blanket carried over my shoulder.

Once in Varanarse, I walked to the small park on a hill overlooking the river to sleep. I awoke early and joined the many pre-dawn shadows squatting along the misty riverbank answering nature's call, then slipped off to the river as the last stars disappeared in the east. Stripping to my underwear and saying a fervent prayer of gratitude, I plunged into the waters of the sacred Ganges, dead bodies and all.

I felt as if I had returned. After sitting for a long time absorbed in observation of thought and reading the *Gita,* I made my way to the Shiva temple where I had had my first encounter with God. I stood transfixed looking at the Shiva idol engaged in his cosmic dance. Great waves of joy overcame me as I heard from within, *Your training has now begun. Be faithful to your vision.*

I roamed about that day watching the chaotic activity of the 'city of Shiva', the holiest of cities in India, with millions of pilgrims bathing daily in the Ganges River and worshipping at thousands of temples and shrines. The streets were lined with beggars wrought with every imaginable human affliction, some being little more than a torso with a head crawling in a contorted fashion from one place to another.

In addition to the beggars, there were thousands of *sadhus*, who also lived off of the generosity of the pilgrims but did not sit in the street soliciting handouts. They sat around fires in the parks or along the river in small groups reading holy books or practicing meditations and chanting. Pilgrims would stop for advice on spiritual or worldly matters. They were the counselors, advisers, and shrinks of Indian society, performing a valuable service for the multitude and receiving gratitude and small contributions of food and money in return.

Early the following morning, after sleeping in the same park overlooking the river, I was having tea and observing the beggars lining both sides of the street, waiting for pilgrims to return from their bath. As one approached, they would all thrust the most grotesque part of their human anatomy into the air and contort their face as if suffering, displaying a certain professionalism.

An impulse to see the world from their perspective sent me out of the tea stall and behind the line until I found a place near the end where the throngs had thinned out. I sat down on my blanket. Front row seats being hard to get at that hour, I had to settle for a few rows back, but I still had a good view and I settled down to wait. At first, the people in front closed ranks thinking that I was going to move in on their territory. But when they saw I was willing to hang back they began to talk to me and slowly we became friends.

They seemed to be together in a group of five or six, all dressed in discolored rags, some of who had serious deformations and others intact. They appeared to be pooling rice but guarding any small coins they received for themselves. I placed my yellow scarf down in front of me, as I had observed the procedure to be, and began to gather rice and coins myself.

They explained that the rice was for a communal kitchen they belonged to where each would give a handful and a few coins to receive a meal in the evening. For their noon meal, they would beg from one of the restaurants or go to whichever temple was serving a cooked meal that day and wait in line with thousands of others for a plateful of rice and lentils.

They liked me, so I settled in to watch the dazzling crowds flow by. The feeling was certainly humbling, as a parade of feet and clean white cloth passed by tossing rice and coins to the miserable specimens of humanity sitting in the gutter at their mercy. I felt as if I was participating in some ancient ritual whose purpose and meaning had long been obscured and whose participants, on both sides, had forgotten the essential ingredients of love and gratitude.

After a while I caught on to how to look miserable, eye contact and facial expression being as essential to success here as in any other business. I waved my arms about from the back row and made some sound to attract the attention of the passers-by. Any rice or coins that landed on your cloth were yours and any that landed on the ground belonged to whoever was the fastest, those with hands and arms having a distinct advantage. No one took anything from the cloth of another, as if by sacred code. It was not physically hard work but perhaps the most psychologically demanding thing I have ever done.

About an hour later, a legless beggar came pushing himself along the line on an improvised skateboard and stopped in front of my crew, talking to them in the vernacular of the street while eyeing me with noticeable surprise. My friends pooled some coins and bought some ganja, mild marijuana, from this rolling dealer who continued down the line peddling his wares. In Varanarse, the city of Lord Shiva, alcohol was illegal but anything that would expand the mind was sacred and acceptable. When the crowds thinned out, they took a break and smoked it in a clay *chillum* right there in the street. Their mood picked up as they sang a few chants to attract attention and pass the time.

I cleared my throat and spit out a big hunker behind me, as my mouth had become dry from the dust and heat. This provoked one of the beggars to jab me with the stub of his half-arm, making it clear with animated gestures, to, *spit out there where they walk, not back here where we sleep*. Their world, too, had rules which only one who lived (and died) in the street could comprehend.

A bit of a commotion began over my breach of etiquette, which ended when a women came directly to me — not common in the impersonal parade of rice-tossers — and handed me a coin saying something to the effect that I was a good omen for her today.

At this, my new friends huddled together and mumbled over a new strategy. I was convinced that I was on the verge of being thrown out of the game for un-sportsman-like conduct. After some discussion however, they decided, if I were willing to share my rice and coins with them, they would put me out in front to see if I could attract greater attention. A front-row seat sounded like a great idea, so I quickly moved my blanket forward to the front line, wrapped my white cloth around me and closed my eyes to meditate.

CHAPTER 12

WORLD OF ALL KNOWING

I had been having so many rushes of energy over the last three weeks that to close my eyes and bliss out for hours was quite normal. The first five minutes passed with me being aware only of the ruckus my assistants were making to draw attention to my presence and the grains of rice falling on my head in the hot sun.

Then *Shakti*, in her playful way, chose that moment to send a bolt of energy through my body, stiffening my spine and filling my every cell with bliss and radiance. I lost awareness of my physical surroundings and let go unto a field of energy obscuring all personal identity. I drifted through realms of light and peace until I felt sucked into a powerful energy grid. An unseen presence stopped me and examined certain aspects of myself that even I was not aware of — intention, ancient past, energy systems within my luminous sphere, and connections to other universal patterns of wisdom and guidance.

I felt as if I was in a cosmic struggle with forces outside myself who had found me in their private world and were deciding what to do with me. There was no fear or aggression, just a sense of indecision.

In a flash, something released and I found myself in a world of total clarity. I was there not as body or mind, but an expanded aspect of awareness itself. There was only one sensation: being the experience out of which all knowing arises.

As a boy in grade school, I dreamed in the back of the classroom of a place where everything was known. If I could just get there I could skip all this memorizing of facts to get grades. And here I was! It did exist!

The ecstasy of it all overwhelmed me as I experienced knowing, not as a capacity of mind or memory, but an attunement of awareness. One does not have to know things or information but only feel the origin of concepts and creative principles. It is a matter of sensitivity and receptivity, more intuitive than rational.

Then I became acutely aware that I was not alone, though I could see no one else. Through an extreme effort of will, I formulated the thought, *Why can't all people know this realm? It would all be so much easier.*

"*This is why,*" came a thought-like voice from all around me. "*Watch!*"

The subtle emanations of the golden fog that appeared to define this world began to activate along lines of force until a mathematical equation appeared before me. I knew from this new place of certainty that it was a form of energy more powerful than the destructive atomic force now in use on the planet. My question had been answered: *We are not ready.* I felt great relief that no one could get here.

I thought again, *Why am I here? Why me?*

"*Your intentions have been sufficiently aligned with love. Masters beyond your awareness are transforming your consciousness through this experience,*" came the unseen voice.

After a time, I realized that *all-knowingness* is not information about many things but one thing, one source, one experience. An immense gratitude settled over me and I asked in sincere humility, "Who are you, my unseen guide?"

"*I am the part of you that is never separated from this place,*" came the reply.

"*Who you are becomes relative as you explore these realms. Not even I know why you have been allowed this perception. Your reaction to it will someday determine its value and meaning.*

"*Come, let's take a moment to absorb the vibrations of this place together before they call you back,*" continued my guide.

Our journey consisted not in moving through this new world but in aligning our personal frequencies with distinct currents of movement that presented themselves as ripples upon the etheric sea of consciousness. As movement passed by, we aligned with it by allowing our vibrations to be absorbed in its flow until wisdom made itself known within our awareness. It was a passive, receptive act of receiving, not seeking — a level of awareness more subtle than feeling.

At one point in our mystical voyage, we became attuned to concepts about fields of force and electromagnetic consistency generated through rapid fluctuations of polarity. As I integrated this normally incomprehensible concept, new formulas of negative gravity fields and the technological and social ramifications of such technology made themselves known to me. I saw devices, some small enough to be held in the hand, capable of neutralizing the effects of gravity by generating an opposing field, as well as various ways to move objects within these new fields.

"Why doesn't someone discover this and change the world?" I asked, stunned by the clarity and simplicity of it all.

"Just as we are now receiving knowingness through alignment, the process of tapping into this storehouse of wisdom from outside is similar. One's imagination, always guarded closely by one's beliefs, must create an affinity with the concepts contained here before attunement and understanding can result.

"The mind must first conceive of flow, not thrust, as the essential movement of the universe and the use of natural forces of attraction and repulsion before concepts and principles of such advanced technology can be realized," my guide informed me.

"The idea of using a force to overcome natural conditions of creation is where the present civilization has become confused. Alternative technologies developed around the principles of flow first require understanding the energy fields created by relationships between different patterns of movement interacting with one another. The development of technologies using combinations and interactions of fields of force existing naturally within the universe is safer, more efficient, and infinitely less destructive to the environment.

"A sense of reverence and respect for the Mother Earth would be the first atti-tude essential for any scientist seeking to align with such advanced ideas. The self-importance of scientists causes them to create their own limitations in the form of laws they discover *or theories they devise to try explain creation in some rational way. These laws become cages of their own conceptual learning process. They think they discover or own truth and become blinded by their own desperate attempts to see things the way they believe them to be.* **Reality can always be made to conform to one's beliefs because thought and form are one and the same thing in different stages of manifestation.**

"There are no limitations. The speed of light is infinite and space never ends!"

I was struck by the powerful sensation that mysticism and science share a common origin. But since science does not seek knowledge through vision, it does not *feel* that which it is observing. To explore in order to dominate does not always advance the harmonious co-existence of the whole and may not be an efficient attitude in terms of energy expended or use of natural resources.

"That is part of the truth," commented my guide, knowing my every thought. *"The scientist accepts the atom and its complex composition as the basis of life while the mystic sees movement as the essence of all life. Vision arises out of inten-tion, which is a complex combination of personal and cosmic alignments. One cannot penetrate the world of all-knowing through concentration and determina-tion alone. Certain preliminary synchronizations of human feeling and intention must align with universal harmony and unity. Every movement of life is taking place within a process of creating perfection out of cooperation and co-existence.*

"Do you remember what happened when you passed the threshold into this world?" my guide asked.

"You were screened by *The Preceptor*," he continued at my silence. "*That Preceptor is not human intelligence but universal sensitivity. What is screened are the electro-magnetic frequencies created by your intentions, and these are compared to your past, your future, and your alignment to human potential and evolution in general.*

"*Humanity can deceive through words because they belong to their domain. But human intentions have been obscured by desire and remain largely outside of their awareness, even in most attitudes of prayer.*"

"Now that I have been here, will I always be able to return?" I asked, humbled by the potential of the place.

"*To know of its existence will influence your destiny. The extent of your free access, however, depends on the coordination of your will and intention as focused through dedication to the principles of human unity.*

"*You have created certain affinities by your presence here. The part they will play in your life depends on you, not The Preceptor*".

"Then what is the purpose of it all?"

"*That is your choice.*"

CHAPTER 13

OM BABA

Of all the way-out, mystical voyages I had had up until then, none was to have such a lasting effect on my life as my trip to the 'world-of-all-knowing'. Once having experienced its existence, I would forever look for ways to incorporate its potential into my life, aligning my intentions with the proper use of this wisdom. This was the first real parallel reality to hold any form or consistency for me and, unlike my other mystical bliss-outs, it contained a thread of meaning that tantalized my entire inner being. Until that moment, bliss and euphoria were discordant themes being played out on a chaotic backdrop of confused perception and misunderstanding. But now, the hippie paradigm of other dimensions of reality was taking on meaning and substance beyond just another trip. My imagination was usurping the throne of the rational mind as the ruler of my life and destiny.

The clarity of this reality quickly dissolved into emanations of light and sound and once again I felt the density of my physical body surrounding me. Regaining awareness of my breathing and becoming aware of the sounds and smells of the street, I opened my eyes to find a crowd of people staring at me. I was covered in a mound of rice, coins, and flowers, which tumbled down from my head and overflowed into the street as I began to move. People came and touched their heads to my feet, while others looked on in bewilderment. I must have glowed again.

Quickly my associates began to gather our hoard and prepared to leave the street saying, "We have more than enough for today and for us, today is all that matters."

Still dazed from the transcendent voyage, I sat motionless, beginning to feel the excruciating pain in my knees from sitting cross-legged for too long.

My friends finished collecting the rice and coins, tying my share in my cloth, and insisted that I go with them. As usual, I didn't care where I went, so, with difficulty, I stood up and followed them through the crowd to a back alley that was obviously their home. They motioned for me to take a seat on the curbside saying I could live here in the gutter with them. I sat staring off into space while my friends circulated among the few old people no longer able to beg in the streets who lay about on rags in the shade of a giant tree. I could tell by the way they propped themselves up on one arm and looked in my direction that my friends were relating the recent miracle of rice and coins.

Time passed there in another corner of Wonderland with me spacing-out on my latest hallucination. It was a narrow cul-de-sac off of the main street with no shops or doorways. The street people had obviously established camp here many years ago, perhaps generations, judging by the makeshift shelters, piles of rags, and open-air kitchen tucked into the far corner. As I was to find out later when the full tribe of beggars and street people returned from their *work*, every inch of space was the property of a tribal member, relinquished only at death or ostracism for stealing from the clan. No one had the right to sit or sleep just anywhere and all members strictly adhered to this unwritten protocol.

This was the world of the untouchables and lepers, the outcasts of society forced into a bleak existence at the mercy of humanity. Yet in their own sub-culture, their relationship to the rest of humanity was not as important as the daily struggle to beg the rice it would take to survive that day.

My presence required a council that evening, the result of which awarded me a spot to sleep alongside my friends and the rights to a meal from the kitchen, if I contributed my two handfuls of rice and three small coins. As the word spread among them about the about the hoard of rice and coins we had gathered that day in such a short time, I was given a special place of honor among them, as if I had brought good luck to the entire tribe. They produced a battered tin pie plate, scrubbed shiny clean with river sand, and presented it to me with great ceremony. Women insisted that I touch their babies in a form of blessing and they, in turn, touched their foreheads to my bare feet, hoping, I imagined, that good luck would rub off and stick to them. The holy men among them — for each street tribe had their own priests and *sadhus* — questioned me at length about my relationship with God. Understanding almost nothing, I just made my little bow with hands joined, uttering OM to answer all questions and to give all blessings that were asked of me.

They began to call me OM Baba and, from that point, my identity as Tom slipped further into oblivion and I was reborn as OM Baba.

The tribe seemed to be made up of maimed beggars, young thieves (in posses-sion of all their arms and legs and capable of running when trouble began), and women who traded off babies and roamed the streets all day looking for handouts. Waiting seemed to be a way of life for them. The younger children played a form of hopscotch while the thieves hung around under a tree and smoked cigarettes and the disabled beggars, who were the majority, sat in a row and chanted together, using their plates and cups as musical instruments.

Once I adjusted to the horrifying poverty and the presence of every form of human affliction and deformity, I began to realize that they were neither sad nor suffering. Religion and its cast system helped them to accept their situation. Rotting away with leprosy, blind or lame, in rags and without shoes, they were living. They had, among themselves, their own healers, dentist, psychiatrists, and priests. Their fascinating sub-culture functioned on a system of barter and favors that was an organic outgrowth of the conditions they lived in.

As the days unfolded, it appeared that my friends had some rights over me. They took me along with them in the morning to the begging lines, as if I were an asset they were guarding from the others. I was always given a front-row seat and, while nothing so spectacular as the first day reoccurred, we always gathered a mound of rice and coins faster than other beggars, and everyone seemed content.

I spent two weeks living among my newfound family, sharing the morning ritual of begging in the street and the evening meal under the big tree. One morning, I was jolted to attention by a loud cry of "*Bum bum boli*! Man man standing up! Me Mataji tea taking! You man coming!"

It was Mataji, who yanked me to my feet with surprising strength, stared down the others when they tried to protest, and hustled me off to the tea stand where our friendship was instantly renewed. She insisted that I was not to sit in the street with those people. I was, she said, a *sadhu*, not a beggar and if I wanted to live in India, I had to take my proper place in society.

"You man, man, Shiva knowing. No street sitting! All mans no beggars," she emphasized, obviously having heard through the grapevine what had happened the other day.

I told her I had been experiencing intense cramps from the chronic dysentery that had become part of my life and she gave me some of her black mixture to take away the discomfort. She told me that John was still in town and had a houseboat moored a ways up river. She mentioned a guru and many other things I only partially understood, concluding with, "You man houseboat going. Me Mataji coming.

"Man man," she went on in the soft way she used when requesting something, "Mataji one rupee giving?" she asked, grinning through missing teeth, true to her old self.

I passed her the money, the first I had used in many days, and paid for the tea, agreeing to meet her at the houseboat in the evening. I walked in the direction of the houseboat, weaving my way through an unfamiliar maze of narrow alleyways, until I came to the riverbank and located the boat. John was out so

I climbed a steep hill overlooking the river and sat under a tree near a small temple to wait.

I must have daydreamed because a short time later I was aroused by the ruckus of an angry pilgrim screaming at a monkey in the tree, jumping from limb to limb with a leather sandal in his hand. A priest of the temple intervened, explaining something to the man who, in obvious frustration, walked over to a nearby vendor and bought a banana. Returning, he placed it on a high branch and moved to the temple to wait. The monkey cautiously swung down, grabbed the banana and tossed the sandal in the direction of the man. The same drama repeated itself several times with other unsuspecting worshippers who were obliged to remove their shoes before entering the temple, until the ingenious monkey had finished his breakfast and moved on to other adventures for the day. Not only the human beggars of this town had become resourceful.

With still no sign of John by noon, I bought some bananas and peanuts from the same vendor and returned to the tree to read, write, and wait. Eventually John returned with an old man he introduced as Ganesh Baba, his guru. John opened the louvered windows inside the cabin to allow the afternoon breeze to chase away the stale heat of the day while the old Baba and I arranged ourselves sitting cross-legged on grass mats. John lit a few sticks of incense and went to the back room to change his cloths.

Ganesh Baba was dressed in impeccable light saffron robes, typical of the holy men of India, and carried only a tiny bag hanging under one arm and a light woolen shawl draped over one shoulder. His long silky-white hair and beard were combed smooth and gave him an air of wisdom and serenity. His sparkling gray eyes glinted with humor and lightness. I guessed him to be in his early seventies but he moved with agility uncommon for a man of his age and when he began to talk, in perfect English, his voice resounded with strength and confidence.

Sitting ramrod straight, he told me that his guru had been Albert Einstein and that they had been together in Germany for many years. He went on for over an hour, as most professional gurus in India were capable of doing, about scientists being the real mystics and how Einstein had received his theories and insights into the nature of the universe from dreams and meditations. He talked of how Einstein had proven the illusionary nature of time and space, substantiating the ancient Hindu scriptures, and established the speed of light to be the limits of the universe.

"The speed of light is infinite and space never ends," I said, during one of his brief pauses to change his position. "It is not the limit of the universe but perhaps the limit of our present awareness or means of perception. The speed of light will one day be seen to vary in relationship to perception. And human perception is stabilized by the electromagnetic frequencies of the Earth."

"And who told you that?" he asked, his eyes widening and fixing his gaze intensely upon me.

"Vision," I answered.

"Ho! And who gave you such a vision, young man?" he replied, taking on even a greater air of importance and glancing at John, as if they had a secret together.

"No one gives a vision," I replied, feeling a new surge of inspiration. "It arises out of the synchronization, through intention, of one's personal vibrations with the emanations of other realities. It is not a thing to be given but an event or happening."

He looked at me for a long minute, contemplating what to say next before asking, "What then, my young fellow, is light?"

"The emanations of consciousness," I heard myself answering. "When consciousness becomes excited or activated, a movement takes place which is perceived as light.

"The speed of light, as we now know it, is only the limit of the material dimension. Each exclusive dimension of consciousness has its own speed of light. Human awareness has been conditioned, through repeated identification with only what its senses can perceive, to a limited spectrum of total reality. There is more."

I had perceived all this during my voyage to the 'world-of-all-knowing' and it had left me with a residue of realizations that poured out of me.

Ganesh Baba was reflecting on what I had said, repeatedly glancing at me and nervously raising his bushy white eyebrows, obviously contemplating something. Then shifting his position so as to bring his eyes closer and staring intensely, he said, "Tell me of your vision, my young mystic. My master once spoke of the possibility of light being something like a movement of energy, but the field that it was moving through eluded him."

I told him briefly of my experience the other day and of the apparent common origins of science and mysticism I had perceived. He questioned me about the sensations in my body before and after the experience, not showing much interest in what I had learned.

Breaking another short silence, I asked, "What is this energy that fills me up and transports my awareness to other dimensions? A friend told me that my body shakes and I radiate with golden light."

"That is the goddess *Kundalini*, she who opens the mystical gates to immortality," he answered, straightening his spine and half-closing his eyes, as if imitating someone in trance.

"I will teach you of her ways," he went on, putting vibrato in his voice. "I will take you as my disciple and train you. We will travel to your country where I will reveal this truth to many."

I asked Ganesh Baba to explain what he could about the *Kundalini* and why it happens but he went off on a tangent about how he would guide me and how only he could help me.

"You must have a guru to show you the way!" he insisted. "It could be dangerous."

Something about the tone in his voice and the expression on his face reminded me of the high school guidance counselor who had said I could never be a doctor and I instinctively became cautious. I politely thanked him for his offer explaining that I planned to travel around India before settling down in one place to study with one person.

"I know she has called me. But I must respond the way I feel from within my heart," I concluded just as the cry of Mataji echoed out from the riverbank.

The door flung open and she burst in, faded white tunic wrapped about her wiry, black-skinned body and a mass of dread locks coiled on top of her head. She and Ganesh Baba greeted each other with respectful disapproval as they exchanged words, which John later explained were the equivalent to humorous insults.

Mataji had always considered John to be her disciple and, in many ways, it was comparable to taking rice off of someone else's cloth to move in on her territory. In India at that time, gurus were many but Western disciples, who might take you to their country, were few and in great demand. The dream of most gurus was to be taken to the land where rich disciples walked the streets of gold.

A tension-filled hour passed with Mataji and Ganesh Baba vehemently discussing, in Hindi, many points of disagreement, one of them being who had the rights on John and myself as disciples. Finally, Ganesh Baba announced in English that he was leaving if she was going to be allowed to insult him in that way. Mataji stood up, opened the door and, bowing slightly, said, "Then leave."

Neither of them left but rather they went at it with greater ferocity than before. John and I went to the roof to watch the sunset and let them work it out.

"You sure are different, Tom. What's happened to you in the last three months?" he asked, after we'd spent some time in silence.

I gave a brief account of the various experiences that had transformed me, concluding with, "Now I'm floating around in a mystical fog most of the time, never knowing when the next 'bolt of *Shakti*' might strike me."

"Shit, man, I've been here over five years now and nothing like that has ever happened to me!" he emphasized with frustration. "You must've done something, some powerful drug or something. It can't just happen lifting a stick of incense!"

"I see it more as though I broke a habit that was blocking the flow of my potential. Like bursting a dam and letting the water flow. Maybe we all have some basic pattern inhibiting our greater expression. If, through some effort of will, we can choose to be different, a new vision will appear. There is so much more than just the mystical. I feel creative, intelligent, and alive."

We sat in silence for a long time watching the light-show of the gods in the western sky and listening to the cacophony of bells, conch shells, and chants echoing out over the siren waters of the holy river. I had grown to appreciate these moments of common joy and prayer, a pause in the flow of my mind and a reminder of the divine presence all about me.

After a short meditation, John told me that Jasper had gone off with Bhagavan Dass, an American *sadhu*, and the now legendary Dr. LSD, to see some guru in the north. Most of the others had gone with Eight-Fingered Eddy to sun their auras in Goa. He had met Ganesh Baba a month ago and felt he was the one who could teach him the secrets of yoga, although he had no intention of taking him back to Australia.

"He's a little glory-hungry," he said, "having spent most of his life in search of God and wisdom. Now he wants to be with people who are looking for what he has to teach and who will give him the respect he has earned.

"We all need a guru, Tom. It can't be done without one. That's what all the scriptures say."

"It's like crossing this river," I replied, pointing to the rippling waters of the Ganges, now shimmering with a soft pink glow. "You need a boat to get to the other side but once there, you have to get out and walk to wherever you want to go."

"In that case, I'd better go and attend to my two boats below before they sink each other," he said. "You can sleep here tonight if you want. They'll just steal whatever you have left sleeping in the street like that."

"Thanks John, but I have very little left," I replied pointing to my small bag and blanket. "When they steal that, I will either be free or destitute and it really doesn't matter much at this point which it is"

"That's great, Tom," he said, shaking his head. "Meet me at the tea stand in the morning. There's something I want to show you," he concluded with a look of seriousness in his eyes.

After tea in the morning, John led me to a small rise overlooking the morning carnival of tens of thousands of beggars enacting their ritual of destitution and suffering before the procession of pilgrims parading by. He searched the mob looking for someone while I became absorbed in the living movie before me. I had lived it, if for only for a few weeks, and knew that there was order and protocol among them and that this act of misery was, in some strange way, their livelihood.

"There he is!" called John, pointing to the line of beggars not far from where we were standing. "Let's get closer."

We slipped down the embankment and walked behind the begging line, coming to a stop behind a group of beggars sitting in the street.

"There," said John, motioning with his head in their direction. "Look at that one!"

At first I couldn't see what he was trying to show me among this typical group of disheveled beggars banging on their tin pots and pleading for rice and coins from the pilgrims passing by. Then I saw him sitting on a tattered burlap sack with matted, filthy hair, bleached from the sun, hanging down his back and torn rags, patched together and wrapped about his emaciated body. Flies swarmed around open sores on his arms and legs while he sat motionless, holding his plate in the air and staring like a zombie off into the distance. There were thousands of beggars in the same condition in the lines but he was different. He was a Westerner.

"He's been there for years, Mataji says. No one knows where he comes from and he doesn't talk or relate to this world at all," commented John, as I watched in amazement.

"Maybe he needs help," I replied, feeling brotherly concern rising within me. "Has any one tried to do anything for him?"

"Go ahead and try."

I made my way to where he was sitting and, requesting permission from the other beggars, squatted down next to him. Long fingernails sprouted from his bony fingers and his dirt-caked body was covered in oozing sores. A close look at his decaying, insect-ridden body and hollow, lifeless eyes made me sick in my stomach. I tried to talk to him but he never moved from his catatonic pose. No one home. I tried to grab his hand to get his attention, which caused him to growl like an animal and pull his arms tight against his body in contracted fright. His companions motioned for me not to touch him and made me understand that they were taking care of him. I left and walked in shock back to the tea stall with John.

"That crazy beggar freak is one of the possibilities out here," commented John while we sipped our tea. "He's living his private hell and God is taking care of him, also. Be careful!"

I was shocked. Even in my extreme condition of not caring, I could see the similarities to my situation. Even his tin plate was exactly like mine. Compared to that, repatriation was a better choice, but I wasn't going to give up my vision. What was my next move?

I closed my eyes and prayed for guidance. *Go to the river,* I heard from within. *A boat awaits to take you to the other side. You will be leaving the city now.*

I was the last of fifteen passengers to hop onto the old wooden rowboat shuttling people across the river. While watching the sun reflecting off the towers and domes of the many temples lining the river and listening to the bells and conches echoing across the river in praise of God, I scooped a handful of water from the center of the river. Holding it to the sky, I shouted out *"Shivaji qui ja."* I was off, once again, into the unknown but I did not feel alone.

PART THREE

THE TRAINING

WHEN THE STUDENT IS READY
THE TEACHER WILL APPEAR

CHAPTER 14

HARDWAR

During the next three months, I traveled throughout India as a wandering pilgrim telling anyone who inquired I was a white Indian from the hippie tribe of the United States of America here in search of greater communion with God. I walked along the roads crowded with people, animals, and oxcarts, observing the people of this great land in their daily routines of tilling the soil and attending their lean animals. I was no longer accosted by hoards of raucous children because my presence was now that of OM Baba, a *sadhu*, not a tourist. Everywhere I was offered meals in humble huts or shared what people had to eat right in the fields by the side of the road.

The parched, clay-like soil had been plowed and sowed for so many thousands of years without a rest that its responses to the demands upon it were meager, at best, sometimes hardly making the effort worthwhile. But the bottom line was survival, not production, and most people, having never heard of the *miracle* of chemical fertilizers, remained grateful, celebrating their small returns as gifts from the gods.

The children constantly amazed me with their ingenuity in inventing games with sticks and stones, that would require a $50 bat and ball for a kid from the US. They combined play and exploration with herding the goats, cows, and water buffalos, carefully collecting every drop of excrement in baskets to be mixed with straw and dried in the sun to make fuel for the cooking fire. I felt a little ashamed of bargaining with my father over how much he would pay me for cutting the lawn on the weekend after seeing the contribution and coopera-tion of Indian children.

The competitive values of the American way of life seemed unproductive and inefficient compared to the interaction and co-existence of the people of this *underdeveloped* country. In this nation of over five hundred million people, with no unemployment insurance, social security, or welfare assistance, there appeared to be a coordinated functioning of the whole, which depended more on looking after each other rather than keeping up with or getting ahead of one another. I realized that these *safety nets* of government assistance and selfish attitudes in general really retarded natural creativity, ingenuity, and human caring.

There was the overwhelming feeling of being welcomed by the people and honored in their simple dwellings. Religion seemed to be the central pulse of their lives, giving them a code of ethics by which to live, as well as organizing the social structure of their homes and villages. I asked many questions about their religious customs and beliefs and slowly began to understand that Hinduism is a complex pantheon represented by the many personalized aspects of the one God Brahma. Brahma also had Its' own variety of philosophic and metaphysical interpretations, giving rise to different schools of thought and seemingly infinite forms of worship.

The people often asked about my purpose for seeking God in India. An insignificant question seven months ago when I set out for India, it now put me through some real soul-searching. Meaning, purpose and motivation had become blurred concepts of my past. The flows of ecstasy and wisdom from my inner world now tantalized my imagination and intuition and this new dimension had become fertile ground for my exploration of meaning and purpose. Life had again become a supreme mystery, as it must have been when I was a child in the crib watching the patterns of light appear and disappear before my developing rationality. I felt like that at times now as I peered through the etheric veil into other dimensions of reality.

Some afternoons were spent rocking back and forth atop an overloaded truck seeing India as few Westerners ever dared. These mechanical beasts of burden, decorated with bright paintings of religious figures playing in splendid gardens and alongside of cascading waterfalls, were christened with titles such as 'Rama's Revenge', 'Chariot of Krishna', or 'Shiva on Wheels'. Each was staffed with a driver, a mechanic, and the owner, usually a bearded Sikh under a great turban riding along to insure his investment and take care of business at both ends.

They lumbered down the narrow roads at a top speed of forty miles an hour, living in outdoor truck stops and making all repairs on the side of the road with a few wrenches, some wire, and a big hammer. Universal joints were wired back together, bearings and axles changed, injectors repaired by making parts out of old inner tubes, and tire casings riveted together with leather patches and filled with air from an old bicycle pump. I was more awed by these mechanical miracles of ingenuity than by the man lying on the bed of nails or the cobra coming out of the basket.

After two months, I caught a truck heading toward Goa and decided to see

Eight Fingered Eddy and his phantom disco of enlightenment at its winter stop-over. The scene at Eddy's was intense, with thirty spirit-struck hippies gathered in a small adobe house, dancing, singing, and playing music as if all the answers to life had come together in the phrase: 'Let it be'. Guru-mania was spreading like a fire in dry grass as the Beatles, Mick Jagger, and other prophets of the rock age were declaring meditation to be the 'ultimate turn-on'. Most people held secret hopes of soon meeting the mystical magician who would instantly enlighten them with just a touch on the head. Wild tales of the Beatles in Bombay, Maharishi and his new airplane, Mick Jagger on his way to India, and Mary Anne Faithful right there in Goa, were so distorted by the hippie telegraph that everyone expected John Lennon to walk through the door any minute.

I wandered the coconut groves and white sandy beaches of this paradise until the restless impulse to search urged me onward. Many people, both in Goa and along the road, had talked of a great spiritual celebration taking place in the north, saying that many great saints would be coming down out of the mountains. I thought I might be able to find one who could guide me.

Traveling truck-express, I arrived in Hardwar in time for the last few days of the great festival of *Khumbhamela* and became enraptured in the energy of millions of worshippers bathing, chanting, and making offerings at the thousands of temples and shrines along the Ganges (closer here to its source in the foothills of the Himalayas). Hoards of beggars lined the streets enacting their ritual of destitution as an endless stream of pilgrims flowed by, shouting out praise to their gods while tossing them alms of rice and coins. The contagious devotion of the euphoric multitude carried me away in its tide. I poured holy water from the river over the idols and phallic *lingams* and chanted among clouds of sweet smoke and booming cries to all forms of God.

This rush of energy occasionally caused claustrophobic panic and drove me out of the epicenters of religious furor to the more peaceful banks on the far side of the river. There I would sit in quiet meditation and read my copy of the *Gita*. I now opened it at random several times a day for inspiration and guidance. Its teachings represented a simplified path to self-realization clothed in a symbolic conversation between Lord Krishna and the warrior Arjuna. It advised a path of devotion and renunciation to attain liberation from the illusionary quality of the material world. It helped me assimilate what I was so intensely experiencing.

> The man who sees Brahman abides in Brahman: his reason is steady, gone is his delusion. When pleasure comes he is not shaken, and when pain comes he trembles not.
>
> He is not bound by things without, and within he finds inner gladness. His soul is one in Brahman and he attains everlasting joy" (*Gita* 5:20, 21)

I was also finding my first guidance on the mysterious process of meditation, of great interest to me in that moment.

> "Day after day, let the yogi practice the harmony of the soul: in a secret place, in deep solitude, master of his mind, hoping for nothing, desiring nothing.
>
> With upright body, head and neck, which rest still and move not: with inner gaze which is not restless, but rests still between the eyebrows:
>
> With soul in peace and all fear gone and strong in the vow of holiness, let him rest with mind in harmony, his soul on me, his God supreme.
>
> And whenever the mind unsteady and restless strays away from the spirit, let him ever and forever lead it again to the spirit."
> (*Gita* 6:10, 13, 14, & 26)

I met many holy men from all over India during these festival days. Some invited me to sit with them by their fires and join in their evening prayers. Not given to many words, they asked few questions and appeared to live day-to-day, following some form of discipline, or what they referred to as their yoga. All, regardless of sect or form of worship, followed renunciation of all worldly possessions to some degree. I was making a strained entrance into this guarded subculture.

I began to experience, in the presence of these men, something strangely familiar in their way of life. At times, when we would chant mantras or prayers around the fire at night, I seemed to know the words and rhythms as if I had lived it all before. At first I attributed this to their lifestyle — somewhat hippie — but after several nights of haunting familiarity, I began to suspect something deeper.

Within a few days, the crowds began to disperse but I still hadn't found my teacher from out of the mountains. I began to think we must have missed each other in this crowd of only a few million people. Each morning I would bathe in the chilly waters of the sacred Ganges, wash my white tunic and sit to meditate and read while it was drying. Many people would pass by and some would stop to ask questions and encourage me in my spiritual quest. Whenever I asked where to find a teacher, they would invariably repeat the ancient adage: When the student is ready, the guru will appear. Some would tell me of a famous yogi or swami living near-by and insist I should pay them a visit.

After fruit and tea I would tour the ashrams of Hardwar listening to these holy men. Each ashram had its *swami*, or great wise one, and they each praised the wisdom of their *secret* brand of yoga. Most required seekers to become initiated into their path and practice certain disciplines in their ashrams. They all assured me that they could guide me and that I should become a devotee of their yoga.

Sitting by the banks of the river one morning after an exhausting week of searching for a guru, I felt as if the hunter had become the hunted. Gurus outnumbered Western disciples a hundred to one. The Beatles had created 'disciple mania' by giving Maharishi an airplane, so every would-be teacher was hoping that he would be discovered next and whisked off to the land of rich disciples. My visa was about to expire and my only options were to find a guru who would arrange with the authorities for me to stay in his ashram or leave the country.

Part of me wanted to give up my search for someone to teach me and return to the West, but the thought of the Vietnam War or, even worse, nine-to-five in a jacket and tie brought strong resistance from within; yet years in an ashram twisting my body into contorted positions and chanting prayers in an unknown language began to appear as a poor alternative. I knew I wanted greater communion with this mysterious force within me, but how and where continued to elude me.

I wrestled with this chaos of my uncertainty until I couldn't stand it any longer. Jumping to my feet, I collected my clean clothes and made for the market to have breakfast. Feeling frustrated, I spaced out and passed the footbridge and continued up river to an unfamiliar bathing place. When I realized my error, I turned to retrace my path and found myself face-to-face with a young Indian boy who bowed, hands folded in respect, saying, "*Namaste*".

"*Namaste*," I replied, surprised by his presence.

"Please come. Babaji is waiting for you over there," he said in perfect English, pointing toward a tree a little ways off from the river.

I could see several *sadhus* sitting around a smoldering fire in the shade of a small tree. One was waving his arms indicating I should come. The boy, whose clothing suggested he was from a well-off family, insisted once again. Impulse directed me to follow him to where the *sadhus* were sitting.

"*Om Namo Narayana,*" they greeted me in the customary salute of the wandering *sadhu*.

"*Om Namo Narayana,*" I replied, as Shiva Baba had first taught me at the Monkey Temple.

Two of them were naked except for a loincloth, their bodies smeared in ashes, foreheads streaked with fresh colored paint, and dreadlocks down around their waists. The third *sadhu* was considerably older and was dressed in a white cotton cloth with long, neatly combed white hair falling past his shoulders. His skin was smooth and deeply tanned with a distinct shine to it. His eyes glowed with a glint of mischief, as if he was about to tell a big joke and didn't want to laugh before he got to the punch line.

"Please sit down," came the authoritative voice of the oldest, stroking his long white beard and pointing to an empty spot around the fire.

"I have been waiting two weeks almost for you." he went on in unpracticed English as I was laying out my blanket and taking my seat.

He appeared to be at least seventy and sat cross-legged on a thin wool blanket with his spine perfectly straight and his head held high. A certain dignity surrounded him as he talked to the others in Hindi. From his gestures, I gathered that he was telling them I had arrived at last.

"I saw you in my dream nine months ago and I knew you were coming," he said, turning to face me.

"Yeah, sure," I replied, thinking he was disciple hunting and would soon start in on how much he had to teach the people of my great country. Before long, he would have himself on a plane to America, at my expense.

"You live on an island. I saw water all around," he continued, as I looked around at the others who were taking great delight in him speaking English.

"No. I never lived on an island," I replied. "Guess again."

Showing little concern for my sarcastic reply, he went on, with his English improving considerably, to tell me that he had been waiting to take me to his ashram in the jungle, three days walk to the south. There I would learn the secrets of yoga from a real yogi.

He said that he had learned his English in the Indian Army as a corporal — a sergeant maybe, I thought. He was a bit different from other would-be gurus, with certain lightness about him that I liked. A bit of a showman, he began referring immediately to me as his *American disciple*, calling friends who were passing by to introduce me.

We drank tea together, prepared on the last embers of the morning's fire, as he told me more about his jungle ashram, switching between Hindi and English to keep his friends informed. He talked of being a friend of Maharishi Mahesh Yogi and denounced him for having an airplane, something he considered off-limits for a man of renunciation. This made me feel more comfortable about my bulging shoulder bag but left me with the strange sensation of being suspended between belief and disbelief about his jungle ashram.

I wasn't taking him too seriously, since he didn't look like he was going to walk three days through the jungle, but something about him wouldn't let me completely disregard what he was saying. If he did have an ashram in the jungle, something I was far from convinced of, it could turn out to be just what I was looking for to continue my inner quest. Everyone had told me that the real yogis were to be found deep in the jungles and mountains.

"We march at zero eight hundred hours sharp! Tomorrow. Here." he said, standing and putting on the tone of a practiced drill sergeant.

"I'll be here. Zero eight hundred sharp!" I replied, clicking my bare heels together and half-saluting, which raised a chuckle from his friends.

We'll see in the morning, I thought to myself while turning to leave.

"Remember where you were nine months ago. *Shakti* has called you," he said, using the same expression as Shiva Baba. "Your body must be prepared, now," he concluded, as our eyes met in a gentle embrace before parting.

CHAPTER 15

JUNGLE BABA

During a breakfast of mangos, yogurt, and tea, I retraced my life and reached the shocking realization that nine months ago I was on an island off the coast of Istanbul trying to decide whether to accompany Todd to India. I could vaguely remember a dream, or maybe it was wakening up from a dream, where I saw the figure of a man in white flowing robes hovering over the sea and smiling at me. He said nothing but I was left with the impression that we would meet someday.

I spent the rest of the day in a state of mental gymnastics, seesawing back and forth between wanting to go with him to the jungle and believing he was just another guru looking for a ticket to the United States. By late afternoon, I had decided that I would be there at eight in the morning. If he was ready to leave for the jungle, I would go with him. If he started to come up with excuses to delay our journey, I'd consider him a phony and be on my way, to where, I wasn't quite sure.

No one could have been more surprised than me when I arrived at his camp the next morning and he stood up, looked at his watch, and said, "Zero eight hundred sharp. We shall march."

We walked around town for the next three hours making offerings of flowers and Ganges water at various temples and taking a late morning meal at the home of one of his devotees. Everywhere I was introduced with a great air of importance as his American disciple, bestowing the utmost prestige upon him and making me feel I was being used. Just when I was beginning to think that we weren't going to get out of town that day, he stood up and announced: "Now we march for the river!"

Arriving at the riverbank sometime before noon, hot and tired from the long walk in the midday sun, we climbed into an ancient wooden boat as the last of thirty pilgrims preparing to cross. At the signal of the boatman, a scrawny donkey began to pull the boat up-river taking advantage of an eddy created by a large boulder. When we reached a certain spot where the main current was racing by close to the shore, the towline was released and we began to drift out into the raging river. The bow swung abruptly about as our overloaded craft took off down river among cheers and screams — of panic or delight I wasn't quite sure. The boatman put all his frail body into the great rudder at the stern, attempting to steer us towards the opposite bank.

The full force of the current hit us as we reached the middle of the river and water began to splash over the gunnels of the bobbing craft, causing my heart to sink. Just as I was sure that we all were going for a swim, people began to stand and toss flowers and rice into the turbulent waters, causing our fragile craft to rock and tip further toward disaster.

I looked around to see Babaji, who was perched proudly in the bow like an Admiral surveying his fleet, not showing the least bit of concern. My reaction was controlled as I released my bag from around my neck, freed my feet from under the person sitting next to me, and prepared to swim.

At that moment, the boatman leaned hard on the rudder, causing the boat to spin around in the raging current. A feeling of being suspended in time came over me once again as the sky above spun round, filled with flowers and grains of rice, accompanied by shouts of, *"Gungaji qui ja."* In a devotional furor that would not abate, the pilgrims were making their last offerings to the sacred river, assuming that God would get us safely to the other side.

Among greater shouts, mostly of panic this time, the boat shot out of the main current into the gentle backwaters of the opposite side and we drifted to the safety of the shore. My legs were shaking as I stepped onto solid ground and made my way to the shade of a nearby tree to recover my cool.

"Look, Babaji," I said, after rearranging my cloth, which had come untied from my waist in my frantic effort to disembark, "next time let's wait for another boat. We could've gotten ourselves killed in that overloaded antique out there."

"It's not that easy to get yourself killed," he remarked, unfazed by the experience. "A man of wisdom is aware when his time of death is near and meets it with a dignity. He doesn't waste energy worrying about what *might* happen," he went on in a tone of total seriousness.

"But look" I interjected, "we were both near death out there in that river. I'll bet you can't even swim!"

"No, I can't," he replied calmly, "and therefore I don't have to waste time thinking about how I'm going to save myself.

"There's no such thing as near death," he continued stroking his beard, and slowly formulating his words "You're either dead or alive. And if you're alive, your responsibility is to be aware of your aliveness all the time."

I calmed down, reflecting on the meaning of, 'to be aware of your aliveness'. I knew that he was right. What's more, I had known from some obscure place within me that I wasn't going to die in the icy waters of the Ganges that day. Why the panic?

"A man must be able to feel the pulse of his life," he continued, after sometime in silence, "and learn to live in accordance with certain positive expectations if he is to conserve energy and increase awareness of his divinity. Knowing you are divine is but the first step. Living that reality requires practice and determination."

"Babaji," I asked, after another time of reflection, "would you have gotten into that boat if you'd felt that the pulse of your life was in a certain relationship with death today?"

"That depends on the state of my personal energy at the moment," he replied, without hesitating. "There are times when the crossroads of uncertainty are met with force and determination in order to gain new momentum within the flow of life. And there are other moments when lack of personal strength and clarity require caution and respect for the conditions at hand. Someday you will perceive death as a choice, not an accident."

We walked the rest of the afternoon in the hot sun along a gravel road leading away from the river and through thick undergrowth. The sergeant, or Jungle Baba as he preferred to be called, was carrying only a bamboo walking stick, a light wool blanket, a small bag tucked under one arm and a brass pot and cup that he kept filled with water. His walking stick seemed to be part of his anatomy. It swung in a soft arc at his side, keeping pace with his quick steps. With the accuracy of a professional golfer, he could flip small stones and sticks out of his path without missing a step. When standing, he would often cross one foot over the other, leaning casually on his gentleman's cane. At all times he held himself with such poise and dignity that it was hard to believe that he wasn't acting the part of a great statesman.

Walking barefoot, he set an unbelievable pace for a man of seventy-two years that he claimed to be. I found myself unable to keep up. I had been walking barefoot for over three months, but mostly on the soft beach sand or the regular surface of roads and city streets. Now, the sharp stones dug into my still-tender feet and the sun baked the top of my head, torturing me further. I struggled along for several hours before dropping to the ground in the shade of a tree, frustrated and tired. My severely parched throat hardly allowed me to say, "I can't go any further!"

"Then we must rest here," he replied calmly, not reacting in the least to my attack of self-pity. "There's a village an hour or so from here where we can spend the night. Tomorrow we shall continue our march."

97

After spending the night in the nearby village, where I once again became the *American disciple* of the great guru Jungle Baba, we continued our trek along narrow foot trails through cultivated fields and into the jungle of dense underbrush with giant trees spaced several hundred feet apart, tangled in climbing vines. At first I enjoyed the soft dirt trail under my extremely beaten-up feet and began to feel the adventurous spirit of the lush surrounding forest. Soon, however, thorny twigs began to appear on the trail and several times they embedded themselves in my feet, forcing me stop every so often.

"Shit man, I don't see how you do it," I said, as we paused under a tree for me to pluck another thorny twig from the heel of my foot. "We're both walking along the same path and I step on every damn thorn yet nothing happens to you."

I was becoming extremely frustrated, reverting to a sub-personality of expressing myself in coarse, sarcastic language. He didn't react but showed me by the movement of his eyes that I was off base again.

"It's because of what you're thinking," he said slowly, rising and preparing to continue on.

"Now come on, Babaji," I replied, "you can't tell me that my mind is causing me to stomp on these thorns!"

"You're afraid of them. You don't give them the right to exist on this trail," he insisted, grabbing my eyes with his penetrating stare. "You resent their presence, which distorts the clarity of your mind so you don't have enough awareness to avoid them.

"You expect to step on them and suffer in the process, so that is exactly what's happening to you," he said, now visibly restraining his laughter at my obvious frustration.

"Try to walk in confidence that you will not step on them and see what happens," he concluded, turning and heading out along the sun-baked trail once again, swinging his walking stick merrily.

Now I know you're an old fool, I thought, rising slowly and gently placing my battered feet on the hot earth again.

"Why are you following me then?" came the sarcastic voice of my guide, followed by his roaring laughter. I snapped out of my self-pity and scurried after him shouting, "You're reading my thoughts! How did you do that?"

"Don't talk while you walk. It wastes energy and we have a long way to go," was his only reply, as he quickened his pace and left me scrambling to keep up.

I stumbled along the rest of the day, the old man pausing every so often to let this athletic youth catch up. I had to admit that he was right. I didn't like the thorns and wished that they weren't there so I could relax and enjoy the walk. But I couldn't see how that was causing me to step on them. By the time we stopped in mid-afternoon at a group of thatched huts by some open fields, I was collecting fewer thorns in my feet and had even created a game of hopping around them when they crossed my path.

We were greeted with great respect by the women of the village and served a hardy peasant meal, after which we laid on rope-strung cots in the shade to rest. The men came in from the fields in the late afternoon and Babaji began his American disciple routine, impressing these simple peasants to no end. I nodded my head on cue, reaffirming, I think, that I was indeed his Western disciple. By now I was getting into the game as well, feeling that it was the least I could do to cooperate in our joint venture.

Our hosts insisted that we spend the night, something I was in complete agreement with, not wanting to take another step on the hot earth. Babaji wanted to go on, saying we could reach the ashram before dark. He gave up his plans when the women of the village offered to prepare a special milk-rice dish, which must have been his favorite. It was obvious he was well known and respected by the people in this area and they all talked as if he did, indeed, have an ashram nearby.

I was beginning to see him as a wise man whose comments on life constantly amazed me. My skeptical nature was definitely softening and, despite my tired body and aching feet, I was glad I'd accepted his offer. What was ahead left an uncertain feeling in my stomach but my quest was at least moving forward.

Refreshed by a good night's sleep and a cup of warm tea, we hit the trail early in the morning and moved out over an ancient flood-plain of tall grasses, marsh reeds, massive trees entwined in creeping vines and, of course, thorny underbrush. Birds and insects serenaded us as we walked along in the cool morning. Occasionally, the piercing cries of peacocks punctuated this chorus of insects as they took flight before our approaching footsteps. It was the jungle all right. I could hardly believe that I was strolling along the same path that a big cat might take, though in reality I was more concerned about the tiny thorns than the king of beasts.

Around midday, Babaji stopped under a tree by the river and I came stumbling along several minutes later, hot and tired from the morning's march. Stripping down, I prepared to bathe my weary body when he shouted, "Stop! Don't enter the water with your body hot."

"Come on Babaji, I'm beat!" I replied, dropping to the ground. "Why not?"

"Sudden temperature change is bad for your internal organs," he calmly replied without looking up. "And don't drink any water until your body has cooled down. You can rinse your mouth out if you want but don't swallow any water yet".

"How much further is this ashram, Babaji?" I asked, settling down in the shade and deciding to accept his advice on not bathing or drinking.

"Just there," he said, turning to his left and pointing off in the distance.

"Under that great spreading tree on the hill over there. Another hour at the most and we will be there."

We bathed, after our bodies had cooled down, and walked the last hour at a rapid pace. When he reached the steep embankment that led up to the giant tree, Babaji again waited for me to catch up and we walked the last five minutes together in silence. The steep footpath opened out onto a flat clearing of about a hundred square yards, surrounded by thick jungle on all sides. On a low rise to the left stood a small, whitewashed shrine with the typical dome-like roof and low arched doorway. On the side of the clearing opposite the temple, stood a small thatched hut closed on all sides with a low doorway facing out toward the jungle. Under the massive tree was a rectangular shelter, open on three sides, with smoke from a central fire pit drifting upwards and filtering through the thatched roof.

Following the custom of paying respect to the local temple upon entering any ashram, we walked first to a small shrine. Babaji poured water from his *comundle* (brass begging bowl) over the phallic stone that stood in the center of the chamber and enthusiastically recited a prayer while I looked on in silence.

I was exhausted and a little dizzy from the sun, so when we entered the long open-air hut under the big tree, I dropped to the ground and propped myself up against a post supporting the roof.

"*Om namo narayana*," came the familiar greeting.

"*Om namo narayana*," replied Jungle Baba, entering and selecting a seat around the fire pit.

Too tired to say anything, I took in the scene through my sun-blurred vision. I could discern a three-foot square fire pit dug into the floor with two smoldering logs sending wisps of smoke toward the blackened roof. The hard-packed dirt floor was impeccably clean, and the area surrounding the fire pit was covered with thin reed mats. At one end of the hut stood the massive trunk of the ancient tree that had guided us there. Neatly fit into the fork of its lower branches was the ridgepole, supporting the structure of the roof. The entire hut was lashed together with a crude natural fiber without the evidence of a single nail. At the base of the mighty tree, nestled in a natural alcove formed by its gnarly roots, was a simple shrine of ancient origin, blackened by centuries of smoke from incense and oil lamps. The shrine contained a single picture of Lord Shiva sitting on his cobra throne, the heads of many snakes shrouding his meditating form.

Through the haze of smoke gently rising form the fire I could make out the figure of a small man, with a great coil of matted hair balanced atop his tiny head, hopping around on his haunches and staring at me. He and Babaji were engaged in conversation, looking toward me and roaring with laughter from time to time. Was this real? Could a scene like this exist in the twentieth century, or was I even still in that time reference any more?

I stretched my feet out and tried to relax, consoling myself with the thought that at least this was some semblance of an ashram and it certainly was in the middle of the jungle.

Suddenly a tall, dark-skinned figure, naked except for a small piece of cloth covering his genitals, came bounding in from behind me, grunting and waving his arms in obvious disturbance.

"Attention!" came the urgent voice of Jungle Baba. "Do not point your feet at the fire like that!" he shouted.

"This is our sacred fire," he spoke quickly while looking at the naked grunter. "It has been kept going continuously for over four thousand years on this very spot. You are *never* to point your feet at it like that or throw anything into it. Do you understand?" he concluded authoritatively.

I pulled my knees to my chest, placed my head on them, and looked out through the smoky haze of my latest predicament. Another young man with unusually short hair and delicate body joined the others and they huddled to one side of the fire in deep discussion, glancing at me from time to time as Jungle Baba did most of the talking. In my imagination I could hear them saying:

"What is that?"

"It's an American disciple."

"Where did you get it?"

"I found him in Hardwar walking along the river."

"Sure is a fat little thing. And all that white skin. What did you bring him here for, anyway?"

"We're going to train him to be a yogi."

"Not that one! Look at his spine. He's bent over like an old man. No he'll never make it. Looks too lazy."

"Look, there aren't too many American disciples walking around free these days. Maybe they're all like this."

Feeling like a trapped disciple, I thought of trying to make a run for it, but to where? Into the mouth of a hungry tiger, most likely. Besides I didn't think I could run more than ten feet.

How could I have been so stupid as to walk right into this set up? I berated myself, exchanging cautious glances with my captors.

Jungle Baba and the tall one approached me and stared close up at my face, as if looking for something special. The tall one bent over and scribbled something on the dirt floor and the others gathered around, gazing intently at my face. They reached some agreement and retreated to the fire for another round of discussion.

"What are you all looking at me like that for?" I challenged, overcome with frustration. "What are you going to do with me now that you've trapped me?"

"Calm down. Don't let your self-importance get the best of you," replied Jungle Baba, who was obviously the only one who understood me.

"Yogi Baba," he said, pointing to the tall one, "has confirmed what I thought. You have the mark of *Shakti* on your forehead.

"He can't imagine why she has chosen you," he went on, pointing to my body disdainfully, "but there is no mistaking the sign. You have been called," he concluded, turning to the others and resuming his conversation.

What he said reminded me of the ancient one in the teashop in Herat, who had said something about a mark of Allah on my forehead, and I calmed down a bit. There was really nothing I could do. Imagination or not, I was deep in the jungle with little or no chance of finding my way back to Hardwar. I reached into my bag and pulled out my copy of the *Gita* and opened it at random to a verse which read:

Face to face with what must be, cease thou from sorrow." (2:27)

What else is there for me to do? I thought. *I went looking for it. Now that I've found it, I can't run away.* I wanted to blame Todd for putting these crazy thoughts into my head about yoga but, after all I had experienced in the last six months, I could no longer consider myself on his quest.

I looked up to see Jungle Baba and the one he called Yogi Baba standing over me again, peering with great curiosity at what I was reading.

"May we see your book for a moment?" asked Jungle Baba in a respectful way.

"Sure. It's called *The Bhagavad Gita*. Do you know it?" I replied, happy that we were getting on as friends again.

He took the book and handed it to Yogi Baba, who began quickly leafing through the pages. Without saying a word, he handed it back to me, pointing to a certain verse.

"He wants you to read that," said Jungle Baba smiling slightly at his friend. "It's your lesson for today, if I'm not mistaken."

Those who themselves have seen the truth can be thy teachers of wisdom. Ask from them, bow unto them, be thou unto them a servant.

When wisdom is thine, Arjuna, never more shall thou be in confusion; for thou shall see all things in thy heart, and thou shall see thy heart in me. (*Gita* 4:34, 35)

"Go now and bathe in the stream we passed on our way up the hill and think about what is being asked of you," said Jungle Baba before I could make any comments.

"And if you want to run for it, your best chance is to get to the river and follow it until you come to a village." Bursting into laughter, he added, "If the tigers don't get to you first!"

Feeling like a child caught with my hand in the cookie jar, I picked up my bag and retraced my steps until I came to the stream and sat down. This time I was sure he was reading my mind but how did he do it? Burning with curiosity, I resisted the urge to run and ask him. Instead, I opened my book and read their selected passage over several times until I thought I understood what they were trying to teach me. If I wanted to learn, my first lesson was to respect and submit myself to those who could teach me.

I remembered my father saying, "Why do you always resist what is good for you while running headlong into anything that will get you into trouble?"

With my first lesson still running through my head, I slowly bathed in the icy waters of the trickling stream and returned to the camp. I had resolved that this was my destiny and I was going to make the best of it. I had been in search of a yogi without having the slightest idea what they might be able to teach me. Now that I had found one, I realized that I had only been feeling good about myself for having such a lofty quest without having any real purpose behind it. Trapped myself again.

That night, after an hour of singing prayers in Sanskrit, Jungle Baba called me to one side of the fire saying, "We must talk.

"Up until now, we've been playing a game," he began, "but now is the time for a serious discussion. I really brought you here because you need help. God, in the form of a dream or the fantasy of an old man, has made that clear to me.

"Yogi Baba quite honestly considers you to be some kind of freak. You see," he continued, speaking slowly and choosing his words with a certain care that I hadn't experienced before, "you have the mark of a wise and ancient soul on your forehead yet you play the game of a fool. You are overweight, out of shape, and your thoughts are those of a man who knows not what is good for him.

"Yet if *Shakti* has marked you, you must be ready. It is not our responsibility to teach you anything. It is your duty to learn. Here we can guide you to strengthen your body and calm your mind so that the real work, that of total surrender, can begin.

"We are not perfect beings, as you will discover if you stay with us. But we have traveled the path further than you in this present lifetime and can show you the way as far as we know. The end of the path is always walked alone.

"You will have three days, as is the custom, to decide whether to accept our training. If you decide to leave, I will guide you out of the jungle, but you will not be able to return."

The stillness of the moonless night blended with the chorus of insects calling out to the spirits of the jungle. I closed my eyes to ask my inner friend what to do when I heard my own voice, strong and confidant, saying, "I don't need time to think about it, Babaji. This is where I want to be. Thank you for bringing me here."

CHAPTER 16

Sidh Kuti

Thus this reluctant disciple became the willing student of the most unlikely bunch of teachers imaginable and the next year of my life became a mind boggling collage of practical, esoteric and mystical lessons that would take over twenty years to assimilate into my understanding. I became an eager student, constantly seeking experience while learning to acquire knowledge through service and humility.

"You will have three principle teachers while you are with us," said Jungle Baba, who started my training the next day.

"Ram Dass Navarn, you may call him Navarnji out of respect," he continued, introducing the short *sadhu* with the tremendous coil of matted hair perched on top of his head, making him look a foot taller than he was, "will instruct you in the sacred code of the *sadhu*. This will include, not only all kitchen etiquette and the preparation of holy foods, but also the proper conduct and procedures for the ancient rites of fire worship.

"He is an illusive master whose conduct and mannerisms are his teachings. His training will require the utmost of patience and trust. If you learn well, his wisdom will become the foundation of your devotional life and your entrance into our inner society of people who renounce all for God.

"I know that you did not come here to learn how to cook and that will make your comprehension of what he has to teach you that much more difficult. He is a hard and exacting teacher and will bring you to new levels of frustration. We all see that your major battle is with your own self-importance that prevents you from learning. Navarnji will cure you of that, I'm sure."

Navarnji and I exchanged glances as my mind began to squirm within my consciousness, looking for a way to cop-out of this whole thing. His extremely thin body was firm and agile like a young boy yet his dark face was furrowed with age and his hazy black eyes were deeply set under thick bushy brows. He paddled around the fire pit looking like a caricature of a top-heavy dwarf, hardly ever rising from a squatting position. He wore only a faded black cloth about his waist and sat on a worn black blanket, indicating that he was a devotee of the Goddess Kali, the female, destructive aspect of the Supreme Godhead. He only nodded in my direction, not knowing what Jungle Baba had said, but the look in his time-glazed eyes told me that he would be a tough master and an adept teacher.

"Yogi Baba will be in charge of strengthening your physical, mental and spiritual bodies," he continued, while introducing the tall, lean man who had kicked up such a fuss when I pointed my feet at the sacred fire. "He is the greatest of yogis in this part of the world, as he might slowly allow you to perceive, depending upon your development of the proper attitudes and intentions.

"He does not speak and has not for over twenty years," continued Babaji, as Yogi Baba and I locked in guarded eye contact. "It is his way of conserving energy and developing greater concentration, which are the essence of all yoga."

He was tall for an Indian, about six feet, with lean yet powerful legs and arms. He was apparently a young man in his early fifties, whereas Ram Dass Navarn was as old as Jungle Baba, if not older. His shiny black hair was neatly combed and hung down past the middle of his straightened back. A long pointed beard hung from his angular chin and his mouth was held firm and serious, except when he broke into one of his child-like grins.

A smile broke upon his face, as if he had understood every word that Jungle Baba had said, and he gave me my first lesson right then. He slowly began to whistle, starting with a low tone and ascending upwards in pitch, while subtly moving his index finger towards the sky. I instinctively straightened my spine from its customary slump and he smiled in approval. It was a lesson he would repeat many times each day during my stay there.

"I am in command of all areas of your development," announced Jungle Baba in his military jargon. "My job is to teach you how to learn. The vision of God makes you feel important so you cannot learn. You must learn humility, patience and total surrender.

"I don't want you as my disciple for what I will gain, as you're constantly concerned about," he emphasized with that knowing twinkle in his eyes. "I see it as my duty; a calling from within, you might say. I am also learning to accept the opportunity that has been given to me. You think me to be an unlikely guru and I also see you as a difficult student. We're made for each other. So you must be a bit of a rogue, pleasure seeker, and lazy on top of it all, because that is the kind of teacher that has been chosen for you."

I dropped my eyes to the ground, shocked that he could know the real inner-me so well, things I was just beginning to realize about myself. I could see that, accident or destiny, I was in the hands of real masters and it wasn't going to be easy.

The routine of ceremony and work, teaching and play in this jungle retreat slowly unfolded as the days turned to weeks and weeks into months. At first nothing was expected of me as I rested, adjusted to my new surroundings and intensely observed the customs and rituals that outlined each day. Everyone was awake before first light and some fresh wood was added to the banked-up fire before heading off to the plains below to answer nature's call and bathe in the small stream. Returning sometime later, invariably just as the fire was bursting to flames, they would perform the morning ritual of offering clarified butter, flowers, water, and wheat flour to the fire. A long prayer was then chanted aloud to Agni, spirit of the sacred fire and transformer of all material reality, followed by a long silent meditation, each in their own universe.

Teatime, a ritual in itself, was next, with Jungle Baba as the master of ceremonies. Heating water in his *comundle* on the glowing coals remaining from the morning fire, he produced a sweet, stimulating brew which was first ceremoniously offered to *Agni,* while repeating an ancient prayer in Sanskrit, then meditatively poured into exact servings for all. This event was repeated several times throughout the day, especially when visitors arrived with gifts of sticky raw sugar or fresh milk, the most cherished item in our diet. One main meal of spicy vegetable stew and fresh hot *chapattis* (unleavened bread), prepared exclusively by Yogi Baba, was served sometime in the early afternoon, followed by a short nap. Another round of bathing and prayers in the evening concluded the day.

All activities centered around the three foot square fire pit, or *dhunie*, where specific sitting areas were designated by slight rises in the dirt floor, forming four distinct levels. The highest, and ruling seat, which was shared by Yogi Baba and Navarnji, faced east and all rituals and ceremonies were conducted from there. Each level was integrated through a specific protocol, rigidly hierarchal in structure, with each place becoming the temporary domain of the person laying their blanket there. They could invite others to join them according to well-defined rules of respect for age, wisdom, friendship or caste. For the same reasons, some people could be refused certain positions and even entrance to the *dhunie* itself.

All food was prepared ceremoniously over this fire, which was kept smoldering day and night. Ram Dass Navarn, the sternest and most serious of my three teachers, was in charge of the kitchen, overseeing all activities of food preparation. But, as with all other aspects of running the ashram, Yogi Baba was the supreme authority. They all looked to him as the one who had the last say in all matters and no one ever questioned his decisions. Yet in his humble way, he would always serve us *chapattis* hot from the coals of the fire as we ate, then take his meal alone while one of the other *sadhus* served him in the same way.

Jungle Baba referred to this forest retreat as Sidh Kuti, named after Sidh Baba, who sat at the first *dhunie* four thousand years ago. He insisted that the fire had been kept going in this ashram continuously since that day. Throughout many ages, it had been attended and worshiped by many great saints and *sadhus*. Gradually I began to understand the etiquette and ritual of this most ancient and revered traditions of India and feel my place within it.

In addition to my three teachers, there were two other resident *sadhus*, both in their late twenties or early thirties. One, Ragana, was the personal attendant of Yogi Baba and looked after his needs like a friend and valet. He didn't appeared to practice any particular disciplines and was considered more a devotee of Yogi Baba than a renunciate. He came and went but when he was in the ashram, he spent all his time with Yogi Baba and didn't join in the other routines of work or worship.

The other, Suriya, a young man with short black hair and a stocky, powerful body, had recently taken vows of renunciation and was, like myself, learning this unusual and demanding lifestyle. He was a student and disciple of Navarnji, who put him to the test in many ways, often making me wonder if I was in for the same treatment. He was a willing student, knowing much more than I about the preparation of food and of the complex protocol that took place around the sacred fire. But, as Jungle Baba later explained, he didn't have the determination to explore the deeper mysteries of the path of yoga.

After I had adjusted to my new surroundings and displayed a willingness to integrate into the routine, my three teachers slowly began their training. Once every other day, Jungle Baba, always jovial and fun to be with, would stroll about the garden with me, which was about a hundred square yards and just beginning to be planted by Yogi Baba and Suriya. He would ask me how I was doing, and then begin a short lesson, mostly concerning the philosophy of yoga. Each day we grew closer and our relationship grew more like father and son than master and disciple.

One day during our walk, Jungle Baba asked me if I had ever been with a woman, using the appropriate four-letter word, showing that his English hadn't all been learned in the classroom. When I assured him that I had, he said, "If not, it would be better to live that experience first before making a deeper commitment to the path of yoga."

"But Babaji," I insisted, confused by his statement, "I thought yoga was to overcome all worldly temptations?"

"That is a common misconception that is due to the impurity of the science as it is practiced today," he replied, laughing a bit to himself while stroking his silky beard. "Yogis today believe that restraint creates dominance over worldly desires; that suppression and control will lead to freedom from attraction and temptation.

"Yoga is not an achievement but an awareness," he went on after having been distracted by a flock of parrots chattering in an overhanging tree. "One must have a greater purpose than just control over the natural inclinations of the body. Yoga channels energy into new areas of healing, health, mind control and divine awareness.

"If your purpose is control of any kind, you may experience greater life force in your body and even better mind control in general, but where does this take you? He who escapes into yoga to be free from the world will have to return to the world to find his freedom through yoga in the end. Even sex can be yoga, if one knows how to direct its energy properly.

"Consider why you're here, not just what you want to learn," he concluded, as we reached the old hand pump at the edge of the garden. "Now pump some water until you understand what I have said."

Yogi Baba was equally obscure in his teachings. Even though he didn't talk, we had intuitive communication from the beginning. Being the most disciplined of the three, he expected me to sit the entire time with my back straight and was uncompromising in his demands on my endurance. He would spend at least half of each day, and I can't say how much of the night, sitting in the full lotus position, meditating in the temple or in special places in the forest. He seemed to have complete control of his energies and could work for hours in the hot sun, prepare chapattis for the midday meal, then retreat into the temple to meditate before taking his meal. He had, through Jungle Baba, insisted that I arise before the sun each day and take a bath in the icy waters of the stream that flowed just below the ashram. I argued that I wanted to wait for the sun to come up but Jungle Baba commanded me, saying something to the effect that the cold water would rearrange the electro-magnetic field surrounding my body, completing the cycle of sleep and readying it for meditation. In addition, I was to join in the morning and evening prayer and chanting sessions, keeping my back straight the entire time, and work with him in the garden two or more hours a day.

I kept asking him about the energy rushes I was experiencing and the sudden loss of contact with the material world, which still punctuated most days, but all he would communicate, through gestures and a few words scratched in the ground interpreted by Jungle Baba, was that my body wasn't strong enough to be instructed in anything that would cause an increase in energy at this time. The energy channels were weak and misaligned, so that was my first priority.

Ram Dass Navarn was, for me, the most difficult to understand. He seemed more inward and serious than the others, fussing and complaining about my oblivious lack of familiarity with Indian customs and showing his disapproval through stern looks and exasperated gestures. He insisted that I learn everything he wanted to teach me by watching. Rather than tell me when to wash the dishes, which was all he allowed me to do for the first month, I would have to be aware of every movement of the kitchen so as to catch the dishes the moment they were ready. If I spaced out, he would get up and do them himself, or ask Suriya to do them — a failure on my part either way. He was an exacting master, often having me rewash the dishes for 'improper concentration' and expected me to be an amateur mind reader to keep up with his teachings.

We were apparently deep in an isolated part of a jungle reserve, but many *sadhus*, wandering merchants and peasants from nearby villages passed by, so there was a constant exchange with the outside world. I could hardly understand anything that was being said and Jungle Baba would only fill me in on what he thought was essential for me to know, saying, "Keep your mind clear of preoccupation of worldly matters and it will flow more easily to your eternal spirit."

One day I brought the clean cups from the morning's tea to the kitchen and Navarnji, without even looking at them, told me to rewash them. I tried to argue that they were clean, but he indicated through a few simple gestures that I had been looking at the monkeys playing in the trees rather than concentrating on what I was doing, which was true. Gritting my teeth, I returned to the pump and rewashed them, going through the entire procedure of scrubbing them with powdery ashes from the fire before rinsing them in clean water. As I was in the middle of this labor of frustration, squatting out in the hot sun, four peasants entered the ashram in an unusual hurry and went straight to the kitchen. An excited discussion followed, with Jungle Baba laughing loudly at times, while Yogi Baba and Navarnji looked on with great interest.

When I arrived back to the kitchen, everyone was in a heated debate over something. I took up the small hand-broom made of branches and busied myself until Jungle Baba was finished and I could ask him what was going on. Soon, Yogi Baba got up and walked to the temple and Jungle Baba started preparing another round of tea, showing me a clay jug of fresh milk.

"What is going on, Jungle Baba?" I asked, once everything had settled down. "What do these people want?"

"They've lost one of their prize water buffaloes and they want us to find her," he answered, humming happily to himself about something.

"Why all the discussion?" I asked, looking over at the four peasants, who had lit a few *bidies* (hand rolled herbal cigarettes) and were sitting around the fire talking among themselves.

"About how much milk they will give us each day when we find the animal!" he confidently replied, looking at me with a glint of mischief in his eyes. "We're going to receive four cups a day for as long as she's milking!"

"Then why don't we get going and find her?" I suggested, happy that sweet, spiced tea might be in abundance for a while.

"Relax," he replied, "Yogi Baba is doing that right now."

I took up my broom and went to sweep around the temple while waiting for tea to be ready. As I passed the temple door, I could see Yogi Baba sitting in his customary place, legs crossed one upon the other, back straight, and eyes closed in deep meditation.

"Yogi Baba didn't leave yet," I said when I returned to the kitchen. "He's sitting in the temple."

"We'll talk about that later," he answered, pouring the tea and motioning for the visitors to come and share a cup with us.

After tea, I gathered the cups and went to the pump to wash them. Yogi Baba came out of the temple and walked to the fire. There was a brief discussion before the peasants went hurrying off. I was dying of curiosity but didn't want to hurry my task, knowing I would have to repeat it if not done to certain *unspecified* standards.

"Now please, Babaji, tell me what is going on," I said, entering the kitchen and placing the tray of sparkling clean cups on the ground.

"Yogi Baba found the buffalo. Now we're going to have milk for a long time," he concluded, rubbing his hands together in anticipation.

"But Yogi Baba didn't go anywhere" I insisted. "How could he have found the buffalo?"

Jungle Baba, laughing at my insistence, told me in a few words and motions of his arms, that Yogi Baba had flown out of his body and seen the buffalo in a certain place in the jungle and the farmers had gone to get her.

Todd had talked about astral projection, where advanced yogis could leave their bodies and travel to other places. It had been a favorite theme of the spiritual seekers in the Blue Tibetan Restaurant. I had experienced a brief out-of-body journey on the houseboat in Varanarse but it was far beyond my understanding and control. My interest in Yogi Baba's teachings picked up immediately, but I decided to see if he really did find the buffalo before asking him to teach me.

An hour later, the farmers returned saying that they had found the buffalo exactly where Yogi Baba had told them to look. This news prompted an enthusiastic celebration. Yogi Baba took the jug first to the temple, pouring some milk over the stone in the center of the shrine, and then to the fire, where he dripped a small amount onto the embers, raising hissing plumes of vapor in gratitude. Then Navarnji lead us in a long chant, praising all forms of the one God, *Brahma,* until Jungle Baba declared sweet milk rice for lunch and we all started to prepare it.

That evening, as a cool breeze began to stir up the stagnant air of the hot summer day and we were all preparing for evening prayers around the sacred fire, I asked Yogi Baba, with the help of Jungle Baba, to teach me how to leave my body and fly through the air. They both looked at me seriously. Then Yogi Baba scribbled one word in the ground and walked away.

"What did he say?" I pressured Jungle Baba. "What does that word mean?"

"It means, 'why'" he answered. "And that is to say you must meditate on why you want to learn it."

I started to say that it seemed like a good thing to know when he silences me with a motion of his hand.

"The deeper mysteries of yoga are learned through the proper alignment of will and intention," he began deliberately, shifting his position from squatting on his hunches to sitting cross-legged. "Yogi Baba cannot teach you that. You must learn it and the key to your learning is 'Why do you want to do it?'

"We know you have experienced moments of yogic travel by the activity of certain energy centers in your body. These experiences have been given to aid you in the development of focused intention, nothing more.

"Be careful," he said, looking me directly in the eyes. "Desire for unusual experiences can be a great stumbling block even to an accomplished yogi. Keep your back straight and let peace come to your mind first. That is the only focus for you at this time."

The flying yogi stunt was not the only strange thing happening around the ashram. While every meal consisted of curried stew and thick *chapattis* toasted golden brown in the coals of the fire, it occurred to me that I had never seen any wheat flour coming into the ashram. While sweeping out the kitchen area one morning, I peeked into the large clay urn where the flour was stored. There was just a sprinkling on the bottom. Several hours later, Yogi Baba went to the jug and scooped out a platter full of flour and proceeded to make the dough for the meal.

Later I looked in again and saw the same sprinkling of flour on the nearly empty bottom. A nifty variation on Christ's loaves-and-fishes routine. When I asked Jungle Baba about this, he replied that knowing such things implied a certain responsibility, which my skeptical nature was not yet ready for. Instead of answering my question, he had me read a certain passage in the *Gita*

> But to those who adore Me with a pure oneness of soul, to those who are ever in harmony, I increase what they have and give them what they have not. (*Gita:* 9:22)

From that day on, I began to scrutinize my fascinating teachers, discovering them to be strong mentalists and even minor magicians. They always seemed to know when visitors were coming, what direction they were coming from, and sometimes even who they were and what they wanted. Jungle Baba later explained that by listening to the insects, birds, and the rushing of the wind in the high trees, he could discern every movement of the surrounding forest. When I questioned him on this self-proclaimed ability, he laughed and told me to just wait. One evening a week later, he told me to stand at the far corner of the garden; someone wanted to talk to me. Thinking that he just wanted me away from the *dhunie* for a while, I took up my place at the edge of the jungle. I had settled into a peaceful vigil and was drifting in a maze of personal thoughts when a piercing roar broke the silence of the night and sent me scrambling to my feet. I fell dead silent, listening to the forest that was absorbed in eerie stillness.

"What was that?" I asked, hurrying back to the fire.

"That was the tigress who shares the jungle with us," replied Jungle Baba, fighting back his laughter.

OK. To have contact with wild animals was a keen sense of perception. But what about spirits that one cannot see?

One of the realities of sitting around a hole in the floor with two smoldering logs was the smoke, which at all times drifted in trailing plumes about the *dhunie*. I often became engulfed in these asphyxiating clouds, which caused stinging irritation to my eyes and sent me out to the garden to avoid suffocation. Yogi Baba, Navarnji and Jungle Baba however never seemed to get caught by these swirling masses and I soon became aware that they could make the smoke go wherever they wanted.

If a villager joined us at the *dhunie* and became too talkative or hung around too long, I could perceive the three of them moving the smoke in his direction. One day after they had sent chattering peasants coughing in retreat and the three of them snickered discreetly to themselves, I couldn't contain my curiosity.

"How do you make the fire send the smoke in that direction?" I asked.

Jungle Baba laughed a bit to himself and started to get that 'it's none of your business' look on his face, but changed his expression and replied:

"The fire doesn't do it, the wind does. Now go to the stream and take a cold bath and think about that!"

CHAPTER 17

YOGA

My training accelerated, with Yogi Baba giving me hints on how to keep my back straight while sitting and helping me with my concentration in general. He softened in his demands after I displayed a greater willingness to learn. He taught me a series of rhythmic breathing exercises, counting my heartbeats to a rhythm of four, sixteen, eight during inhalation, retention and exhalation of my breath. He also insisted that I sit an additional two hours, one in the morning and one in the afternoon, saying that my energy channels were stronger now and *Shakti* could flow more freely.

For a westerner, sitting cross-legged on the ground, with back straight or not, was a formidable task. I was already feeling that the morning and evening two-hour prayer sessions were torturous sitting events. My knees ached and the muscles in my back throbbed with pain throughout every session and often Yogi Baba's whistle would break into my painful daydreams, tempting me to run for the river and never return.

They found a T-shaped stick and instructed me to place the long end between my crossed legs and fold my arms on the flat upper part to support my back when I could no longer stand the pain. This helped with the backache but did little for the crippling pain in my knees and ankles.

Yogi Baba pointed to a passage in the *Gita*, our only real means of communicating, and I read:

> When the mind is resting in the stillness of the prayer of Yoga, and by the grace of the Spirit sees the Spirit and therein finds fulfillment;
>
> Then the seeker knows the joy of eternity; a vision seen by reason

far beyond what senses can see. He abides therein and moves not from Truth. (*Gita* 6-20 & 21)

I enjoyed the breathing exercises and practiced with enthusiasm. Jungle Baba insisted that much time was needed before the importance of breathing would be realized. I had been sitting and concentrating on my thoughts for many months, so I just switched my attention to my breath. At first there was a relaxing sensation from this new discipline but slowly, as the novelty of a different point of concentration wore off, it became the same challenge as trying to concentrate on anything else.

The mind, like a monkey frolicking in the branches of a tree, would not be still. It jumped from thought to image and the slightest sound carried it off on a worldly tangent against my most urgent insistence that it be still. I began, with the help of Jungle Baba and Yogi Baba, to perceive it as the master of my externally focused attention, constantly drawing me away from my concentration on my breath.

I read in the *Gita*:

With soul in peace and all fear gone and strong in the vow of holiness let him rest with mind in harmony his soul on me, his God supreme. (*Gita,* 6-14)

Walking was added to my routine as I accompanied Jungle Baba each day to get the milk at a farm about an hour away, where we enacted our American disciple routine. The settlement was tucked away in a peaceful clearing cultivated in tobacco, corn, squash and lentils. Simple mud houses lined the perimeters of the open fields and huge trees of the surrounding jungle towered behind them, isolating this tribal village. We would often be treated to fresh buttermilk while Jungle Baba talked in the shade for hours. Like many of the wandering *sadhus*, he practiced a basic form of folk healing using a charcoal-opium mixture for stomach problems and a white powder and mud compresses for headaches. He also counseled in the importance of a proper diet, placing special emphasis on food preparation and the time of day the meals were taken. Sometimes he was called upon to help resolve family or village conflicts, which he did, playing Hypocrites or Socrates with equal ease.

Navarnji, my kitchen master and sternest mentor, would sometimes accompany us, gathering herbs to make fresh green chutney and sweet drinks on the kitchen grinding stone. He instructed me, through simple gestures, how to find tender herbs according to the plants and shrubs that grew near them and promised further instruction on how to prepare them when I had mastered washing dishes and pealing and cutting of vegetables, which had recently been added to my training. Jungle Baba was right. It was hardest for me to learn from Navarnji because I didn't consider it necessary to know how to cook. I wanted to learn how to fly like a yogi.

The three of us were returning late one morning with milk, wild herbs, and seedlings and squash cuttings for our garden. Navarnji, with his coiled mass of dreadlocks perched deftly upon his tiny head, was leading and took the shorter trail through open jungle of tall grasses. As we scurried along the narrow trail, wild, deer-like animals would charge through the brush and ugly black vultures took flight from fallen carcasses at our coming. We were moving along at a fast pace and I was trying to keep up without stepping on one of those thorny twigs when Navarnji shot out his arms and stopped suddenly, causing me almost to bump into him. His walking stick was pointing at the trail a few feet in front of us where the scaly head of a large snake was just appearing in the underbrush. We stood motionless, hardly breathing, as it raised its flattened head slightly and wagged its forked tongue at us before slithering across the trail with rhythmic contractions and slipping out of sight.

Although there hadn't been any real danger, I felt just a little frightened. But I was more mystified at how Navarnji could have known that the snake was crossing our path. Did he see it or sense it in another way?

"She warned him she was crossing before she let us see her," interpreted Jungle Baba, after we had arrived back and set to work peeling squash for the day's meal. That left me more confused, but it confirmed what I had intuitively perceived: He had sensed it in some paranormal way.

I began to see yoga not as a bunch of isolated exercises of breathing and concentration, but as a total awareness of all life. Jungle Baba kept repeating that *"yoga is not the disciplines but the state of awareness that results from the disciplines"*. Slowly, my rational mind began to yield to this new concept and I realized that I was seeing yoga in action not the actions of yoga.

My willingness to serve my new teachers became the devotional focus of my life. I looked for opportunities to wash the dishes and even their clothes, which was an honor for one serving any teacher. I put more 'trying attitude' into the torturous sitting marathons and, even though my back and knees still ached, I began to feel a new pleasantness while sitting and praying; a relaxed flow in the energy rushes that raced through my body, lighting up its cells and filling me with the presence of Oneness.

We planted the garden, first chanting an ancient mantra to the Earth Goddess for fertility and prosperity. Then we fashioned a simple shrine out of large, flat stones at the garden entrance where we lit incense and made offerings of wheat and freshly picked flowers. I had never in my life planted anything before but Yogi Baba stayed by my side, patiently showing me how not to damage the roots of young seedlings or plant the seeds too deep, while always reminding me to keep my back straight. I asked many questions about the ceremony: Why the shrine? What was the meaning of the chant? But Jungle Baba would only place his index finger to his lips, telling me to keep quiet.

"Keep your mind on what you're doing and in time you will understand everything," he insisted. "Learning is not knowing something about something. It is a process of recognition arising from within."

We concluded our first day of planting by pumping water and directing it to flow along little channels to our new seedlings while chanting in spontaneous unity. I thought of Christmas Eve at the Mad Hatter's tea party, in another part of Wonderland. Again singing, or chanting was creating a feeling of spontaneous unity

My duties were expanded to include pumping water for the garden. Yogi Baba, turning everything into a discipline, gave me a special exercise of short, shallow breathing, keeping my arms straight while bending at the knees to move the handle. I became a focused student in the art of pumping, enjoying the change from sitting and the invigorating sensation of hyperventilation that it produced, forcing me to pay close attention to my breathing to avoid passing out.

One day near at end of my third month of training, Jungle Baba called me over from one of these yogic 'pump-a-thons' in the midday sun, instructing me to sit by him and get out my copy of the *Gita*. He explained that Yogi Baba was giving an important lesson to some visiting *sadhus* and I should pay attention. I took my position next to Jungle Baba, handing him my book, and watched as Yogi Baba demonstrated a certain sitting position of placing the heel of his left foot directly in the soft fleshy area between his scrotum and anus. He moved his right foot to come over the top of his penis and placed it on top of his left thigh. For me, who could just barely touch both knees to the ground for a short time, it looked impossible without certain castration. The other *sadhus* looked on with keen interest before trying their own version with varying results. From the same position, he demonstrated a type of shallow, rapid breathing while pointing to different areas along the spine. Jungle Baba explained that this was a technique for directing the energy flow upward in the body by closing the gate at the base of the spine and using the breath to control the movement of energy toward the top of the head. He handed me my *Gita*, opened to a certain passage, and told me to read:

> If when a man leaves his earthly body he is in the silence of yoga, and, closing the doors of his soul, he keeps the mind in his heart, and places in the head the breath of life.
>
> And remembering me he utters OM, the eternal word of Brahman, he goes to the path supreme. (*Gita* 8:12, 13)

I had read it many times before but the inner message of this ancient yogic technique caught my attention that morning. "Keeps the mind in the heart and places in the head the breath of life" seemed like trying to concentrate on two things at the same time. I was finding it extremely difficult to just concentrate on my breathing.

I was urged to ask Yogi Baba about one specific reference: "the doors of his soul." When he had uncoiled himself and the discussion had ended among the other *sadhus,* I asked by showing Jungle Baba the passage and having him read it to Yogi Baba.

He looked at me several times and glanced at Jungle Baba, before standing and demonstrating a still more complicated exercise of taking seven deep breaths before retaining his breath within. He pointed to his pelvic area and indicated he was squeezing some muscles in his anus and penis before exhaling. Without releasing the muscles at the anus, he continued the same breathing until he retained his breath and tightened the chest diaphragm, holding the energy in the same way. He repeated the same contraction after deep breaths in the throat, before closing his eyes and making a gesture with his hand like flying out of his body.

One of the other *sadhus* began to demonstrate a position with hands inverted and fingers made to close all of the sense openings of his head, touching simultaneously his eyes, nose, ears and mouth. Jungle Baba disagreed about something and further discussion took place before I could learn from him what was going on.

"Yogi Baba was demonstrating a yogic technique for raising the energy up the spine and holding it there," he informed me, "while the other *sadhu* was interpreting the 'doors of the soul' to be the senses. The answer to any question must always reflect the condition of the inquirer. What Yogi Baba was showing you is called the *bandhas,* or locks, and they are used to accumulate and store energy in certain centers of the body. That must be what he feels is your lesson for today.

"You will find," he concluded "that the teachings of our sacred books cover many dimensions of reality and find their correct interpretation through meditation and inspiration."

"What's the meaning of "the breath in the head and the mind in the heart?" I asked, still uncertain of Yogi's demonstration.

My question created much conversation, during which Yogi Baba's child-like eyes never left me. We were having an intense communication experience involving love and trust across cultural and spiritual barriers. In that moment, I saw him as my master and guide. Moreover, I perceived we had been in that relationship before. All of life was somehow being woven around circumstances that I had come to see as exchanges of energy out of which we gain direction and momentum. Yogi Baba, and maybe all these men, held keys to my further awakening and I could now see pumping water and washing dishes as acts of devotional necessity and justified energy exchanges. I began to perceive that his ability to answer my questions had a mystifying relationship to my attitudes and intention behind my devotional acts, as if our wills were linked together in some mysterious way.

There was a marked silence before Yogi Baba made a sign with his hand, signaling he wanted to write, which was treated as an important occasion by everyone. Suriya hustled to the back of the hut and reappeared with a child's blackboard. Using a crude block of chalk stone, Yogi Baba wrote a series of words in Sanskrit and crossed them out when their meaning was agreed upon, pausing every so often for Jungle Baba to give me his interpretation.

> Consciousness is rooted in the breath.
> Through breath one travels to soul's gate.
> Then leaving breath, through devotion,
> One enters the heart of oneness with all.

"He says that the journey ends in the heart," concluded Jungle Baba, "But by paying attention to the importance of your breathing, in every way, it will lead you to the door of total surrender, even of the process of breathing itself. The difference is like that of breathing or being breathed."

Over the following weeks, we had several exchanges like this. I enjoyed finding obscure passages, which were for me still words without meaning, but they could repeat them all from memory. There seemed to be agreed upon meanings, with personal variations. Most of my questions were answered directly by Jungle Baba with agreement of Navarnji, who had no idea what was being said in English but bobbed his mass of dread locks when in agreement. Yogi Baba, unwavering in his vow of silence, sat quietly through most of these sessions, being called on only when there was some disagreement or lack of understanding.

A few weeks later, I found another reference to breathing. After pumping water and leaving the squash peeled and cut to the precise size in the tray next to the grinding stone, I took it to Jungle Baba for an interpretation.

> Some offer their out-flowing breath into the breath that flows in;
> and the in-flowing breath into the breath that flows out;
> they aim at Pranayama, breath-harmony,
> and the flow of their breath is in peace. (*Gita*: 4,29)

Yogi Baba, who was nearby making dough for the day's *chapattis*, perked up at my question and waited to hear what Jungle Baba would say. Unclear himself, he asked Yogi Baba for an interpretation. Looking at his hands, which were filled with sticky dough, he thrust his pointed chin at me and motioned to Jungle Baba until they reached an agreement about something.

Turning to face me, Jungle Baba said, "He wants you to answer."

My first impulse was to say I didn't know, but the memory of 'questions and answers' with Richard and Leo grabbed my awareness and I began to be possessed by the feeling of all-knowingness once again.

"This refers to how to go from one dimension of consciousness to another," I heard myself saying within the stillness of the moment.

"There exists a relationship between breath and thought. Thought is a process within consciousness and is joined to breath through will. Breath sustains consciousness, the creative potential of humanity.

"When will, taking the thought of the in-breath, merges it with the flow of the out-breath, perception is altered to know the divine."

Jungle Baba translated what he could but Yogi Baba seemed to understand without being told. He nodded in approval, having received an answer to his indirect question: I was in contact with knowingness.

Jungle Baba handed me my copy of the *Gita*, pointing out one verse:

> But those whose unwisdom is made pure by the wisdom of their inner spirit, their wisdom is unto them a sun and in its radiance they see the supreme. (*Gita*: 5,16)

"That is for you. Your light is to wisdom," he said in a respectful way, letting me know that I was more than just his American disciple.

It hadn't felt strange for me to interpret the passage. But that they were interested, even impressed, caught me by surprise. For me, all wisdom was coming from the same source. I told Jungle Baba, in response to his questioning, that I had experienced moments of knowingness like that before, but not in relationship to the *Gita*. It was a moment in which we all recognized each other and all of them recognized something in me.

After that day, my training went into deeper, subtler levels. Pumping water became a joy, counting breaths and thinking of the plants that would use my energy to give life. Yogi Baba, always looking for ways to strengthen my body and quiet my mind, added a jarring movement by instructing me to rise up on my toes, with spine stiff, and drop onto my heels with the last twenty strokes. He indicated that the vibration was good for my spine.

Walking in the jungle became a meditation. Jungle Baba and Navarnji, placing me between them while walking on narrow trails through areas of dense jungle, taught me a new way of walking. It was like gliding with my determination kept in the area of the body below the navel while concentrating on a field of energy generated in the heart. Except for how to breathe and where to concentrate, they told me little about how to do it, insisting that it had nothing to do with the mind and could only be understood by doing.

We would start off slowly counting six steps for every inhalation and exhalation until we were all in the same rhythm, moving along as if we were joined together by an invisible cord. Then without a word of indication, Nivarnji, who always took the lead and set the pace, would change gears, taking more steps per breath until we were moving at a fast clip. Another shift in rhythm and we were floating along, not breathing any faster but lengthening the time of each inhalation and exhalation as the pace quickened to an unhurried scurrying of steps, like dancing

"Don't think about it," insisted Jungle Baba twirling his walking stick like a baton. "Walk as if you're being pulled along on an invisible beam of light."

With not a moment to think about snakes or thorns, we would cover long distances at a great pace and without tiring, stopping only to gather herbs or vegetables donated by farmers. After I stopped trying to see it as a physical trial of strength and coordination, I relaxed and could glide along as if my feet hardly touched the ground. It was a heightened state of awareness that I related to special moments in sports when one's performance is well beyond one's physical capabilities.

I would practice by myself in the afternoons while walking through the floodplain stretching for miles below the ashram. Walking with practiced determination and trying not to think about what I was doing, I traveled in a great circle, gathering peacock feathers to trade to traveling merchants for cooking oil and fresh cow dung to resurface the dirt floor in the main hut.

I was returning, unusually tired, from one of these gathering excursions with three feathers and a fresh cow pie when Yogi Baba took a close look at my face and raced to get Jungle Baba. They immediately placed me in the garden hut, saying I had the fever. I had been tired all day but thought it was the intense summer heat settling over the ashram. But they took it seriously, wrapping me in thick cotton blankets and filling me full of herb teas prescribed by Yogi Baba. By noon the next day, either because of being wrapped in blankets in the jungle heat or the effects of Yogi's fever teas, I was on fire. Alternating chills and fever soon had me in a delirium. Emotional outbursts of wanting my mother and visions of breaking up with my high school sweetheart and wanting to please my father by winning the football game tormented me throughout the night.

Wracked with fever and chills I floated in this space of uncontrolled emotion, moving between my perspiration-soaked physical body and a detached, pseudo-reality pervaded by reverberating thoughts of "Who am I?" At times, I would hover above my lifeless form, vaguely perceiving Yogi Baba forcing warm teas down my throat and Jungle Baba burning herbs in a brass pot to ward off spirit entities, which I could clearly see as semi-luminescent energy forms drifting about the hut. Death was there as a possibility at all times, but its presence did not create fear or sadness, nor was it a choice that was totally mine. I perceived it as the relationship of my personal energies with the greater, macrocosmic flow of life's potential.

Exhausted, I would relax my identification with that physical reality and become something else: A complex series of relationships comprised of desire, fear, memory, and probability, which maintained the consistency of my personal identity through attitudes and beliefs. I saw myself not as a physical being in a three-dimensional space-time relationship, but as an energy field of possibilities sustained by an empathic expression of will like a subtle form of attraction and identification. My being, rather than consisting of anything fixed or determined, was reduced to a movement; a flow of awareness taking direction and form out of the desires and beliefs to which I was, for some unknown reason, attracted to. *Who I was became a moment-to-moment choice of what memories and probabilities I wanted to identify with.*

Somehow, through this haze of mystical awareness, I perceived that Tom, the university graduate seeking adventure, was a fragile consistency that could dissolve at any moment into a number of alternatives. I saw that, at the same time, I was and had been a wandering *sadhu*, rooted in the ancient Hindu traditions of renunciation and devotion, whose relationship to wisdom was derived through many life-journeys of discipline and service. Yet even beyond that, I existed simultaneously on a non-physical dimension as a vortex of guidance and love for other life forms of both biological and etheric nature. I was infinite choice and probability interacting in a dynamic flow.

At some point in this deluge, reality unraveled to where all worlds inter-existed and my identity could hold no consistency except that of LIGHT. I merged into the vibrational sea of the infinite OM.

CHAPTER 18

ABANDONED

This *clear-life* experience, as I would later come to relate to it, had a profound effect on my inner being, a turning point in my adventure and life. I had released a great stress of attachment to my fixed conditioning created by family and culture. I felt different, lighter but extremely disoriented, not only from fear and weakness of a near-fatal illness. Something in the core of my personality had been altered. From that moment on, I was not going away from my old life but toward my new one.

I reentered awareness of my physical body to see shafts of sunlight shining though the thatched roof creating patterns of angels out of the dust particles suspended in the air and, for a moment, I thought I had transcended. Jungle Baba, leaning majestically on his cane near by, assured me I had not, but I had been gone for several days, after the fever had peaked. My physical body was exhausted. For a long time I lay around doing little, experiencing some transitory stage of awakening to my new identity. My visa had already expired, but so had my old self. Nothing of my old life retained importance.

Jungle Baba went off with my passport to arrange with the authorities for me to stay and I was cut off from English communication for a while. I used my pocket guidebook to learn more Hindi and, slowly, greater communication opened up with Navarnji and Suriya. It was a month before I was back to full strength and could pump water, pull weeds, and cultivate the young plants in the garden. In Jungle Baba's absence, I was put in charge of the milk run and spent hours walking alone through the jungle, collecting feathers and the common herbs we used in the kitchen. I began, with greater enthusiasm than before, to repeat to myself the eternal sound of OM aloud while walking or sitting around the fire. Navarnji, who had resisted calling me by the name OM

Baba, feeling that I was unworthy of a *sadhu* name because I had received no real training the sacred rights, began to call me OM Baba; and Tom became a faded memory.

I became an attentive student of Navarnji, serving him like a devoted and admiring son. My training continued in the customs and rituals of the *sadhus* as well as the preparation of the holy foods. His stern and demanding ways could now be seen as a facade covering over a gentle and wise interior. As I displayed more willingness, he responded with greater patience. About this time, I was introduced to the large rectangular block of stone used to grind herbs and spices into drinks and chutney. At first, it was extremely difficult to add just the right amount of water for the proper consistency and to work the smaller stone at the correct angle to make the paste really fine. The most essential part of all Indian cooking was getting the spices just right, neither too hot nor too bland. The rules of holy cooking did not permit one to taste anything during the preparation, food being essentially first an offering to God. This made it a combination of intuition and experience. Regardless of whether Suriya or I did the actual grinding, Navarnji always choose the quantities of specific spices to be used and placed them on the stone for us. In the same way, the consistency of the dough for the *chapattis* was considered more important than who actually cooked them. With only a few exceptions, Yogi Baba would always prepare the dough, carefully kneading just the right amount of water into the mixture and letting it sit for an hour before cooking them on the fire.

Mealtimes were acts of devotional worship. When the food was ready, a small tray was prepared with a silver dollar-sized *chapatti* and small dab of *subji* (spicy stew). These were first offered to the fire while repeating a certain prayer. After being served, each of us would take a small amount of our serving and make another personal offering to the sacred fire before eating in absolute silence.

I had been allowed to place my blanket in the spot occupied by Jungle Baba and from there I slowly incorporated into the rhythm of maintaining the fire just right to cook, yet not burn, while stirring the stew and toasting the *chapattis* in the coals with metal tongs. The fire became a central part of my life and I learned to make the proper offerings and devotional chants used in this form of worship. Most nights I slept next to the fire with just my light cotton cloth pulled over me. A few times, I awoke in the middle of the night and joined in silent meditations with Navarnji and Yogi Baba of which I hadn't been aware of before.

Yogi Baba refined his teachings by requiring me to sit in one of three acceptable positions while around the fire. When I could no longer hold my back erect he would signal, with a movement of his head, for me to get up and find something else to do. He showed me how to make a flat roll out of my small yellow cloth and sit on it so as to lift my tailbone and create a soft, upward pressure on my spine. Alternate nostril breathing was added to my morning routine, along with the eight, thirty-two, sixteen rhythm of counting during inhalation, retention and exhalation.

He showed me three different breathing techniques to be practiced slowly over many years before I would master them. The first was the *long breath* which consisted of inhaling and exhaling as slowly as possible, lengthening the time for one complete cycle, until each inhalation and exhalation could take up to three minutes for a beginner and up to an hour or more for a master yogi. The *still breath* was practiced by inhaling and exhaling at a normal rate but prolonging the space between breaths as long as possible by retaining the breath after each inhalation. This produced a pleasant floating sensation and distinct stillness of body and mind. The last and most difficult was the *infinite breath*, practiced by drawing one's attention away from the breathing process and surrendering to an infinite wave that was breathing you. At first the concept of being breathed rather that breathing was difficult for my rational mind to accept. But after a few months of practice and a few glimpses of this reality, I accepted that this awareness did exist and, slowly, experiences of my infinite self began to emerge from these practices.

The sound of OM now reverberated even stronger within the wellspring of my being. I spent most evenings chanting the eternal word while walking by myself around in the garden. I felt a great lightness of mind and body, having no ambitions or plans. The identity of OM Baba, worshipper of the One Eternal Spirit through service and surrender, crystallized more into my being every day.

Nothing was a chore or discipline any more. My actions sprang out of joy and service, seeking nothing in specific, only greater awareness of life's flow in general. Desire for social justice, personal achievement, and even mystical experiences became vague background impulses, part of another me who had relinquished his identity to the racing tide of personal transformation. A new sense of peace accompanied me in my daily routine and thoughts of spending the rest of my life without leaving this jungle paradise replaced all other restless needs to create a future. I read with great devotion my *Bhagavad Gita*:

> He whose undertakings are free from anxious desire and fanciful thought, whose work is made pure in the fire of wisdom; he is called wise by those who see.

> In whatever work he does such a man in truth has peace; he expects nothing, he relies on nothing and ever has the fullness of joy.

> He has attained liberation: he is free from all bonds, his mind has found peace in wisdom, and his work is a holy sacrifice.
> The work of such a man is pure. (*Gita*: 4-19, 20, & 23)

On a physical level, my body felt lighter, taller and more flexible. Over the last six months, its flabby consistency had been firmed and toned through my new diet and abundant exercises. The skin itself was smooth, clear and tanned dark from hours of daily exposure to the sun. I had stopped experiencing the violent attacks of dysentery. The simple diet of mostly vegetable stew and *chapattis*, heavily supplemented by sweet, spiced tea, gave me more energy and stamina than the protein-laden fast foods of my American past. I required less sleep, about six hours a night, which was still more than the others. The cold baths in the chilled morning air and long hours of sitting became more enjoyable each day.

I talked little, confining my communication to that which was absolutely necessary. I slowly noticed that a great amount of my talking arose out of an internal anxiety or fear of not being accepted by others and, as I resisted the urge to impulsively repeat empty words to please myself and feel important, my mind became calmer. My voice, however, rang with a new strength and confidence, surprising me at times as words were now instinctively chosen to convey imagery and meaning in a more precise and poetic way. The most obvious result of all this was the heightened awareness of my thoughts. When I wasn't always looking for the next thing to say, a greater percentage of my thoughts could be disregarded as unimportant. I found it easier to maintain focused attention on what I was doing, whether it happened to be walking in the forest or preparing food.

Of all the changes within this process of transformation, none had a more profound effect upon my being than the rise of a genuine attitude of devotion and service, which emerged as the dominant aspect of my personality. Since all aspects of food preparation were supposed to be performed in an attitude of worship, something I now felt from deep within, I found myself praying and chanting throughout, as if I had been doing it that way all my life. I went several times a day to the temple to make offerings of water and flowers and joined enthusiastically in the morning and evening ceremonies, feeling the spirit alive within me. God became a sea of total unity and harmony in which I was blissfully floating. The presence of oneness grew stronger each day as I dedicated my life to the service of God through the service of others.

> Offer all thy works to God, throw off selfish bonds, and do thy work. No sin can then stain thee, even as the waters do not stain the leaf of the lotus.

> The yogi works for purification of the soul: he throws off selfish attachment, and thus it is only his body, or his mind or his reason that works. (*Gita*: 5-10 & 11)

Just as I was fully adjusted to the routine of ceremony and ritual, work and play, Yogi Baba, in his uncanny way of noticing the moment I became comfortable with anything, as if I were on a crash course to learn everything he could teach me, switched the rules of the game again. After our noontime meal and a short rest, he whistled me to attention and communicated with a few gestures that I was to pick up my blanket from my spot around the fire and prepare to leave. Since we hardly ever went out at that time of the day except to take a bath at the river, I immediately suspected something.

We left the ashram by a faint trail that took off from the far end of the garden with Ram Dass Navarn in the lead, carrying a clay pot of coals from the main fire, and Yogi Baba behind me carrying a sack of something over his shoulder. We walked for an hour through thick underbrush, along an indiscernible trail, until we arrived at an unkempt clearing of 100 square feet and a tiny thatched hut open on three sides. The site felt abandoned but with a certain air of being used from time to time.

Since one of us didn't speak and the other two of us were capable of only one or two word sentences in the same language, what they told me is still vague today. Yogi Baba set the sack in the center of the hut and Navarnji set the pot of coals in the fire pit and they made me understand that they would be back in ten days. And that was all!

I watched as the bushes waved a last good-bye. My fleet-footed friends disappeared and I breathed an anxious sigh of resignation. What was the meaning of all this?

I resisted the temptation to run after them and sat in the middle of the clearing realizing that the sun was low in the sky. If this was to be my home for ten days, there was lots of work to do before sunset.

Before nightfall, I had fashioned a hand broom from dried branches laced together with thick strands of grass, cleaned out the hut and placed my blanket in front of the fire pit. I gathered firewood, in great abundance on the edges of the clearing, and managed to start a fire with the coals. I examined the sack Yogi Baba had left and found whole wheat flour, a squash, some onions, black tea, raw sugar, salt and a cup, bowl and metal plate for cooking chapattis. All in all, the bare minimum one could survive on for ten days.

When I opened my eyes after my evening prayers and meditation, blackness pressed in all around the fragile hut and the droning buzz of insects was amplified a hundred times over the sounds in the ashram, making it feel as if the jungle was encroaching upon the hut, ready to swallow me up in its tangled web of life. The sensation wasn't a common fear of death or loneliness, but an all-encompassing certainty that this experience depended on total awareness, as well as surrender to the situation at hand, or I would soon fall deeper into the pits of human madness.

That first night was spent in an anxious vigil listening to night creatures prowling about in the underbrush, expecting the deafening roar of the lioness to precede her leap upon me from out of the blackness. My greatest concern was the fire. Would the pile of firewood I had gathered see me through the night? Could I keep the fire going for ten days without matches? Could I survive this test, if that's what it was, and if so, what was the purpose behind it all?

CHAPTER 19

NATURE SPIRITS

I awoke long after the sun had risen, having succumbed to sleep unable to sustain my fretful vigil another minute. My first concern was the fire. Once I had coaxed it back to life with the last of the dry twigs and branches I had on hand, greater concerns assaulted my mind. Hunger? I had some food and could cook in the clay pot they brought the hot coals in. Thirst? I had heard water trickling somewhere nearby last night. I was sure I could find it in the daytime. Of course survival was possible on a physical level but what about the jungle at night, wild animals and perhaps the most frightening of all, the solitude; the fear of being with just myself?

It is difficult to describe the psychological process that followed as I seesawed about between fear and resolution, trying to order my life within the uncertainty of my new plight. I knew that I had to establish some form of routine or my mind would turn against me, leaving me little hope of surviving even one more night. The first few days were spent in a highly rationalized process born out of survival and everything it might take to bring this about in that small jungle clearing. I divided the day up among the essential chores but it was obvious that these would take less than an hour of each day. Free time became the biggest challenge. To busy myself and keep my mind occupied, I cleaned up the clearing, repaired the thatched hut, set a row of green branches in place to make a second wall, cleared the path to the water and set a broad leaf in place under the trickling stream so I could duck my head under it and resume my cold baths morning and evening.

I was sure I could follow the trail back the way we had entered, but two hours of exploring only led me deeper into trackless jungle and I felt relieved to find my way back to the hut. I thought I could find the river by following the direction of the setting sun, but after several attempts, ending in impenetrable jungle, I gave up exploring. The hut, the clearing, and the watering hole became my daytime world.

Meals became the centerpiece of each day as I ceremoniously prepared my squash stew and two *chapattis*, chanting and praying throughout the process. Although I had been instructed in sacred food preparation, it wasn't until I was completely on my own that its deeper esoteric meaning reveled itself to me. My body became a temple nourished, not only by the material food, but also by the spiritual disciplines that accompanied its preparation. Mealtime was not just the twenty minutes it took for me to fill my stomach but began when I first washed my hands to start the preparations and continued until I washed my hands at the end of the meal. I needed less actual food because I was being nourished on so many levels that I was full to overflowing almost before I ate anything.

The other part of my routine that finally took on new meaning was meditation. Before coming to the ashram, what I called meditation was a drifting through random thought patterns with little or no control over the process. By shifting my attention to my breath, Yogi Baba had given my meditations more form and self-control, but there was still enthusiasm and discipline missing from the entire process. Once alone and forced to establish my own discipline, I took to it with a renewed determination to find peace within my eternal spirit. Sitting and watching my breath became the main activity of every day and I eagerly looked forward to finishing my other duties so I could return to my blanket, close my eyes, and drift to my inner sanctum.

It was during this time of retreat that I first noticed the flow of energy that accompanied each breath rather than just the rising and falling of the lungs themselves. Every time air moved down into my lungs, a subtle current of energy moved up my spine to the point between my eyes. On the exhale, this subtle energy flowed back down to the base of my spine completing a kind of circuit. Jungle Baba had talked at great length about the Sanskrit concept of *prana*, which he insisted could be translated as breath, energy or light depending on the context and level of awareness it was referring to.

As the focus of my meditations became the energy patterns related to the breath and not just the movement of air in and out of my lungs, the importance of many of Yogi Baba's teachings of compressing the muscles at the base of the spine and locking the energy in became clear. According to Yogi Baba, the problem of my uncontrollable energy attacks of bliss and light originated from weak or blocked energy channels. With this new insight into energy flow in meditation, I had found the way to strengthen these channels and slowly, from that moment on, energy and light became balanced within my body. I had never been told how to attune to these subtle energy currents but I guessed they knew the process of following my breath would lead me there; they knew

129

that I was ready for this experience and that this time alone in the hut would be the catalyst in my own awakening.

Without intentionally making any changes, I began to concentrate on the flow of this newly discovered energy, which, unlike the breath, pulled my awareness deeper within and further away from bodily sensations. Soon a soft light accompanied the flow of energy and at last, after over a year of practice, access to my inner being was born. Breath, energy, and light, the constituents of consciousness, became my inner guides leading me on a tantalizing trip to self-realization.

I attributed this breakthrough not to any magical technique, but to my earnest determination and dedication to the process itself. Being told to do something, or doing it to please someone else, is not the same as wanting to do it yourself. I began to look at it as if some intelligence was monitoring my intentions and rewarded me with these revelations.

The nights, however, were another trial by anxiety and anticipation. By the fifth night, I had resolved that most likely the lion wasn't going to gobble me up for her midnight snack and that I was as safe here as in the ashram, but I still kept late night watches breathing, chanting OM, and listening to the choirs of the jungle. It was then, in the black stillness of the night, listening with great attentiveness, that I began to perceive a specific flow and rhythm to the sounds of the jungle. I could actually tell when an animal entered into the surroundings and from where it was coming by the way the night sounds stilled in waves and then resumed again as my visitor moved on to different territory. Certain sounds would become hushed for smaller visitors and others would become stilled for larger ones.

These observations led me to perceive that the forest itself was, in some mysterious sense, a living being capable of communicating to me if I could learn her language. The jungle was talking to me and the exuberance of this realization quickly replaced my fears of supposed dangers.

Then I was blessed with yet another realization. The jungle was breathing as an immense being and its breath was giving me life. All living things were linked through breath. The trees and plants took in the carbon dioxide, which we expelled and in return gave us the oxygen necessary to sustain our lives. On the deepest level we were one being, one breath, one life.

I found sleeping in two hour stints convenient to keep a careful watch over the fire even though I was, by now, confident that it would last through the night. Whenever I had awakened during the night in the ashram, there was always someone awake sitting by the fire. Jungle Baba had tried to get me to see the value of these middle of the night meditations but, even though I did sit up at times, I never entered into the rhythm of the jungle as now. The nights were no longer restless vigils awaiting the security of morning but intense sensual explorations of my surroundings, feeling the presence of a new spirit coming alive before my awakening imagination.

It was on the night of the ninth day that another inner realization shocked and thrilled me, perhaps even more than my new communication with the forest. I had slept longer than anticipated and a restless feeling, as if I had had a dream experience that was not quite clear yet, pursued me to wakefulness. In that moment between the world of dreams and wakefulness, I could hear inside my head, *push the big log further into the dhunie.* It was clearly only a thought, but a remarkably clear one. When I came to full awareness, I was shocked to see that the big log I had placed in the fire before going to sleep had indeed burned away and all that was really needed to keep the fire alive was to move it further into the hearth.

Within my flowering imagination, I was sure that the fire was telling me how to keep it alive. It also was talking to me!

When I awoke to the grayness of early dawn and the chorus of birds singing the sun into the sky, I received yet another twist of fate. There at the edge of the clearing was another sack, with provisions for another ten days, I guessed. I had been aware this was the tenth day and that I would be going back to the ashram. After last night, I did not really want to go just yet, but this whole thing had not been my idea in the first place.

The second ten days plunged me even further into the mysterious world of intuitive communication with nature spirits. The jungle now talked to me both day and night. I became keenly attuned to the slightest change in her rhythm and could intuit the movement of her creatures and changes in the weather and hours of the day by paying attention to the way her voices shifted. During the day, I could perceive certain distinct rhythms; certain animals moved about at random times while others sang and chirped at specific times of the day and night. What were discordant sounds within a chaotic whole became an orchestrated symphony whose conductor was the coordinated interaction of the whole.

The fire, my nighttime companion, ceased to be tool or convenience dominated by humanity and revealed herself to be an actual spirit, alive with consciousness. It would awaken me at night when it was in need of tending and, when I added more wood it, seemed to take note of the new arrangement of sticks and set about to burn its fuel in the most efficient manner, sometimes asking that I shift one stick or another to aid in this process. I perceived that it could shift its heat center at will to make the most efficient use of the fuel at hand and, in all ways, it was programmed to keep burning.

These revelations shifted my relationship with the fire. The fire spirit and I were in a symbiosis; it wanted to keep burning just as much as I wanted it to burn. It truly became something sacred. Wood was never just tossed onto the fire but offered with care and reverence to a living spirit who would always, once I had learned its ways, reply back with a glow, sparkle or pop in apprecia-tion. I began to realize that the fire could announce visitors, as Jungle Baba had suggested, and perhaps reveal secrets of the universe as well.

As the nights passed, the moon rolled on toward full and the sounds of the jungle took on a new intonation, as the night creatures became more active and the forest itself celebrated. I had awakened to tend the fire and was squat-ting on my haunches listening to the pure stillness when something seemed to shift. The wind blew through the high branches and a solitary call of a night bird rang out as if announcing an arrival. Minutes later, the few lonely insects still chirping near the clearing suddenly hushed and I felt that someone was watching me. This sound pattern was different from any I had experienced before and I couldn't shake the feeling that someone was nearby.

Two nights later, the same sound sequences occurred but this time from out of the shadowy moonlight Yogi Baba and Nivarnji appeared. I jumped to my feet, shocked they had gotten so close without me hearing even a rustle of the bushes. Yogi Baba motioned for me to come to where he was standing. When I arrived he started off on the path and Nivarnji motioned for me to follow. My mind balked, refusing to believe that we were going to walk through the jungle at night, something I couldn't even do in the daytime alone.

Yogi's whistle broke into my mind-struggle and, without considering how I was going to do it, I started off down the invisible path trusting more than seeing where I was going. My attention was fixed on the faint glow of Yogi Baba's cloth still visible in the moonlight as we moved through dense, almost impassable jungle, lightly touching branches now and again. Within minutes I was in some kind of a spell and resisted all temptation to tell myself that I could not do this. Even this slight struggle was distracting and when the pace picked up, as if Yogi Baba was floating more than walking, I surrendered fully and floated after him.

He was gone, or at least no longer in sight, but I couldn't stop. I kept going at an incredible pace, seeing nothing but a faint trail of light that I unconsciously followed. Suddenly Yogi Baba was in front of me again and I could intuitively feel Nivarnji behind me, although I didn't turn to confirm it. We moved along still faster, a sensation I was accustomed to from the walk of power in the daytime, until I wasn't walking any more. All voluntary control had been surrendered to some higher consciousness. My instincts and sensual perception became those of a night creature and I moved with a will of another kind.

Then Yogi Baba was gone again, but this time it didn't matter at all. He was no longer guiding me. Some strange pattern of jungle consciousness had taken over and I glided along. Strangest of all, I was not really aware of my surround-ings as if I was floating along in a tunnel of suspended consciousness. I had stopped thinking about the impossibility of what was happening, stopped imposing rational fears upon the experience, and accepted it as a paranormal experience that was happening to me.

Time and distance had no relative importance, nor did the absence of my guides or any rational orientation. When I came out into my small clearing sometime later, I snapped back into bodily awareness to find Yogi Baba and Nivarnji sitting at the blazing fire. I started to laugh uncontrollably. I had no questions. I didn't even want to understand what had just taken place. I bowed, hands folded in front of me, and sat down at the fire.

CHAPTER 20

THE SWAMI

We all walked back to the ashram as the sun was peeking over the jungle canopy, lighting up a new day. They said nothing about the previous night — not that our communication was based on words — and I, wanting to hold on to the mystical sensation, did not care to define in rational terms its magic. After much reflection, I came to recognize it as a state of heightened awareness, beyond rational sense perception yet within the domain of human experience. This intrigued me as to the capabilities and limits of human perception but I realized, more than before, that no amount of questioning could reveal these limits. I had to explore the frontiers of this twilight zone myself.

Jungle Baba returned a few days later saying that they had taken my passport because my visa had expired. I was now illegally in the country and could be arrested and put in jail at any moment. This news, which should have been a source of considerable concern, hardly fazed me. I was, at that point, so devoted to the will of God (the manner in which I had began to relate to the flow of my new life) that, if jail were to be my fate, there must be a divine reason for it. Instead of causing greater anxiety, I felt more resigned to living out my life in the jungle and became even more peaceful within.

Jungle Baba also brought news that sent an air of expectancy flowing throughout the ashram. The Swami, who he said was over four thousand years old and had been the first great yogi to light the sacred fire here in Sidh Kuti, was coming in a few weeks for some special celebration.

For me, this meant little. I could not, even in my new state of mystical bliss, conceive of a four thousand year old person, and thought there must be some misunderstanding. Expressing my doubts to Jungle Baba, he laughed and had me read a passage from the *Gita*:

I have been born many times, Arjuna, and many times hast
thou been born.

But I remember my past lives, and thou hast forgotten thine.
(*Gita*: 4-5)

"Do you mean that he's a reincarnation of the first *sadhu* to live here and
attend the fire?" I inquired, after reading the passage. "How do you know
that?"

"Yes, that's what I mean," he replied, "You will see."

By now the entire concept of reincarnation and past lives had become more
than just an intellectual belief. Even my identity as OM Baba now seemed like
just another step in a continuing process of universal awakening.

That was the last we talked of the imminent visit of the Swami but everyone
worked a little harder for the next few weeks. Yogi Baba put a fresh coat of
white wash on the little temple and completed his project of building a small,
open-air altar near the entrance. Upon completing it, he produced a long,
phallic-shaped stone, worn smooth by the river, and erected it with mud in
the center of the altar. Then we all joined in a spontaneous round of lighting
cones of sticky temple incense and making offerings of flowers and water while
chanting a prayer to Lord Shiva.

While walking in the garden in the cool evening air, I reflected on the worship
of God in the form of a stone, remembering something about Jesus telling his
followers to abandon all idols of stone. I greatly enjoyed the acts of devotion
and worship, doing everything with concentrated thought and intention, and
tried not to question the wisdom of these ways. I hadn't questioned the value of
prayer, offerings, and rituals to stone idols since my first mystical awakening a
year ago. They all seemed, not only natural, but also necessary.

Jungle Baba joined me in my walk, informing me that the *Swami* would be
coming tomorrow and we were going to have a big celebration commemo-
rating the first lighting of the sacred fire. We had talked little since his arrival.
My mood had become more devotional and my endless stream of questions
had just about dried up. I took this moment, however, to express my doubts
about such things as stone idols, fire worship, and human forms of God, as I
had heard them referring to the Swami.

He quoted a verse from the *Gita* in English, something I never heard him
do before.

Even those who in faith worship other gods, because of their love
they worship me, although not in the right way.
For I accept every sacrifice and I am their Lord supreme.
(*Gita*: 9-23 & 24)

"I'm proud to see your new enthusiasm for the devotional life," he continued, once we had stopped to sit on a fallen tree trunk at the edge of the garden.

"You are on a long and challenging quest that must take you over diverse paths before there will be total understanding. Devotion is not a form but an attitude that must be thoroughly cultivated, as we are cultivating this garden," he insisted, speaking in his slow and deliberate way, as if weighing each word. "As we have talked about discipline being but a tool to build focused intention, devotion is an attitude that frees the mind of doubt and fear, the adversaries of wisdom. Devotion is not the end of your quest, but one cannot reach the end without it."

"What is the end then, Jungle Baba?" I asked, after some reflection.

"That I cannot tell you," he replied, slapping his knee in an unusual display of animated excitement. "It is different for each person, depending on his or her particular arrangement of destiny. Knowing God is not only a personal experience but it may be reacted to and interpreted in a variety of ways, all of which will create a slightly different *end* for everyone."

We sat in silence for some time. Jungle Baba seemed to be deep in thought concerning his last statement and, although I was ready with my next question, I chose to savor the moment of our mutual contemplation. My awareness shifted to the chorus of insects calling to the moon swelling to fullness in the evening sky. Its radiance created a crown of light around Jungle Baba's head.

After a long, peaceful silence, during which my next question lost all importance, Jungle Baba slowly rose and placed his hand warmly on my shoulder, saying, "Tonight I understood why we two rogues seeking God have been brought together. To remind me of the end once again."

"But what is that end, Jungle Baba?" I asked, sensing his emotional mood.

"It will be expressed differently by all souls, but in essence it is the same: *To love yourself and others as you now love God,*" he replied with a wink and a chuckle, spinning his walking stick around in a full circle and heading off towards the main *dhunie.*

I sat alone for a long time thinking about his last statement then drifting further off on the sounds of the jungle at night. As I was floating on the sound of the wind in the high trees, the faint rumble of a train way off in the distance caught my attention and the thought flashed within my mind: *Go there.* With that specific intention, I concentrated fully on the distant sound for half a minute and then, bang! I was there. I could hear distinctly the *click-clack* of the steel wheels and see a mass of bodies huddled below me.

I started to look closer at the people when one of the faces lit up, as he saw me floating there in the semi-darkness. In that instant, I became aware that I was a glowing orb of light for him, as if, through his recognition of me, I had become aware of my own presence. The next moment I was back in the garden listening to the sounds of the insects and the wind in the trees.

The entire experience had taken less than a minute but it had been so real that I was positive that I really had been there. I returned to the main fire and told Yogi Baba, through Jungle Baba, that I knew how he had found the water buffalo. I told them how I had tracked the sound of the train and with a willed-thought appeared in the coach and had seen the people sleeping on the floor. Jungle Baba, who seemed surprised by the tale, leapt to his haunches and peered over Yogi Baba's shoulder as he scratched words in the dirt floor with a piece of charcoal from the fire. They agreed upon their meaning before wiping them out and writing another until Jungle Baba understood his full reply.

Laughing to himself he said, "Water buffaloes don't ride on trains."

Returning home alone from an early milk run the following morning, I was shocked at the sudden transformation of our peaceful paradise. It had become a center of frenzied activity, like any festival city of India. A line of beggars, chanting and banging on their bowls in discordant rhythm, stretched from the temple to the main entrance. Hoards of other people were scurrying about lighting cooking fires in the field, carrying firewood from the surrounding jungle, and arranging mountains of pots and pans, bundles of foodstuff, and makeshift lean-tos for shade. A crowd of half-naked *sadhus*, with matted dreadlocks and streaks of bright colored paint drawn across their foreheads and arms were gathered at the main temple, chanting and making the traditional offerings of water, flowers and sweets.

My presence went unnoticed as I made my way to the main fire, looking for a familiar face to reassure me that I was still in the same time-space dimension I had left an hour ago. At last I saw Jungle Baba sitting in his habitual place around the fire, which was packed on all sides by the unfamiliar faces of *sadhus*, talking and drinking tea. The noise and level of chaotic activity was more than I had experienced since leaving Hardwar over nine months ago. I was, by that time, feeling panicked and disoriented and desperately wanted to get to Jungle Baba to find out what was going on.

"What's all this?" I asked, half-shouting to be heard, after slipping in behind him and getting his attention.

"Swamiji is on his way," he answered, while taking the milk from my hand.

"These people are here to pay their respects to him and celebrate the day this sacred fire was first lighted four thousand years ago. There's going to be a great feast. More people are on their way, so prepare yourself," he said, laughing to himself while turning his attention to preparing the next round of tea.

My dependence on the routine and tranquility of this place became frustratingly obvious as my attempts to pump water were constantly interrupted by people wanting to fill pots for the improvised kitchens dotting the garden. Sweeping was impossible as people moved about everywhere raising dust and bumping into me. I became distracted, unable to follow my breath while pumping or chant my OM mantra while sweeping. By mid-morning I had retreated to the far end of the garden, placed my blanket under a tree and remained far from the center of chaos, reading the and practicing my sitting and breathing.

By late afternoon, I returned to the *dhunie* and managed to squeeze in next to Yogi Baba on the upper seat just as a great commotion began out near the main gate. A tall, slightly heavy-set man, with shaven head and bright orange streaks of paint across his forehead, appeared in the slanted rays of the sun with a stream of people following behind. Carrying nothing and walking briskly, he went straight to the main temple. The crowd gathered there dropped to the ground and people reached to touch his feet as he passed by and went inside. Emerging a few minutes later, he eyed the new altar with expressions of approval and ran his hand over the smooth stone in the center.

As he approached the main fire, everyone stood up, bowing and repeating in near unison, "*Om namo Narayana!*"

"*Om namo Narayana!*" he replied in a booming voice that sent cheers up from the people now pressing in all around him.

There was a punctuated stillness, marked only by the steady eyes of the Swami carefully surveying the crowded sitting arrangements. He looked in the direction of Yogi Baba, who motioned with his hand for him to take the appropriate seat at the head of the fire. Turning toward the rear of the hut, he made a slight movement of his head and the people directly behind him devotedly hurried off to lay out a thick wool blanket, a tiger skin, two large pillows, and a small brass bowl with water. He moved with polished authority through the admiring crowd and took his seat on the modest throne. People immediately began to file past and place flowers on his blanket, touching their foreheads to his feet while he mumbled a nonchalant blessing and continued to astutely observe his surroundings.

I returned to sitting at the head of the fire, enthralled in this truly grand performance of calmness and total control amid what was, for me, claustrophobic madness. It was easy to see that he was not your average *sadhu* with a begging bowl. His smooth, glossy skin and round, full face with piercing eyes created a certain mystique about him. But most shocking of all, he looked truly ageless. Neither old nor young, his countenance was marked, not by time, but by strength and authority.

His admirers, mostly *sadhus* in their traditional orange or white clothing, barefoot and carrying only a begging bowl and blanket, continued to file by, some stopping to say a few words and many taking seats around him. Jungle Baba and Navarnji left their seats around the fire to sit with the Swami. After a time, two unknown *sadhus* dressed in black, one carrying a large metal trident and wearing a necklace of shiny black prayer beads, came and occupied their seats. Meanwhile, another *sadhu*, wearing the same black cloth and prayer beads as the other two, crowded in on the top seat next to Yogi Baba, who stared in his direction without yielding an inch. An air of tension came over the *dhunie* as the newcomers removed Jungle Baba's and Nivarnji's blankets from their customary places and replaced them with their own.

Yogi Baba displayed his vehement disapproval by making several forceful gestures, catching the attention of the others before picking up the begging bowl of one of them and placing it at the far end of the fire pit. The large *sadhu* with the trident gave a challenging look at Yogi Baba and, with cocky defiance, stood up to retrieve his bowl, his body language saying, 'You can't do that.'

Before he could as much as take a step, the lightning hand of Jungle Baba, who had snuck up unnoticed from behind, snatched the blanket from under him and tossed it in the direction of his bowl. His friend sitting beside him turned to confront Jungle Baba, only to have his blanket pulled from under him and tossed aside by Navarnji, who had approached from the other direction. Humiliated by the slick teamwork of my three friends, they retreated to the far side of the fire to retrieve their blankets. But the intense look of pride and determination on their faces said that the matter was not settled yet.

The ousted *sadhus* went directly to Swamiji, who was laughing aloud over the entire incident. A long and heated discussion ensued between the Swami and the three invading *sadhus*, which ended when he stood up and made a short announcement, causing almost everyone around the fire to pick up their blankets and prepare to leave. The three *sadhus* who had started the ruckus stomped off towards the main entrance, taking several others along with them.

"What did he say?" I pressured Jungle Baba, when things had settled down. "Why is everyone clearing out?"

"He declared that only Yogi Baba and the *sadhus* he chooses to attend the fire may sit at this *dhunie*." he said, still chuckling to himself as if some victory had been won.

"Who were those men, Jungle Baba? And why did they try to take over the fire that way?"

"The tall one with the trident is Hanuman Navarn and this was his *dhunie* before Yogi Baba," he replied, starting the preparations for another round of tea. "He left many years ago to sit at another temple five days walk from here. People have been saying that he wants his position back, but the code states that he can have it back only if the *sadhu* now occupying it willingly returns it to him. Swamiji did the right thing by passing the authority to Yogi Baba."

"Then where did they go?" I asked, only partly understanding the incident.

"They have refused to join in the celebration tomorrow and have gone to set up their own *dhunie* a short way from here in the jungle."

A marked silence caused me to look up and see the Swami standing before me, scratching his head in a comic display of bewilderment. Laughing with restraint, he motioned to one of his disciples, who came forward and bowed with noticeable enthusiasm to be of service.

Still controlling his laughter, Swami said something to his disciple in Hindi, who turned to me and said, "Swamiji would like to know who you are, and why you are here?"

Caught by surprise, I turned to look at Yogi Baba, who only motioned with his head for me to answer the question.

"I'm here to find out who I am," I answered in words that flowed uncensored from my mouth.

He looked with greater interest as his disciple carefully translated my reply.

"Would you tell the Swami what you are called and how long you have been here?" asked the translator, at the bidding of his master.

"I am called OM Baba," I replied, looking directly at the Swami.

"I have been here for over nine months," I added, looking to Jungle Baba, who nodded in an affirmation but without further explanation.

The Swami took a step closer and stared hard at my face before turning to Yogi Baba and saying something I couldn't understand. Yogi Baba smiled and nodded approvingly at me, then directed his gaze at Jungle Baba, who started in on a somewhat nervous explanation of how I had come to be there. Swamiji stared intensely at me during the rundown, nodding positively at times, until, with a final gesture of approval, he turned and walked out of the hut.

"What was that all about?" I asked when things had settled down.

"He has recognized you as a *sadhu* of this *dhunie* and has given you permission to sit in any seat around the fire as long as Yogi Baba is in agreement," he warmly announced, turning his attention to the tea, which was in that minute ready to come off the fire.

He began to look about for the cups, which I could see were still out by the pump, unwashed from the last round. We seemed to spot them at the same moment and I thought for sure he would scold me for not making sure they were ready on time. Instead, he leaned over to Yogi Baba and whispered something in his ear. He, in turn, immediately looked in the direction of the pump and closed his eyes, as if he was concentrating hard on something.

At that same moment, a young disciple of the Swami's passed by the pump, stopped suddenly, looked at the tray of dirty cups, and went immediately to wash them. The coincidence was too great. I was sure that these men had been reading my mind during my entire stay there and I expected them to know what I was thinking all the time. But this new display of thought projection caught me off guard. Could they really put thoughts into my mind?

"Hey, I saw that," I said, leaning over to Jungle Baba and half-whispering, as if we were sharing a secret. "How did he do that?"

"What are you talking about?" he answered, trying to make me think that nothing had happened.

"You know, Jungle Baba," I replied, letting him know that I was not to be easily fooled. "How did Yogi Baba make that boy wash the cups?"

"Now don't you worry about that," he said, as if it was none of my business. "To do that you have to know what is going on in your mind first. Pay attention here!" he said, pointing to my head.

CHAPTER 21

THE TEST

Throughout the night people kept arriving. I awoke, just as the eastern sky was presenting the first pink glow, to find crowds everywhere, bathing, chanting, and moving about with pots and pans, firewood and water. After our prayers around the main fire, where many of the visiting *sadhus* enthusiastically joined in, Jungle Baba cancelled the milk run saying that there would be plenty of milk for everyone that day.

"Swamiji has requested that sweet milk rice be prepared for all in his honor," he informed me, showing his approval by rubbing his hands together. "And tonight is the full moon of Shiva. We shall have a special ceremony with the Swami, so there's lots to do.

"Now I must find Yogi Baba to send for the main ingredients of our feast. You start the tea and don't let it spill over into the fire!" he emphasized, reminding me of my earlier lapse in concentration.

I completed my task with exacting movements, following the correct procedures as Jungle Baba had instructed me and amazing several of the older *sadhus* sitting around the fire. Jungle Baba returned just as I was tipping the pot slightly to make the last offering to the fire and he joined in shouting the customary phrases to Lord Shiva and Agni, the fire deity. We shared a cup of tea, a familiarity reserved only for special relationships in the fussy sub-culture of the Indian *sadhus*, while discussing preparations for our celebration. He told me that Yogi Baba was getting the milk, sugar, and other ingredients and sent me to gather two herbs growing in abundance on the lower plains.

Happy to be away from the center of activity, I wandered slowly among the tall grasses and ancient trees looking for the herbs and picking up a peacock feather I discovered in a thorny bush. I sat for a while in the shade of a giant tree to listen to the sounds of the jungle; a special meditation I had invented all by myself that consisted in watching the movement of my breathing while concentrating only on the sounds of the forest. At first only the most obvious sounds such as the crying of birds, wind in the trees, or the background drone of the multitude of insects could be heard. With the passing of time and greater effort to not become distracted into the collage of personal thought, one sound, or a pattern within the overall soundscape would grab my attention and I would seem to become that sound on a deeper level than my ordinary sense awareness. I would cease to identify with myself as the listener and the process of trying, and become part of the greater whole, breathing in unison with the rhythm of the jungle and integrating into the greater life-system of nature.

I must have spaced-out in my meditation longer than planned because the sun was high in the sky when I became aware of my surroundings. I quickly made for the ashram using the 'walk of power' to cover the distance in the shortest time. While cutting across a thicker part of the plain, I almost tripped over the body of Yogi Baba, sitting naked among the bushes beside the almost nonexistent trail. He sat motionless, showing no signs of awareness of my presence or that he was even breathing. I thought he had gone to another part of the jungle to get the other ingredients so I tried to say something to him but he remained motionless, as if there was nobody home in his body at that time.

The ashram was a sea of activity when I returned but, thanks to the decree of the Swami, the situation around the main *dhunie* was fairly calm, with only a handful of visiting *sadhus* sitting and talking. I tried to tell Jungle Baba that I had seen Yogi Baba meditating in the forest, inferring that he had not gone anywhere yet, but he disregarded me, saying it wasn't the time to explain anything. He set me to work separating the fresh leaves of the herbs saying, "Be attentive to what you're doing. Many eyes are watching you."

The Swami sat all day on his tiger skin at the back of the hut talking with the *sadhus* and householders, some of who had come to ask personal questions, others just to sit for a time at his feet. He seemed to have a great deal of patience and compassion for his disciples and his periodic outbursts of laughter indicated he was enjoying himself throughout it all. Sometimes, passionate discussions would develop concerning certain passages of the holy scriptures or certain metaphysical points, causing more people to gather about to hear the interpretations of the swami.

It was during one of these discussions that Yogi Baba, motioning with his arm and pointing to a spot next to him, called me to the back of the hut to join in. After reminding me to straighten my back, he had me produce my copy of the *Gita* from the little bag that always hung under my left arm and turned to a passage for me to read.

With almost imperceptible movements of his eyes, Swamiji had his English-speaking disciple move his seat next to me, making me wonder what was going on. Swamiji motioned to Yogi Baba to give a demonstration of two different meditation postures, which seemed to be exactly the same except for the position of his eyes. In one his eyes were turned upward and toward the point between the eyes, and in the other, the point of concentration appeared to be the tip of his nose.

Further discussion followed and I could now perceive that there was some disagreement, either as to which position was correct, or possibly something more complicated than that. Yogi Baba had made several slight movements of his head in my direction as if to say to the Swami, *Ask him.* I was beginning to feel uncomfortable and started to rise and return to the fire when the eyes of the Swami caught me, ordering me to stay seated.

At a nod from the Swami, his English-speaking disciple began to explain in a low voice that they were having a disagreement about an interpretation of one of the lines in the *Gita.* "One interpretation," he explained, "is that the point of concentration is on the place between the eyes and the other suggests that it is on the tip of the nose.

"Swamiji would like you to comment on this from your own knowledge," he concluded, looking to his master for further instructions.

My uncomfortable feeling was fast turning to panic as I looked around to discover all eyes on me and even the Swami was leaning forward in anticipation. I quickly read the passage that Yogi Baba had indicated and closed my eyes to concentrate on what I could say. I had played this game several times with Yogi Baba and Jungle Baba and knew that all I had to do was feel the answer coming and open my mouth to talk, but the pressure of the situation was overpowering me. Just then, Yogi Baba's whistle broke into my confusion and I let go:

"*The reference is to the origin of the nose; where it begins, not where it ends,*" came the slow and deliberate words from my mouth. "*There one will find a resting place for the senses and a source of peace for the mind.*"

When I opened my eyes, the disciple had finished translating and the Swami was resting back against a post conveniently positioned behind him and staring intensely at me. A restless silence followed during which I looked to Yogi Baba, who only smiled and nodded his head in approval, as if he was in agreement with what I had said. The Swami said something to his disciple who then asked me, "Who told you that?"

"No one," I replied. "It comes from a place of knowing beyond me personally, yet it seems to be part of me or maybe all of me at once, I'm not sure."

"You may go now and attend your fire," he translated for the Swami. "Swamiji will talk with you later when the moment is more appropriate."

These sudden bursts of wisdom were now unquestioned by me and their slow and effortless development had left me feeling quite comfortable with the whole thing. Jungle Baba had explained that this type of knowing was part of their ancient tradition but little known these days, so people reacted strangely at first. In the depths of my being, I knew that wisdom was recorded somewhere and trusted it would just flow out of me in the proper moments. My experiences of what I called God included a dynamic relationship between energy, wisdom, and love. My identity was intricately woven of these three expressions, which were, in essence, my true self. Energy and wisdom both required love to be in harmony with the divine.

A short time later, a group of peasants entered the main *dhunie* bearing gifts of rice, raisins, nuts, and a big sack of raw sugar. My mind right away wanted to know who told these peasants to bring them. Not Yogi Baba, because I had carefully watched him all day and there was no time he was gone long enough to make the trip there and back. And even if he did run all the way there, why didn't he bring the provisions himself?

"Stop thinking someone is trying to fool you all the time." came the voice of Jungle Baba, "and let's get to work!"

"Only if you tell me how you sent for it!" I shouted back in playful defiance, while lifting the sacks of food and starting for the fire.

"Thought may be seen as a vibration set in motion by an act of will," he began, after he had set the milk to heat and started to pick through the rice, removing stones and chaff. "When the mind has been trained, not only in concentration, but in maintaining focused *intention*, thought may be directed within consciousness by your will. As with all things within the metaphysical world, your belief in the possibility is essential".

"Why is it always Yogi Baba who does these things?" I asked, as we were finishing the cleaning of the rice. "Is he the only one who can do it?"

"Yogi Baba is in training, you might say," he replied, adding the rice to the sweetened milk and arranging the fire to cook slowly and not burn. "He is a great yogi who has mastered his mind and has the least amount of desire compared to the rest of us. That makes it easier for him.

"When talking about thought, power must be realized as the result of clarity and calmness, not strength and control.

"But remember, my young yogi, it all begins with why you want to do it and knowing what is going on in your own mind. The process of becoming aware of your own thoughts is the same process involved in *sharing* the thoughts of others," he concluded, placing special emphasis on the word sharing by pointing directly at me in that moment.

Filled with greater interest than ever, I wanted to question him more but I knew that, for now, our conversation was over. Together we mixed kitchen spices with the herbs I had gathered and ground them into a fine paste. Jungle Baba put the final touches on the consistency, saying it had to be ready to dissolve when it enters the milk rice.

Ram Dass Nivarn had been conspicuously absent all day, something I could not remember ever happening before. While cleaning the grinding stone in the prescribed way, leaving no residue of our work and spilling not a drop of water on the ground, I asked Jungle Baba where he was and if he was going to be here for the ceremony. He explained that Nivarnji had been a disciple of Hanuman Nivarn when they both sat at this *dhunie* many years ago but they had a falling out over personal matters. He was spending the day in the jungle with his old master to arrange a friendly solution regarding who had the right to sit at the head of this *dhunie*.

"He will be with us if he decides to be with us. If he doesn't, then he will not," replied Jungle Baba, looking out over the garden as if the future of this place depended on Nivarnji's decision.

"You mean he might decide to leave us?" I asked, intuitively sensing what he was saying.

"What *might* happen is for fools to think about," he said, which meant he was about to change the subject or stop talking all together. "The wise person concentrates on what *is* happening. Now go and take your bath in the river. There's nothing more to do here until the feast."

CHAPTER 22

THE FEAST

With great fanfare of devotion and reverence, the feast was served in the early afternoon. Yogi Baba and Jungle Baba first made offerings to all the shrines, gods, and spirits before serving the Swami and his closest disciples, which included all of the *sadhus* at our *dhunie* and many others. At the end of our meal, the Swami's English speaking disciple informed me that his master wanted to meet with me at sundown. I was to rest, go to the river and bathe, and put on a clean white cloth for the ceremony.

I returned from the river just before sunset to find the ashram in a festive mood with crowds of people gathered about the temple blowing conch shells and lighting incense in preparation for evening prayers. The Swami, in his dramatic way of constantly shifting the focus of energy, had moved his seat to the far end of the backfield and was surrounded by disciples in front of a blazing fire. At the main *dhunie* sat Yogi Baba, staring off into space, strangely preoccupied over something. Jungle Baba joined us a short time later also in a pensive mood, only nodding as he took his seat.

"*Om namo narayana,*"came a familiar voice, causing us all to look toward the temple. There stood the top-heavy form of Ram Dass Nivarn, his rail-like legs straining to support the weight of his great coil of matted hair, pouring water over the phallic stone and chanting something. His face was streaked with fresh orange paint and he wore a grin from ear to ear. We greeted him with an emotional salute (hugging not approved of in these circles), as Yogi Baba made room for him on the uppermost seat. No one asked any questions but we all knew that his decision had been made — he was with us.

He and Jungle Baba chatted about the ceremony, which, for reasons I hadn't been informed of yet, had something to do with me. A breeze blew through the hut signaling the beginning of sunset and I started to break a few twigs to build up the fire for the evening ritual.

"No, that won't be necessary, OM Baba," said Jungle Baba. "We will be joining Swamiji at his *dhunie* when he sends for us.

"Where he is sitting is the location of the original *dhunie* of this ashram, first lit over four thousand years ago. Only Swamiji has the right to sit there now."

One of the Swami's disciples came to present each of us with a bright red and yellow cloth and tell us that the Swami was waiting for us. Jungle Baba instructed me to put the cloth around my neck or on my head and to keep it there all night.

"For no reason whatsoever should you remove it or wear it below the waist during the ceremony," he insisted. "It will indicate that you are from the swami's *dhunie* and will form a symbolic unity among us all this night.

"The Swami, it seems," he continued slowly while stroking his beard, "has taken up our special interest in OM Baba and, we think, has recognized you as an ancient friend of Sidh Kuti. The ceremony tonight will initiate you into our inner circle and perhaps remind you of who you are," he concluded, with a fatherly grin of satisfaction.

We walked in silence to the far corner of the garden. When we arrived at the Swami's *dhunie*, we placed our blankets on the ground and took our seats, with me sitting in the seat of honor just to the right of the Swami. There were three other *sadhus*, all with matching red and yellow scarves tied about their necks and long dreadlocks dangling down their backs, sitting about the fire with their backs perfectly straight, either looking at the flames or with eyes focused inward. The Swami's English-speaking disciple and one other person in householder attire were sitting to his left, eyes glued to the Swami, anticipating his every request.

My mind was suddenly filled with questions but I knew it was too late so I concentrated on my breathing and looked at the others in our circle. Swamiji was sitting in a full lotus facing east, eyes closed, his freshly oiled chest and shaven head glistening in the light of the full moon just rising over the tall trees at the far end of the garden. I closed my eyes to center myself and started a slow counting of heartbeats between inhalations and exhalations, concentrating on the hollow between my eyes. The jungle clearing reverberated with the songs of holy praise to the many forms of God — shouting, cheering, and praying for the one spirit to come — as evening worship was peaking at the main temple.

We completed the customary evening prayers and offerings of rice and *ghee* (clarified butter) to the sacred fire, with the English-speaking disciple leading the chants and making the offerings at precise times. Just when I was beginning to think that we were going to go on all night, Swamiji raised his arms and everyone let out a booming cry of *Bum bum boli Shivaji!* We fell into a peaceful silence. All eyes were fixed on the Swami, as if there was more to come. He looked at Yogi Baba and Jungle Baba before bringing his eyes to rest upon me. He smiled a radiant smile then slowly let his eyes focus deep within my heart for an eternal minute.

Speaking slowly and deliberately, as his disciple eagerly translated, he began, "The gods have directed you once again to the place of your initiation. These decisions are not made by any of us but are written in the stars that guide the soul on its journey. It is the general consensus of those gathered here that you are an ancient soul on a sacred journey to remember your origin and responsibility to all humanity. We cannot do this for you but perhaps only prepare you for what lies ahead."

Turning to his disciple, he received a new white cotton cloth and a shining brass *comundle* with a stainless steel cup resting within it. "These are the gifts bestowed upon you by our temple this day. They are our blessings and symbols of the life of a renunciate. With them go the responsibility always to remember God first."

As he placed them carefully in my crossed arms, I held back tears of joy. Something within me was saying, *now you are ready*, but for what, I wasn't sure.

The Swami then reached to his hearth and took a pinch of ashes before turning to face me again. Our eyes met in a new sense of recognition, an unfolding of something old, yet familiar. He touched my forehead with his thumb saying, "Our blessings today join the wisdom that you carry within you. May all know you as OM Baba, the wise," he concluded in a louder voice, which carried out over the silent garden as he sprinkled rose water from a brass saucer over my head.

We sat in silence for a long time before Swamiji started to softly chant and slowly everyone joined in. The chant had a particular rhythm and chorus line, which we all sang with increasing enthusiasm. This went on and on as our concentration and group unity increased with each passing moment. At one point, I opened my eyes and could clearly see light fields around each person. Each face had a golden radiance similar to my first mystical experience in Varanarse. I was chanting, having either learned or remembered the words to the prayer, but I was hearing my voice as if listening to the person next to me.

Suddenly, a wave of love and gratitude swept over me and blissful, light-filled energy began to flood in upon my awareness. In a flash, I saw my body sitting below me just before everything in my vision vanished except the leaping flames of the fire. Mesmerized by its dance of expressive potential, personal awareness faded and found myself sitting before Swamiji and two other men; but something felt strangely different. I heard myself talking in another language and them answering me but I was somehow watching and participating in the event at the same time. The fact that no one else was now around the fire did not seem strange. Time and space had lost their consistency once again; but this time the alternative reality was so vivid that my other self, OM Baba or Tom, seemed like a dream I had just awakened from.

Duality then vanished and I was sitting before the Swami four thousand years ago. The two men on either side of him felt instinctively familiar but I could not take my eyes off the face of the Swami to look more closely at them. I began to talk in a rich, poetic way about the problems of society and its self-destructive ways. I wasn't listening to myself talk but absorbed in the emotions of what I was saying.

"True, Babaji," remarked Swamiji, "but that may also be seen as a creative reaction to the collective ignorance of society. They're not trying to self-destruct, as you see it, but rather to transcend human entrapment through rebellion."

"That may be true, Mahatmaji," I answered, "but why do they reject the order and form of our spiritual practices? Without these, only chaos and ruin can come for all."

"Or within these spiritual beliefs, only stagnation may grow," came the assuring voice of the Swami, talking in a light-hearted way, not as if he knew, but as if we were searching for the answers together.

"This we do not know. It is our minds that cling to the old out of uncertainty of the new. We believe that all of this has been created by Brahma, is sustained by Him and will one day be destroyed by Him in turn.

"For us, this is true, and we must live as we believe," he continued, as I offered no objection to what he was saying. "But there is a remote possibility that even this primary assumption of the reality of God is but a series of inconclusive thoughts held together by our own beliefs and has no more truth than that. We cannot challenge that because it is the foundation of our existence. That task must fall to others who are freer to explore and challenge, to those who still see life as a mystery unfolding each day."

I felt I wanted to disagree and say that we had a specific responsibility to guide the lost souls of the world but I could not. I no longer believed that it was true.

The form of the Swami was suddenly aglow with a brilliance and radiance as if he were not a solid being but an energy field of light. I was filled with a sense of compassion for all beings, seeing them all involved in a process of removing obstacles to human unity by resisting stagnation and going with the flow. I could also perceive that there was no one flow, one way, or one form appropriate for all. *Reality was a dance of possibilities upon the stage of human choice.*

CHAPTER 23

LIGHT BABA

The next moment, I was back sitting around a fire with a gathering of *sadhus* in the twentieth century. The chanting, now reduced to a mellow hum, continued as if each person was absorbed in their private inner reality. I looked toward the Swami. His eyes were open and focused on me. A broad smile flashed across his face as our eyes met in what could only be described as an eternal recognition. I felt the urge to jump up and throw my arms about him; I often wonder why I did not.

Could we have had the same experience, reliving an ancient encounter out of our collective memory? I was sure that we had done just that. Now I knew that he was what others said he was and that I, too, had been part of these sacred encounters thousands of years ago.

I tried to move but my body was rigid. My back and knees throbbed with unrelenting pain from not having moved for what must have been well over an hour. As awareness dawned upon me, I noticed that there was no sound of chanting or talking from the other fires about the garden. An eerie stillness hung over the ashram and the surrounding jungle, like the calm before a storm. It made me feel uneasy, as if I might not have made it back to my accustomed time-space reality.

Enduring considerable pain, I struggled to free my stiffened legs and moved my head from side to side to relieve the pain in my neck. I heard a low chuckle near by and looked to see Yogiji and Jungle Baba sitting nearby by enjoying my strained effort to regain physical mobility. I started to say something or, more correctly, I thought of saying something, when I heard inside my head, *You are not to talk for three days.*

The next three days passed like a vivid dream with me floating about the ashram in a pleasant state of disorientation, doing nothing. Spiritually, I felt wonderful, calm, centered, and meditative. On the physical level however, I was having difficulty getting back into my routine of walking, pumping water, and cooking and was spending more time sleeping and staring off into space from under my tree in the garden. By the morning of the third day almost everyone had left except the Swami, his closest disciples, and a few *sadhus* still camped in the garden. Having missed morning prayers and the first cup of tea, I bathed and went to the pump to do a few hundred strokes to jump-start my sluggish body.

The morning sun beat down on my thinning body, now dark brown from not having worn more than a loincloth for over half a year. I was sweating slightly after the first hundred strokes so I decided to increase my breathing rate, bend the knees, and put some force into it! At two hundred, the rush of oxygen to my brain gave me a 'second wind' and loosened up my muscles. Dripping sweat and hyperventilating, I stopped at three hundred strokes and looked out into the garden to see how far the water had reached.

Standing under my tree was a man in simple white cloth waving his arm, signaling me to come.

"Please come here. I would like to talk with you," came a voice, which sounded like it was coming from inside my head. I wasn't sure if this was my imagination or his voice echoing off the jungle. He waved again so I walked over to where he was standing. *"Om namo narayana"* he greeted me, suggesting by his movements that we sit on his blanket together.

"Om namo narayana," I answered, looking carefully at him. He appeared to be a *sadhu*, walking barefoot and carrying one white cloth and a thin blanket. His short-cropped hair suggested that he followed the custom of shaving his head once a year. His face was smooth with stubble of white whiskers and his eyes were bright with a constant twinkle of aliveness. There was a bamboo walking staff and a small brass bowl next to his blanket but nothing else, not even a little arm-bag, string of beads, or spare cloth for his head. There was something different about him from the other *sadhus*. Some strange iridescent glow about his head and body made him appear as if he wasn't totally there on the physical plane.

"I have been watching you for several days now," I heard, this time definitely inside my head.

"Are you talking to me?" I asked, not sure if he was speaking to me or where the voice was coming from.

"Please sit down. We will have a talk," I heard his thought-words inside my head. He was talking English inside my head but gesturing with his body as if he was speaking out loud.

"OK, Babaji, we can have a talk," I said, taking a seat on the hard-packed ground next to him. "At least we know the same language."

"*You are having a mystical life-change,*" he continued, having got a clear frequency inside my mind.

"How do you know that?" I asked, getting a sense that he was a wise man. It seemed so evident that he was talking that I kept looking to see if he wasn't moving his lips.

He was communicating to me on multiple levels at the same time. No words were being spoken, but thoughts, in English, were going through my head. His facial expressions and the movement of his eyes were in perfect synchronization with the thoughts as they passed before my mind. But more important was the feeling that his words or thoughts, which ever they might be, were bypassing my rational analytical process and going directly to a place of acceptance and understanding.

"*Life force has awakened higher energy centers in your being. I have been observing your moments of forgetfulness, staring off into the ocean of consciousness,*" I could feel him saying inside my mind. "*Life is not always solid and definable any more.*"

I loved it! He knew what I was experiencing and could articulate it better than myself. I looked even harder to make sure he really was there before asking aloud, "Can you tell me the next step in my journey?"

"*The next step is the one you are now taking only with greater dedication of purpose and intention,*" He emphasized his message by holding his arms to the sky before bringing them to rest over his heart.

Never had anyone brought such rest to my mind. His answers were satisfying to me on many different levels. For most of my life, answers to my questions only prompted more questions. But now I had no more questions.

"*That is good,*" I heard in answer to my thoughts, "*because your rational attention still distorts your perception of the unity that surrounds you.*"

Right again! I started to think, how is he doing it? But he cut in saying, "*When you're able, you will know how. Until then, knowing would only be a distraction.*"

I could only bow and would have touched his feet, the respectful honor reserved for true wise teachers of India, but a slight movement of his hand stopped me.

"Why have you come, Babaji?" I asked, feeling him so different from other *sadhus.* "And where do you come from?"

He told me he had been here throughout the festival. He had come to visit with the Swami, whom he had known for a long time — instinctively translated by me as more than one lifetime.

"*I come from the high mountains where the men of wisdom and compassion commune with the Spirit reality,*" I heard his thought projections once again. "*Here, these men practice a yoga of the physical reality, using disciplined and focused mind to influence life's flow. With greater surrender one becomes the flow and there is no need to influence anything."*

The call for the second round of tea came from the main fire and I rose to take leave of my new friend and teacher.

"Will you be staying for some time?" I asked, feeling as if I did not want him to leave just yet.

*"For some days, yes. I will visit with the Swami now that the multitude has left,"*he replied with his thoughts. *"We will talk again."*

When I arrived at the *dhunie*, Jungle Baba motioned for me to sit next to him and served me a cup of tea. I wanted to ask him about the *sadhu* in the garden but wasn't sure if the three-day ban on talking was over. Something strange and wonderful had happened during my short exchange with him. The endless stream of urgent questions that constantly filled my mind had stopped. I reflected, while sipping my tea, that these questions were the result of wanting someone to solve the mystery of life for me; to give me one more piece of information that would make everything clear. I was now experiencing that these questions were not necessary, as I had always considered them to be, and even that they were obstacles in the path of my own inner peace.

Sometime later while I was straightening up around the *dhunie* I saw Light Baba, as I had started to call him for the etheric radiance of his presence, approach the hut and could not resist asking Jungle Baba about him.

"Babaji is from the distant mountains," he replied, pointing off to the east. It is rare to see him in these parts. He must want to talk with the Swami."

"Is he a great yogi, Babaji?" I asked.

"No, I wouldn't call him a yogi," he replied, looking at Light Baba taking a seat near the Swami. "Yoga is a means to a more complete realization of..." He paused, looking for the right word before saying, "totality. I would say that he is known rather as the keeper of the ancient way, as one who reveals clarity to those who seek in earnest," he concluded, speaking with his eyes almost closed, as if hearing the answers himself before repeating them to me.

"Now, no more questions my young seeker," he said, letting me know our conversation was over by handing me the milk jug and pointing to the jungle.

As I walked listlessly along the narrow path listening to the monkeys chattering in the high trees and feeling the late morning sun on my bare back, my mind wandered to the encounter with Light Baba and particularly how he could completely enter inside me, even to know what I was feeling. Everyday there were fewer separations between my environment, the minds of others, and myself. The meaning of his words cut through the analytical process of my rational mind. I felt he was aware of my entire being. Strange, but I felt like he was me or could completely identify with me on some universal vibrational frequency.

It took much longer at the farm than usual because they were not expecting me so late and had sent the milk to another house. Returning by the lower road where the vegetation was thicker and the paths more obscure, I started to bring my awareness to my heart and let my body move automatically, picking up speed as my concentration increased. After three or four minutes I was semi-floating over the ground and the customary sensation of tunnel vision set in, further detaching me from my surroundings.

Snake! I heard a voice call to me from within my head.

The now familiar sensation of time clicking into slow motion came over me as I saw a large snake curled up on the path in front of me. The mental process of seeing the green scales unfolding, deciding I could not stop because my right foot was already moving to land a few inches from her head, and looking for an alternative seemed to take several minutes. My options slowly passed within my mind without the least bit of panic or fear. Time and awareness seemed to be intricately connected, as if the greater the alertness the slower the passing of time.

I instinctively lowered my walking staff to the ground inches from its head and, imitating my pole-vaulting style from high school, thrust my legs up and over the uncoiling snake. Riding the arc of my pole, I pushed off with my arms and landed with a quick skip and a jump on the opposite side of the path. I turned to see her slithering into the underbrush and only then did I realize what had happened.

While wiping a little spilt milk from my body, I noticed that my heart had not accelerated and my stomach had not tightened. Another part of my consciousness had taken over and handled the danger without fear stimulating my reaction.

The experience itself was enough to keep me reflecting for the rest of the day but what happened when I arrived back at the ashram topped even that.

"Quick work," said Babaji, as I handed him the milk. "Your mind has become free of distractions these days."

"Wait a minute," I said suspiciously, "what are you talking about?"

Yogi Baba, sitting near by, was restraining himself from laughing. There were no traces of milk on my body but one of them could have been watching nearby and arrived back ahead of me. I looked at Navarnji and he made a little squiggly movement with his hand, as if he was imitating a snake, and then made a clown-like gesture like he was flying. It was not like him to joke around and it made me all the more intrigued.

"Come on Babaji." I insisted. "What are you talking about?"

"The snake," he replied, looking into the jug while noticeably restraining his laughter. "Not bad. Didn't spill much after all."

He refused any further comment, insisting on silence for the rest of the day. Reading my mind, putting thoughts into my head and now watching me while

I walk alone in the jungle. This was getting to be too much. What were the limits to the invasion of myself, or what were really the limits of myself?

A few days later, the young disciple of the Swami, who had been mentally *asked* by Yogi Baba to wash the dishes the other day, came hurrying into the ashram and went straight to the swami. I was just finishing my pumping meditation and went to join the others, who were, by then, engaged in a heated discussion about something. I waited patiently, hoping Jungle Baba would explain when the commotion was over but he did not. Instead he sent me to pull some dead limbs in from the surrounding jungle saying that it was none of my concern and not to fill my head with unnecessary chatter.

After working in the hot sun for an hour while chanting OM silently to myself and listening to the chorus of insects and birds singing in the surrounding forest, I sat to rest under my tree at the far end of the garden. I had just opened my *Gita* to read something inspiring when I heard within my mind, *"Please stand up."*

I looked up to see the luminescent form of Light Baba standing in front of me. How he had gotten that close without hearing him baffled me but, by this time, I was giving up on trying to understand anything these men did.

We had *talked* several times since our first meeting and I enjoyed his company and his wisdom that always brought peace to my restless mind. I had never really heard him actually say anything other than our standard *sadhu* greeting, not even to the others, but our communication was infinitely more complete than anything I had experienced before in my life.

"Will you tell me what is going on Babaji?" I asked, after standing to greet him.

"That depends on whether you can answer something for me first," he replied inside my mind. *"Come,"* he said, turning and walking towards the edge of the garden.

He stopped at the trunk of a large tree that had fallen into the clearing with one of its larger limbs projecting parallel to the ground six feet in the air.

"Can you climb up this limb and stand there for me?" he communicated with inner words, motioning to the limb.

It seemed easy enough so I scrambled up the trunk and climbed onto the hanging limb. "What next?" I asked, showing him that not only could I stand on it, but could even turn around and make it bob up and down under my weight.

"Good. Now think about where you are. I will be back in a little while to hear what you have to say. If you can answer my question before falling off the log, I will answer yours," he communicated, before turning and walking in the direction of the temple.

It was not hard to stand on the limb whose rough bark offered a good gripping surface for my bare toes, so I began to watch the parrots in the high trees and listen to the drone of insects. Fifteen minutes later he returned and asked me, *"Where are you?"*

"Standing on this log, in this jungle." I replied. "Can I come down now?"

"No, that is not correct. You may have some more time."

He returned several times over the next hour and I went through all the obvious answers — here in the ashram, in the jungle, in India, and even on the planet Earth — but he would only say within my mind, *"No. You may have some more time."*

What was a simple task an hour ago, standing on a wide log six feet in the air, became increasing more difficult as the intense mid-day sun beat down on my sweating body and my legs became shaky trying to hold the two or three possible positions. I lost my balance several times and almost fell off. I decided to try a little longer and began counting my breaths to keep my concentration. On his next pass I tried, "In my body," to which he smiled and walked away without any communication.

He didn't return for sometime and, in my effort to stay on the log, I became absorbed in my breathing to such an extent that I heard inside of my head, *"Where are you?"* without even seeing him approach.

I was counting to seven on an in-breath and instinctively replied, "On an in-breath!"

"Good. You may come down now."

By that time, I was in an altered state of consciousness from the intense concentration and physical endurance it had taken to stand on that limb for over an hour. I could only think, *"What was the meaning of it all?"*

"You are where your attention is," he answered. *"And on an expanded level of reality,"* he continued with a serious twinkle in his gray eyes, *"you are your attention, not your thoughts, your dreams, or your beliefs. Who you are is, in many ways, determined by what you are aware of at any given moment. It is not solid, nor always consistent, but a flexible probability of choice."*

CHAPTER 24

THE ANCIENT FIRE

We walked in silence to the *dhunie* and sat with Jungle Baba and Navarnji. After a short time of rocking on his haunches and staring into the mellow flames of the fire, Jungle Baba explained what all the fuss was about around the fire this morning. He told me that Hanuman Navarn and his followers were coming with a group of farmers from his temple to take this land away, saying we have no real title. They were on their way, twenty or more, and some action had to be taken. He said many things about an ancient dispute over this land, which I could not follow well.

"What will we do then, Babaji?" I asked, not really knowing how to react to the events.

"First we will prepare," he said in a determined voice. "What will be done will depend on the moment and cannot be anticipated. Determination must be accompanied by flexibility if resistance is to succeed.

"You will not be able to ask any more questions. All of my attention must be turned to the situation at hand," he said with a stern face, more preoccupied than I had ever seen him.

"From now on Babaji will be your guide," he concluded, bowing hands folded towards Light Baba.

I could not imagine what 'we will prepare' meant but the general mood had suddenly become more concentrated, everyone carefully guarding personal energies. Yogi Baba went to the temple, which meant he could be anywhere on this planet or the universe. Jungle Baba and Navarnji went to the far side of the garden with a pot of embers from the fire. I could see them from where I was sitting under my tree, making smoke and circling some plants with white bell-shaped flowers. They were there for some time before returning, carrying some plants that I did not recognize. Swamiji sent a few disciples to light his ancient *dhunie* in the far corner of the garden.

Light Baba said nothing the whole time and I could not really make him think to me. I loved being with him whether we communicated or not, so I was happy to be exiled to the back garden and hang out with him. No food was prepared and no one seemed to want any. In the late afternoon, Light Baba and I bathed together at the river and were returning by a roundabout way when we ran into a group of fifteen peasants carrying bamboo poles and heading toward the ashram.

At evening prayers, Jungle Baba and Navarnji were stripped almost naked with faces and bodies painted in colored streaks. Their bodies radiated strength as they sang with greater force and determination than other nights. Swamiji did not join us from his *dhunie*. Yogi Baba was still in the temple.

The fire was also unusually powerful this evening, flames whipping around the fire pit and sending bursts of sparks into the air, charging us all as we sang with renewed vigor. The session never really came to an end as other nights. Jungle Baba and Navarnji continued meditating in silence after the prayers. Light Baba signaled for us to leave and we walked through the dark to the Swami's *dhunie* where we placed our blankets on the smooth earth and sat in silence for sometime.

"OM Baba," echoed the voice of Light Baba in my head, "*it would be good for you to move on in your training now. Our job has been done.*" I looked at Light Baba, who was sitting with his back straight, eyes closed as if in trance, and then to the Swami, who captured my attention with his ancient eyes.

"*You had to pass through Sidh Kuti on your trail of awakening, for memories have been stored here,*"continued the voice. The Swami was talking to me. I could see it in the subtle shifts of expression in his eyes and face, but it was the thought-voice I knew as Light Baba. Yet another note was being played on the chords of my consciousness — three-way mind link-ups across barriers of language and culture. In that moment, I perceived communication as a multi-dimensional process involving intention, will, intuition, and feeling, origi-nating far beyond the words themselves. Words and even languages were only a conceptual framework within which human communication took place.

"*Your friends are arrayed on the battle field of life just as the myth of our sacred book,*"continued the thoughts of the Swami within my head. "*I will be called upon for advice whether to fight or not. Now that both sides have forti-fied themselves with the sacred power plants of war, reason may not prevail. My thoughts weigh heavy on my mind. I ask you, ancient friend and one of wisdom, counsel me in this matter.*"

The intensity of life here in this jungle retreat kept me on a constant edge of multi-dimensionality and all reality had become relative to so many vari-ables that were still far beyond my limited understanding. Therefore, I was

159

only slightly surprised when energy jolted through my spine and out of my imagination appeared Arjuna, sitting in a chariot, bow held limply in his right hand and arrows protruding from the quiver at the back of his head. I made no attempt to hold to my identity as OM Baba. Identity was clearly a choice. I felt like I was playing Krishna in a school play and had forgotten my part. I said nothing, as the lines of force of this new reality crystallized before me, until there was no more Swamiji and Light Baba just Krishna and Arjuna standing between the armies of good and evil.

Part of me wanted to laugh, feeling this reality shift was ridiculous; more than my shattered identity could deal with. But I could not, because the words were already pouring from my mouth.

"The wise man sees that good and evil are extremes of the same unity.

He counsels actions that will create cooperation and sharing among all sides.

He worries not, knowing that self-identity obscures wisdom.

And for themselves they may choose to fight, thinking they are right."

I snapped out of my vision to see Swamiji, clearly before me once again, with his palms joined together over his heart and head slightly bowed, My mind was alert, waiting for the process to begin again.

"You will be going now," broke in the voice upon my poised mind. *"Babaji shall guide you until he feels your paths must part. You have unraveled some of your web of personal identity, woven out of attachments to people, things, ideas, and beliefs. Your destiny will be clearer to you now."*

Tears of joy and sadness rolled down my face and dropped from the tip of my beard onto my folded hands. Light Baba bowed to the swami and stood, indicating I should do the same. Before rising I bowed and heard within my head: *wise grieve not for those who live; and they grieve not for those who die. Face to face with what must be, cease though from sorrow.* Words I knew well from the *Gita*.

My heart was pounding as I passed an anxious moment resisting my destiny. I stood and bowed to the Swami before walking in hypnotic indecision with Light Baba to the main temple. By the light of an oil lamp burning inside I could see the lean form of Yogi Baba, legs crossed in a full lotus and eyes turned inward in deep meditation. He acknowledged me, not with any physical signs, but with a presence in my head, giving me his silent blessing in my quest. I poured water from my new *comundle* over the Shiva *lingam* while saying a silent prayer of thanks and protection for this place of fortification and learning.

"We will be going now," came the thoughts of Light Baba. *"Is there anything you would like to take with you?"*

I thought of my old shoulder bag with my journal and notebook that I hadn't as much as looked at in months and said, "No. I'm ready."

I turned to look out over the garden and said goodbye to the plants now ripe with green vegetables and giant squashes. Through the shadowy hue of a moonless night my eyes could perceive the silhouetted hand pump against the darkness of the jungle and memories of my former self, overweight and out of shape, caused me to chuckle to myself. The farmers, who had assembled at the main entrance, were talking quietly among themselves, bamboo poles in readiness. I admired their loyalty, but was it wise to fight for anything in this material world?

"Karma is but the flow of destiny acted upon by personal choice,"came the wisdom of Light Baba. "Right and wrong are concepts that still bind you to this world of duality. Let us be going."

He turned and headed for the trail leading down to the lower plain and out toward the river. As we passed the main *dhunie*, I stopped and looked at the figures of Jungle Baba and Navarnji, glowing with a strange orange hue. Power and determination radiated all about them. The hallucinogenic power plant was drawing every ounce of strength from their thin, frail bodies and their nervous systems had been converted into instruments of resistance, and possibly war.

I had to struggle hard not to join them around the fire. At that moment came the primitive sound of conch shells echoing through the jungle on the far side of the garden and voices could be heard approaching the main entrance. I looked to Light Baba, who had stopped at the head of the trail, and was waiting for me. All of a sudden I seemed to lose all voluntary control and I remember only the soft glow of his vestments guiding me along an unseen path.

CHAPTER 25

Journey Alone

I awoke before the first rays of the sun to find myself in an unfamiliar place near the river. A strange aura of disorientation hung over me. I could not immediately remember how I had gotten there and the events of the preceding night were a hazy reality within my sluggish consciousness. Struggling to recall, the image of Light Baba flashed before me and I anxiously searched for him. He was nowhere in sight but his brass comundle and blanket on the ground assured me that he did exist and must be nearby.

Staggering the few yards to the river, I stripped and plunged into the current without the customary formalities of prayers and offerings. I stood in the shallow eddy with my toes gripping the sandy bottom and repeatedly dunked my non-responsive body into the cold waters until some degree of wakefulness arrived. Returning to my blanket just as the slanted rays of the newborn sun crested the lush jungle canopy, I sat to meditate, the only part of my addictive routine still possible.

"*Om namo narayana,*" a familiar voice broke into my silence sometime later.

I opened my eyes to see the luminescent form of Light Baba sitting cross-legged on his blanket before me. He untied a bundle in the end of his cloth to reveal two large breadfruits and half a dozen ripe mangos. The sight of the fruit brought my awareness to the gnawing pains of hunger in my stomach. We ate without saying a word, not that our communication was based on saying anything. As I ate, the events of the preceding night became clearer and an avalanche of questions rumbled through my mind. How did we get here through the jungle on a moonless night? Why did I feel like I had been drugged? Where were we?

He smiled, rinsing his hands with water from his begging bowl. He spoke to me for the first time other than his customary greeting in Hindi saying, "Be ready, we will be on our way."

Several confusing moments passed before I realized that I understood him in English inside of my head. Now I was sure he was some kind of wizard of communication able to make me understand in a variety of ways. More questions flooded my mind but he was off on the trail heading away from the river and into the thick underbrush of the surrounding jungle.

We walked all morning in silence through unfamiliar jungle, stopping only occasionally to drink water from flowing streams. He was not a fast walker like Yogi Baba or Nivarnji and I had no trouble keeping up. My body had become fit from the jungle training and I found it surprisingly easy to keep my once-restless mind centered on the combined act of walking and breathing, as Jungle Baba had taught me. I had not stepped on a thorn in months. I was now aware of their presence in advance and either adjusted my stride to move between them or flipped them off of the path with my walking stick without losing my pace.

By noon we had come out of the thicker forest and the trail became wider and well defined. Without the protective canopy of the tall trees the sun was intense, causing me to sweat profusely and tire. We paused in the shade of a large acacia tree to eat the remaining mangos. Babaji was in a reflective mood, often closing his eyes and drifting off somewhere. After a short rest, I regained my strength and asked in English, "What were they up to last night and why did we have to leave in such a hurry?"

"Your teachers were men of great training and discipline," I heard within my mind. *"Yet they had not reached a sufficient degree of detachment to avoid the confrontation unfolding there. Life may be divided into teaching experiences, tests of what one has learned, and the celebrating life itself. I would say they were being tested by the course of their own destinies."*

I didn't really understand what he was saying. I wanted to know what they were doing. How they were going to confront the situation?

"They were engaged in what one might call magic — the amplification of intention through a unified field of thought. Two of them had taken power plants and were using this energy to create a force field about the ashram. Yogi Baba was acting as an amplifier of their thought power, making it impossible for an outsider to penetrate this field."

"What happened then?"

"The others were fortified, most likely with the same plants, but none of them would have the disciplined concentration to break the field of Yogi Baba. He is the only genuine yogi among them but they all have learned a few power plays and will use them when the situation demands it. From what I can perceive at

this distance, all parties held firm and Swamiji will be called upon to resolve the conflict."

"If that is all, then why did we have to leave?"

"You are an awakened being unaware of your own potential. Shakti is alive in you like a high-powered instrument waiting to be fine-tuned. Yogi Baba and Swamiji decided that, because the other side knew of your potential and could have, through certain magic, used your untrained energy to their advantage, it would be best if we left. I insisted that we go so that no injury would result to your flowering energy field. Magic requires an egocentric view of the world; the belief that creation is there to be manipulated by mind power and personal desires. Transcendence, however, requires relinquishing one's personal importance and becoming identified with the whole. Magic is a choice to use personal energies to influence the flow of destiny. It is not without certain costs, regardless of whether one has positive or negative intentions."

"What are those costs, Babaji?" I asked.

"One's destiny is always a fluctuating equilibrium between will and intention. When, for any reason, one chooses to direct one's force to influence that balance, a change in this equilibrium must take. Magic, even if done in jest or ignorance, must create a mingling of karmas and an alteration, if only temporary, in one's destiny. One who repeatedly enters into such acts loses affinity within one's destiny and falls into confusion and weakness of mind."

I was ready to resume our trek, having understood his communication but still confused by why I had to leave. I started to stand when he motioned me to remain seated.

"A short way from here we will come to a road. There we will part," he said, speaking now slowly in his own language, yet conveying the meaning to me in a form of inner understanding.

I tried to say that I wanted to go with him but he only shook his head, placing his hand gently on my knee. He communicated to me that our paths would meet again but that I had other lessons to learn, which only life could teach me.

"Let life be your teacher now," he said within my head. *"I have seen your path and it will be necessary to walk it alone for now. Who can know you better than yourself?*

"A guru implies a dependency; someone to shield you from your own fears. There are people who fear to take the all-important step of self-reliance; who become trapped in the beliefs of others. Sacred duty is unique to each person, choice being more important than obedience. If you surrender your right to choose, all is lost."

I didn't understand. The last ten months had been dedicated to service and obedience. How could he now tell me that I had wasted my time?

"Do not choose self-importance," I heard in my mind. *"You have learned of the effectiveness of discipline and service as tools of greater learning. Now you must*

use them to guide your further awakening without becoming dependent on your teachers or their beliefs."

When we arrived at the road a short time later, I was fighting off depression and felt like crying. He was right. I had become dependent on my teachers in the jungle and was now trying to transfer that dependency to him. *But why not? I reasoned to myself. I was learning and...*

"Ready for greater lessons," he broke into my thoughts. *"Do not become attached to learning. That is most often just another form of personal gratification.*

"Your next lesson is to feel part of a divine plan and to play your part with joy and trust."

As usual, his answer struck a chord of truth within me and I fell silent, further insistence being useless. He explained slowly in Hindi that two days walk to the west I would come to the river Ganges again and on the other side would be the city of Hardwar. He told me that I would pass through several villages where the people would feed me and that there might even be a bus in the next few days that would take me part of the way.

"You're a *sadhu* now and people will treat you accordingly," he said clearly. "Learn to bless the ground you walk upon and all who cross your path. Someday you will understand that your quest is more for them than for yourself."

I was puzzled. I could not make rational sense of his last statement but its truth penetrated my heart.

"Is there anything you can say before we part that you feel is important for me to know?" I asked, feeling sorry for myself and wanting to hold on to the moment a little longer.

"Yes," he said with a knowing smile. "Do not take life so seriously! You have been on the path for thousands of years. What is the hurry? Try to enjoy it more. *There is nothing to achieve, only something to perceive."*

CHAPTER 26

ELEPHANT THUNDER

I walked aimlessly the rest of the day feeling lost and abandoned. I spent the night in a village where people actually fought over the right to feed me and provide me with a hemp-strung cot beneath a spreading shade tree to sleep on. After morning meditation and a cup of spiced tea, I resumed my walk along the deeply-rutted dirt road, stopping at times to watch flocks of parrots and packs of monkeys frolicking in the high trees lining both sides of the road. My mood had improved slightly from the day before but attacks of self-pity and frustration would overcome me at times, causing me to sit and pout by the side of the road.

During one of these poor-me fits, a relic of a Bedford bus, brightly painted with peacocks, flowers, and Krishna playing his flute alongside a cascading waterfall, came lumbering along the road, weaving in and out of the potholes and growling like a mechanical dinosaur. Through the dusty windows I could see that it was packed full and the roof was crowded with squatting figures with turbans were pulled down over their eyes to ward off the cloud of dust engulfing them. It hissed to a stop in front of me and the driver motioned towards the rear door. I jumped aboard and wedged myself in among the pack of people squatting on sacks of grain at the back.

Babaji had said that they wouldn't charge me and they did not. It was only then that I remembered money, not having used any in the last ten months. And my passport? This never bothered me before because I never planned to leave the ashram. I passed an anxious moment as my old addictions to the material security of money stirred up within me, before surrendering for the umpteenth time to the will of the Great Spirit.

A short time later, our rolling icon veered off the dirt track and bounced and clanked along a dried riverbed. The main road had been washed away and this was a difficult alternative to no road at all. The going became rough, plowing our way through loose river rocks and patches of sand. Several times we bogged down and the people riding on top had to climb down and push. Everyone seemed to take it in stride and cheered the pushers as the bald tires spun and the motor growled under the strain. I had learned from my hitch-hiking in India that the capacity of a motor vehicle was beyond my wildest imagination, so I just took this circus act to be normal.

We had just finished one of these Chinese fire drills when the people in the front of the bus began to shout and point toward the far side of the riverbed. I squirmed around and peered through the cracked window next to me. A small heard of elephants, with several young ones toddling along, was coming out of the sparse undergrowth. This was my first time to see elephants in the wild and I stared in amazement, not understanding the reaction of the other passengers. I was fascinated by the baby elephants and paid little attention to what was going on around me until two of the larger cows begin to charge at the lumbering bus. The screaming escalated as the driver tried to speed up, but there was really little he could do to move faster in this terrain. They continued charging out of the sparse undergrowth as the rear tires began to spin helplessly in another patch of sand. We were trapped.

I was still staring out the window when the first elephant slammed into the bus, rocking it forcibly from side to side. The next minute its tusk was jabbing through the window five rows in front of me and I came to my senses. Among terrifying screams, I turned to face a horror scene on the far side of the bus where people were squeezing through the windows as the bus rocked more violently. Bodies flew through the air as the people on top abandoned ship and raced to the high side of the riverbed.

I was next to the back door but I could not move. The terrified human mass became jammed like logs on a river, everyone pushing and shoving to get out the rear exit. By then, both elephants were at the bus, and one grabbed the roof rack with its trunk, shaking the bus like a rattle. Hysteria gripped the passen-gers. We were about to be flipped any minute. I sensed, as Jungle Baba had said, that I was not going to die, but a voice inside my head was shouting, *Be alert. Real danger's at hand!*

It was then, as I was gasping for breath and pushing back to keep from being crushed by the panicked mob trying to get out the back door, that reality cracked and time distorted so that I wasn't struggling for my life but observing a horror show passing before my eyes in slow motion. Several times in the past year events of great danger and fear had caused me to slip between the veils of time and space to experience an alternative reality. These two pillars of the material world had become relative to my awareness in the moment, not fixed or immutable. Among the roars of our savage attackers and the stench of a fearful humanity fighting to escape our metal coffin, I heard a voice inside my head say, *Hang on!*

I grabbed the rack over my head as the maimed bus rocked once more and came crashing to its side, causing a wave of glass, bundles, and bodies to spray in all directions.

Dangling by my arms and covered in glass and rice, I surveyed the heap of bodies below me before curling my toes around the frame of a seat and easing my weight down. The screaming subsided as the attacking beasts, satisfied that they had killed the intruder, moved away, trumpeting thunderous battle cries of victory. The severely mutilated vehicle now lay lifeless on its side. The bottleneck released and people began spilling out the back door. The smell of gasoline reached the interior of the bus and I decided it was time to move fast. Stepping onto the carpet of humanity below me, I took one shaky step forward and jumped to the ground.

From the high side of the riverbed, I could see the herd of elephants heading back into the underbrush. Two people had died, crushed beneath the bus, and several others sustained minor injuries of cuts, bruises, and broken bones. I hung around for an hour helping to clean superficial cuts and carry personal belongings to the high bank before deciding to walk on.

I couldn't help but observe the way others handled the reality of death. The mutilated bodies dragged from under the bus were not cause for sorrow. The soul had not died but had left its old clothes behind and gone on to another journey.

The following day, I made the treacherous crossing of the river Ganges in a bobbing wooden boat and walked into Hardwar. I was a different being than the hippie who had left for the jungle almost a year ago. I stood tall, back straight and head held proudly like Yogi Baba had insisted. My curly brown hair dangled around my shoulders and my full beard hung in two points below my chin. I was thin but full of energy and walked with a new lightness, characteristic of the Indian *sadhus*. I spoke a fair amount of Hindi, which gave me a new sense of integration with the people. Everywhere I went, I was greeted and accepted as a *sadhu*.

Of all the noticeable differences, however, the one that brought me the greatest peace was the control over my spirit energies I was now enjoying. Before my training in the jungle, I was continually assaulted by rushes of energy and bliss, which invariable distorted my perception of the physical world into swirling masses of energy and light and brought on uncontrolled fits of laugher, often leaving me screaming of God and love in the midst of crowded streets and markets. Now, through control of my breath and greater concentration in general, I could sit and relax into these blissful perceptions of the total unity and watch the energy fields of people and nature pulsate before my fixed eyes. I could choose the moment and the place and was no longer overcome by the intensity as before. I had, with the help of my three teachers, integrated my insanity into my being and now understood why I had these attacks in the first place.

I no longer had a problem with too many worldly possessions. I had only two pieces of white cotton cloth, which I could wrap about me in a variety of ways, thin strip of cloth I tied about my groin as underwear, my yellow Shiva cloth which served as towel, turban and support for my spine during meditation, and my blanket; my mobile home, which I carried over one shoulder and spread out wherever I wanted to sit down. I carried a small brass *comundle*, a bamboo walking stick, and my small arm bag, which contained my *Bhagavad Gita*, pocketknife, wooden comb, and a twig from a jungle tree that served as a toothbrush. Everything I carried I used every day. That which I didn't have, I didn't need.

I could now understand the wisdom of Jungle Baba's statement that I would learn the ways of the wandering *sadhus* of India and this would give me a ticket to wherever I wanted to go. It was obvious, after only a few days, I had been well trained. I knew all the rules of the sacred hearth, sometimes better than some of the 'city *sadhus*' that I came in contact with. I could sit cross-legged with my back straight for over an hour with ease and could join into the rituals and chanting, knowing the rhythm and words of many chants. Yet the most useful of my skills was the training I had received from Nivarnji on the etiquette around the fire and the preparation of the temple foods. I could walk into any ashram kitchen and see exactly where I could be of service, be it peeling vegetables, washing dishes, grinding spices, or toasting *chapattis*. No one ever asked me where I had learned but they always observed me scrupulously in the beginning to see that I accurately followed the required procedures. I had learned well.

I decided that I would just travel around India visiting the holy temples and shrines. I traveled by train, having been instructed by Jungle Baba to take a seat on the floor in the third class car and the conductor would never ask me for my ticket.

"You have to feel that you belong," he instructed me. "It is your right as a holy man to ride free but your belief in that right will make it so. Don't feel you're doing anything wrong and always be willing to get off if they ask you to."

Two months later I sat on the floor in a third-class car staring out the open door at the parched farmland stretching off to the far horizon, sighting an occasional lonely tree that had survived the onslaught of human settlement. The rocking motion of the antique wooden car and the rhythmic *clickity-click* of the steel wheels lulled me into a twilight zone of reflection.

Screech! Crunch! The train came to a jarring halt, spilling people and baggage into the aisles. Catching my brass *comundle* just before it rolled out the door, I looked about to see what could be happening. I started to stand up to look outside when two men, dressed in some kind of official uniform, appeared in the doorway shouting something in Hindi. I got the idea: 'Tickets'!

The system on the Indian railway is such that anyone can get on board a train without a ticket and the conductors are supposed to check all passengers. Because corruption was a social cancer and, at times, a bribe was necessary even to buy a ticket at the station, many people rode the trains like playing a lottery. With luck the conductor will miss you among the chaotic mob and, if not, it is still cheaper to pay a bribe to the conductor on the train.

I had been through ticket checks before, but the conductors always let me ride free. This looked different. The words of Jungle Baba echoed within my head, *Don't think you're doing anything wrong. Sadhus have the right to ride free.*

They both looked at me, being the first body inside the door, and we had a split second, wordless encounter, during which time I just focused on the idea, *I am a sadhu.*

"Ticket!" one of them said authoritatively.

I smiled, shook my head to say no and waited.

"Your passport."

I smiled again and told them that I didn't have a passport. It had been lost sometime ago and I didn't have any money to get a new one. They paused and talked among themselves, trying to decide what to do with me. I knew that their game was to get as many bribes as they could during the raid and the people who did not have any money would be rounded up and sent to jail. The problem of having no passport was obviously more serious than that of having no ticket. I was beginning to get the feeling that I was in trouble.

"Stand up and come with us! This is a matter for the authorities."

They marched me through the crowded cars to the head of the train. By the time we reached one of the upper-class cars, I was deep in prayer and hoping for a miracle when a well-dressed merchant gasped in surprise at seeing me and dropped to his knees touching my feet. The security guards tried to get him to move out of the way but he kept looking at me with a stare of disbelief while shouting at the guards to take their hands off of me. A great commotion ensued while the man and his wife argued vehemently with the two guards who then released me from their grip and began to listen to what they were saying.

The guards backed off a bit as the man went to his bag in the luggage rack and produced a fine woolen cloth, which he handed to me with tears in his eyes. Many of the people in the crowded car reacted with audible surprise as I fingered its velvety texture and held it to my forehead in the proper gesture of receiving a gift.

At his insistence, his wife said, "This is the finest *pashmina* cloth he has. Woven only from the fleece of the neck of the highland sheep. God has told him to give it to you." After a short conversation with her husband, she continued,

"About a month ago, my husband was riding another train and he saw you in a vision, confirming for him an important business decision. He was told that he would meet you someday and that he would be able to make this gift. He has carried this cloth for you until now."

In that moment, I remembered my brief out-of-body journey that had taken me to a crowded train car and being recognized by someone before returning to my body. I cried tears of joy for Spirit's confirmation of Its presence in my life.

With tears still rolling down my cheeks, I looked to my two captors who were staring at me, amazement plastered on their serious faces. In that moment, some exchange of energy took place. I could actually sense a voice saying to them: *Let him go. He's all right.* I can not say if it was my thought projections from wishful thinking or, as I wanted to believe, God whispering in their ear. It did not matter. They bowed respectfully, acknowledging my right to be there and moved on. I gave thanks, my heart overflowing with gratitude.

Bowing to my two benefactors, I retreated to the rear of the car and sat down on my blanket to pray.

CHAPTER 27

TEMPLE DUTY

I made my way out the *sadhus'* exit at the far end of the tracks the next morning and felt the explosive rush of New Delhi, a city of eight million people. With the few coins I had been given along the way, I brought a cup of spiced tea from a roving vendor and sat on a low wall watching the mobs of people streaming by. I reflected on the events of last night after the security guards had freed me from the clutches of a jail. In answer to my sincere prayers of gratitude, I had heard, *Get off the train at the end of the line.* It didn't make much sense but with my incredible faith I just asked 'why'? *Stand up,* came the voice from within me. *Walk down the street!*

I obeyed, having faithfully followed this inner guidance since my first mystical explosion at the Shiva temple in Varanarse. As I walked I entered an altered state of awareness, much like the walking trance I had learned in the jungle. I glided in and out of the crowd, my bare feet lightly tripping across the life-stained streets while feeling like an iron particle floating in magnetic field. At decisive moments I would hear, *Left* or *straight ahead,* as my vision became completely blurred and people were transformed into translucent energy fields of various colors and intensities. The cacophony of voices, trucks, animals, and transistor radios orchestrated my dance, as I floated across this congested stage of life.

The spell was broken a half-hour later as I entered the grounds of a temple. I slowly walked to an ancient shrine nestled in the trunk of a mammoth tree whose tangled web of vines climbing its central trunk cast dancing, lace-like shadows on the rough cement platform below. My breathing was calm, showing no signs of the walk, as I poured some water from my *comundle* over the phallic shaped stone in the center of the shrine. I repeated my standard prayer of thanks, asking to be of service, then stood motionless, meditation having overcome me.

*This will be your new home for a while,*I heard clearly within my head.

I opened my eyes and looked around. There were two crypt-like temples directly opposite the gigantic tree, both in need of a good white wash and a few new bricks. A high brick wall surrounded a rectangular space of about two hundred square yards, overgrown in weeds, vines, and tall grass. Only a few rough pathways had been trampled through the over-growth to the corners of the complex. It was a jungle in the middle of the city!

*You will live there under that tree,*came my guidance as I looked to the far corner and spotted a lone, leafless tree alongside a raised dirt platform. I picked my way across the trampled path full of thorny branches and broken glass and surveyed my new home. It was covered in weeds, trash, and other debris and had a foul odor. The entire area was covered in broken glass and bits and pieces of other garbage strewn in among the dead bushes.

What am I supposed to do in this place? I thought.

*That is for you to decide,*came the instant reply.

I found a forked stick and was cleaning off the raised platform to lay my blanket out when I heard from behind me, "Hey Babaji, what are you doing there?"

Startled by a human voice at last, I spun around to face two young men dressed in tight western pants and button-down shirts. They were Indians, speaking good English, but their unkempt western clothes and slick vibrations suggested that they were some kind of street hustlers. One was tall and thin with a pointed nose and narrow-set eyes that made his face seem tight and sinister. His friend was on the short side with a more disheveled appearance with hair jutting out at all angles from his round, jowly head.

"I'm going to live here," I replied with certainty.

"You're what?" they both gasped back before breaking into uproarious laughter.

I said nothing, returning to my task of clearing a place for my blanket. Part of me was definitely having second thoughts but some persistent guidance kept insisting that I was supposed to be there.

"Hey Babaji," called the tall one who had come closer and was leaning on the low brick wall, "You know what this place is?"

"It's a temple and I have been told to live here." I said, pausing and looking toward them both.

"No, I mean here," he went on, laughing even harder and indicating more specifically the platform I was cleaning. "This is the pis corner! This is where we come to take a pee!" he laughed, while making gestures of pulling down the fly of his pants.

Without hesitating I said with certain conviction, "Then you will have to pee over in the other corner because I'm living here now."

By midday I had cleared the platform, scraped a level of tainted dirt away and was resting on my blanket in the shade when they returned with three friends. They hung out in the near corner talking and looking over at me. Finally they approached, placing two bananas and a mango on my blanket.

"Babaji," said the leader, who had been there in the morning, "Why do you want to live here?"

I remained silent thinking, *because I have been told to by a voice inside my heart.* He went on saying, "Look around you. It's too dirty even for us Indians to live here."

I had been considering that when they came in. It was a despicable mess of neglect and lack of respect. I was hoping that before nightfall the voice would come again and say that there had been a mistake.

I surprised myself by saying, "I'm going to clean it up."

"What? You're going to clean the whole place up?" he gasped, spreading his arms toward the far side of the garden.

I looked to the far wall through the dead limbs and dried underbrush and remembered my father forcing me to clean up the yard to earn my allowance. I was having a slight karmic attack by this time and had to breathe deep before replying, "Well I'm going to start where you're standing and work my way to the far wall. It doesn't matter how far I get."

They retreated to the near corner again for another round of talks while I relished the bananas and mango as the first foods of the day. I couldn't shake the feeling of being a drafted-volunteer for a karmic clean up duty. My father had loved gardening and had often obligated me to stay home on Saturdays to help him. I had never enjoyed it but, looking out over the sea of trash and entangled foliage, I felt that this was going to be different.

Then, in the eye of my imagination flashed the vision of a magnificent garden with flowers spotted like jewels along winding brick pathways and fountains cascading water into glistening lotus ponds. *Bang!* That more certain feeling of 'having been here before' rocked my time-space coordinates, flooding me with feelings of wisdom and teachings of times a thousand years ago. I saw counsels of wise beings, kings and queens drawn together to guide the destiny of civilizations, taking place under the canopy of the ancient tree. Tents of bright colors ringed her far perimeters. Reed flutes and stringed instruments blended with the exotic fragrance of jasmine and frankincense.

I felt related to the images drifting in the etheric fog before me. For a split second, I experienced my identity as a vibrational affinity with a specific frequency; a choice inspired by attraction. Past, present, and future all danced together as probability coordinates within the timeless web of my destiny. In that moment of identity suspension, life was definitely more electro-magnetic than organic and thought more real than form.

Then I was part of the image itself. My long flowing garment of brightly colored silk danced in the light breeze as I walked with other men and women about the magnificent garden teaming with exotic plants and birds. We entered a spacious green and gold colored tent and walked across the carpeted floor to take our seats on over-stuffed pillows awaiting us. The frail figure of an ancient wise man entered from another direction followed by several people carrying embroidered cushions and an ornate water pipe.

Clang! Clang! The ringing of the temple bell burst my vision and I was staring at the cluttered mess before me, my half-eaten banana resting in my lap. No wonder I had been an excellent c+ student, who excelled in daydreaming in the back of the classroom. A shame imagination never played an important part in my education.

"We will come by tomorrow, Babaji," interrupted my tall benefactor, as he and his friends filed by on their way to the main entrance. "What do you like to eat?"

As if someone else was answering for me using my voice I heard, "I eat fruit, peanuts, and milk." These had become my preferred foods, but I ate anything that was properly offered, except meat. By late afternoon, I had cleared the area in front of my platform, placing all glass and other non-organic refuse in a deep hole I discovered at the far end of the garden and piling anything that would eventually decompose in a corner. I went to the pump and rinsed my sweat-drenched body.

This is a heavy one, I thought, looking at the abandoned rose bushes hidden in the tangled mat of dried grass and vines. *Why was I supposed to be here? Why do I feel like I have come back to somewhere?*

Many mysteries flooded my mind while I walked about those parts of the garden accessible. Returning to my corner, I was preparing to meditate when a young boy about sixteen entered the grounds and came straight to where I was sitting.

He placed two bananas and a handful of peanuts on my blanket in front of me, saying, "I will come tomorrow. Thank you."

I thanked him in Hindi and watched as he went quickly to the main temple, rang the bell and hurried out the entrance.

Over the next week, my life organized itself around a routine of scraping and cleaning pathways and flowerbeds in my corner of the temple grounds. The temple itself was located behind a well tended park of several acres, whose brick pathways wound through mammoth astronomical instruments constructed of stone and mortar, some more than 40 yards high. They had been used by ancient civilizations to calculate the movements of the sun, moon, and planets in order to measure the changing of seasons and length of each year.

After evening meditations, I would stroll about this ancient observatory chanting softly to myself, often stopping at these epic calculators to ponder their uses. I knew that other gigantic stone observatories had been built by prehistoric civilizations possibly more advanced than ours today. I felt that aligning oneself in relationship to other heavenly bodies of fixed positions was a highly advanced concept, possibly arising from the genetic memory of human origin beyond this world. I sensed through my developing psychic antennas of imagination and intuition that the inhabitants of Earth were actually an intermixing of life forms (perhaps not all of Earth origin), spanning millions of years of evolutionary development and influence one upon the other.

During the early evenings, the park was full of students of all ages walking about anxiously and mumbling to themselves, trying to memorize their lessons. The Indian education system was based on the tried-and-true British method of memorizing facts and regurgitating them at particularly stressful moments in life without understanding their meaning or significance in relationship to anything else. Creativity and imagination had been purged from the system and replaced by competition and fear of failure. I could not help feeling that the students were engaged in a useless task, forced upon them by an educational system that retards the expansion of human consciousness into areas of creativity and intuition and rewards only rationality.

"Babaji," came a soft voice, breaking into my daydream as I stood before one of these gigantic structures one evening. "I brought you this bottle of milk."

The boy who had given me the peanuts the first night was standing before me holding a bottle. Before I could say anything, he said, "I have an exam tomorrow morning and I want you to help me."

"Why do you think I can help you?" I asked, laughing inwardly at the thought of me helping anyone with an exam.

"I know you can, Babaji. I have been praying for someone to come to this temple and help me and I know you're the one. I'm not a good student. My mother is sick and if I fail, it will be too much for her. Here take this, and I will come for the bottle tomorrow."

"But don't you think you should wait until tomorrow and see how you do on the exam before giving me this?" I asked, half-teasing but quite impressed by his conviction.

"No. You will surely do it if I leave the milk tonight." he replied with absolute faith, having thought out his strategy well. "I will come again tomorrow and remember, my mathematics test in the morning, please," he concluded, hurrying out of the park.

I prayed hard for the young boy and his test while drinking my warm milk that night. The next day at noon he came for the bottle, thanking me for my help. He was sure he had done well and that I'd had something to do with it.

CHAPTER 28

PISS CORNER BABA

Three weeks later, I had reached halfway to the far wall in my effort to reclaim the garden from human neglect. I worked two or three hours in the morning and the same in the afternoon, scraping grass from the pathways and clearing out weeds and dead plants. My hands, although hardened from my work in the jungle, were red and sore. My back ached from walking around on my haunches for hours at a time. What started out to be a project to kill time while waiting for my next orders from heaven had become a source of great joy and satisfaction. Yogi Baba had taught me to work with a certain detached enthusiasm; to use physical activity as a means of directing my mind and developing focused attention.

I chanted my OM mantra as I squatted and scraped away, slowly restoring the garden to its former beauty. The words of the *Gita* gave me hope that my madness had a spiritual foundation:

> Set thy heart upon thy work, but never upon its reward.
> Work not for a reward, but never cease to do thy work.
>
> Do thy work in the peace of yoga and, free from selfish desires,
> be not moved in success of in failure. Yoga is evenness of mind –
> a peace that is ever the same.
>
> Work done for a reward is much lower than work done in the yoga
> of wisdom. Seek salvation in the wisdom of reason. How poor those
> who work for a reward! (*Gita*: 2- 47, 48 & 49)

By this time, I had my first disciples. Remembering the words of Jungle Baba, 'the disciples fit the teacher', helped me to laugh and accept it all. Some were a group of street hustlers who hung around the American Express office and big hotels, buying and selling black market dollars or stolen travelers checks. Others specialized in stealing anything that they could get their hands on.

At first I tried to reform them with moral arguments of karma and justice, to which they would only reply: "But this *is* our karma, to have to steal for a living. I'd love to work in a bank, but it's not possible." I settled for guiding them not to harm others and to help those with less than themselves, lessons they were responsive to.

They looked to me as their *Baba* bringing me food each day and producing a few hand tools to make my work easier. Sometimes they would help by carrying rubbish to their respective corners, even pull a few weeds, but I never asked them to do anything. They used the temple as a hangout to eat lunch, smoke hash-laced cigarettes, and retreat from the midday sun. Most of them spoke English, being in the tourist business, and many evenings we would sit and talk about religion, God, and the hardships of life. They discussed their problems, which apart from money (like the rest of the world), were mostly about sick relatives and friends, problems with the law, and the rising cost of bribes.

My other set of devotees were a growing number of students enticed by the success of my young friend Pretan, who now brought me milk two or three times a week and spent considerable time at the temple. The students would greet me on my walks, bowing with folded hands. A few even asked me to touch their notebooks for good luck. Many brought me fruit and peanuts and would stop by my *dhunie* the night before exams to touch my feet and remind me of their test the next day.

For me, it seemed like some karmic joke to be playing the part of Piss Corner Baba, the patron saint of thieves and reluctant students, but it did fit the Buddha's guidelines for right livelihood. I took my role seriously and counseled them in their needs, praying for whatever they asked.

For all of its apparent neglect, the temple had a constant stream of visitors, mostly women of determined faith coming to make offerings, light candles, and pray to a higher power for guidance or help. Throughout the day, people came to sit under the majestic tree, talking, lunching, and napping. The boys told me that the smaller, most visited shrine honored *Lakshmi*, the Goddess of Prosperity and Fertility. The glossy-orange, vaginal formation at the center of the crypt was believed to grant the boon of a child and money of course.

The larger temple was dedicated to *Vishnu*, sustainer of all material creation. This was the favorite of businessmen, who dashed in first thing in the morning to say a quick prayer and toss a coin through the bars before hustling off to work.

There was a lay priest, or *pundit*, who came by once a week to clean the shrines and collect the coins. He never said anything to me directly but often stood off to one side observing my work with palatable distaste. My gang told me that he was not pleased by my presence because, according to custom, he was responsible for feeding me, providing me with clothes and other material necessities, and sharing the money with me. I told them I wasn't interested in these things, feeling that God would provide me with whatever was necessary.

"Yes, Babaji" said Prem Lal, the leader of independent tourist association. "But having a Western *sadhu* living here is considered good for the prosperity of the temple. Many more people are coming because you live here now."

"Then the pundit should be pleased I'm here." I said, having just taken my seat after an evening bath at the pump.

"You don't understand this country, Babaji. Everyone's stealing from someone. For now, he hasn't bothered you. I think he sees something different in you."

"Who are you stealing from, Prem Lal?" I asked, crossing my legs and rolling my scarf under my spine for meditation.

"I steal from the government. They make the money market their monopoly.

"I perform a service, Babaji," he bragged, bringing his thin body erect and making a comic gesture of dignity with his angular face. "I help people get more for their money than the government will give them."

I said nothing, reflecting on discussions I remembered with my father. We saw life so differently and could never see the other's perspective. Life was repeating itself on so many levels at once. Events of a thousand years ago intertwined with lessons of the present moment, separated only by veils of awareness within my mind.

"Good night Babaji" came several voices from the devotee section as they filed out the gate. "Pray for us to have good luck tomorrow and we will bring you fresh milk."

I smiled and said nothing, having heard the request before. I prayed for all the pilgrims and devotees of the temple. As they stood before the shrines, I would send them a loving OM charged with the intention to help while visualizing a ray of light surrounding them. It had become a habit in Sidh Kuti under the direction of Jungle Baba and here I had taken it up again with disciplined regularity. Prayer remained a compulsive necessity, preformed not out of fear or hope but from the absolute conviction that compassionate thoughts did influence material reality and help mold personality.

Closing my eyes and entering into the rhythm of my breathing, I prayed a soft request, thinking of the jug of milk: *Help them if it can be so, oh Great Spirit*. I continued my evening breathing routine, until the rhythm of my heart and lungs felt in harmony. Turning my attention to the altar between my eyes, I became absorbed in the peace of another meditation. Since coming to the temple, my times of meditation were cherished moments of devotional union. My intention for each meditation was to create a charged atmosphere of prosperity for the temple and I put special emphasis on this projection in my prayers. I read with enthusiastic joy the counsel of the *Gita:*

> Offer to me all thy works and rest thy mind on me the Supreme.
> Be free from vain hopes and selfish thoughts, and with inner peace fight thou thy fight.

> Those who ever follow my doctrine and who have faith, and have good will, find through pure work their freedom. (*Gita:* 3-30, 31)

I reached the far wall after another month and turned to see most of the brick pathways clean and debris cleared away. I strolled proudly back to my corner thinking of my father, whose presence was constantly with me, and the importance he placed on 'a man's work'. I reflected on how a man's relationship to life is so integrally involved in his work and from that he derives his major identity and purpose as a provider. A woman, however, was identified with her role as mother and nurturer and could assume her purpose from more abstract and creative aspects of life.

In my labors, I had gathered bricks fallen from the surrounding wall, a few sturdy poles buried in the underbrush and giant palm branches from the observatory. With these I wired together a classy lean-to under the now-blooming mulberry tree. I had resurfaced the dirt platform with a mixture of fresh cow dung and straw and dug a brick-lined fire pit. I admired my *sadhu dhunie* and again the feeling of living the rest of my life in this garden brought a sense of peace to my mind.

The *pundit,* who had not shown up for weeks, entered the gate as I was preparing to take my evening bath. He did a quick double take when he saw the patchwork structure that had sprung up in his absence. He quickly splashed some water around the entrance to the shrines and gathered the coins from inside, glancing from time to time in my direction. I walked to the pump along my freshly cleared path and was preparing to pump some water when he approached me. Speaking nervously in Hindi and avoiding eye contact, he stammered, "You cannot live here, Babaji. You must leave within three days!" he screamed, thrusting three fingers in my direction to make his point.

I replied in my best Hindi, "God has told me to live here. I will stay until He directs me somewhere else."

He stared in frustrated amazement, definitely having understood that I was not going to leave.

"You can't stay!" he half-shouted before turning and stomping out the gate.

A few students sitting nearby under the big tree had overheard our exchange and came to ask me not to leave. "He doesn't want you to live here because he wants all the money for himself," one said. "He is not a good man. Please stay and help us. Our final exams are coming and we need you."

"I don't plan to leave." I said, turning my attention to my bath. "We'll find a way to live together, I'm sure," adding a positive note to the otherwise unpleasant encounter.

I talked with Prem Lal that night about our meeting and he agreed that I should not leave.

"He's been stealing money from this temple for years. We all know this but nothing can be done about it. The government of Rajastan owns the temple and they pay him to do the work you're doing. I think he's afraid that if you stay, the people in charge will see what's going on and his abuses will be exposed."

"What can he do, Prem Lal, if I refuse to leave?" I asked, sensing the situation to be more difficult than I imagined.

"Almost anything, Babaji," he replied, looking to the others for confirmation. "He's an angry man. People say he has cancer from stealing from the temple. I don't know, but we'll protect you.

"In two weeks, there will be a big celebration here for *Lakshmi*. If he doesn't get you out of here by then, he may give up and start to treat you with proper respect and share some of the food and money with you."

I worked hard during the next two weeks pruning the hundreds of rose bushes with only a pocket knife, trimming shrubs dotted about the garden, and clearing the secondary walkways. The pundit had made several attempts to get me out of there, but my entourage of students and hustlers had stood in my defense, threatening him with exposure to the authorities if he tried anything.

On the morning of the big celebration, many women arrived early to set up cooking fires and prepare the feast of milk rice, *puries,* and *subji.* I had decided not to work, anticipating a festive day. The boys had just finished their morning 'pick-me-up' cigarette and were about to stroll down to the American Express when the pundit entered the gate with three police officers and made directly for my *dhunie.* The boys, seeing their nemesis with bamboo clubs in hand, indiscreetly scattered in all directions and I braced myself for another adventure.

"Your passport please, Babaji," asked the senior officer in a stern but polite way.

"I don't have a passport. It was lost some time ago and I don't have the money to get another," I replied honestly.

"Then you will please come with us. This is a matter for my superior," he softly commanded.

CHAPTER 29

CLUTCHES OF THE LAW

We entered the cramped, windowless room of police headquarters some time later and I was politely asked to take a seat in a corner opposite the door. With a certain exaggerated ceremony, I spread out my blanket and placed my begging bowl and walking stick next to it before sitting up straight with my legs crossed under me. During the next two hours I was politely questioned and convincingly threatened with up-to life imprisonment for violating several legal restrictions by three different officers, each with an improving command of the English language. Tea was then served, English style, with china cups and saucers. Then I was left alone for several hours.

Indian jails, for people without money, were infernos of wasting humanity, the horrors of which had circulated along the trail ever since Istanbul. I fluctuated between faith that some miracle would happen to get me out of this and rising anxiety of being swallowed up by an Indian prison for the rest of my life. Several times I considered making a run for the door but my inner guidance told me to hang tight. I had a better chance facing this thing with courage than becoming a fugitive on the streets of New Delhi.

In face of the outstanding odds against any possibility other than jail, I straightened my back, surrounded myself with light, and breathed myself into deep meditation. I prayed to be accepting of my fate, but insisted that I preferred something outside of jail. *Let me be surrounded by light and whisper in their ear, oh Lord. Let thy will be done outside of prison, OK?*

A long time later, judging by the stiffness in my back and knees, a soft voice called me from my meditation.

"Babaji, May I talk with you?"

Slowly I opened my eyes and adjusted my awareness to the physical surroundings of the hot, stuffy office, with the clanging of typewriters and the whirling of antique ceiling fans. Sitting in a chair that had been placed in front of me was a well-dressed man in a Nehru jacket and white cotton pants. His slightly overweight body, neat appearance, and perfect English distinguished him from my previous interrogators, who now stood anxiously behind him with various expressions of expectation on their faces.

He went on to say that he was head of this office, called in from his home for this meeting. He did not ask anything about my passport but only wanted to know how I came to be in this country living as one of 'our holy men'.

"I have experienced God," I began, hearing myself speak from a slight distance. "Here in your country there is a place for one who has had such a vision. In my country I would be considered insane and be locked away in a hospital and subjected to violent treatments to make me forget. I'm living like this," I went on, gesturing to my begging bowl and clothing, "because this is the only life for me now. I would like to stay in your country."

"Babaji, you have no passport and the law says that now you must go to our jail. What are you going to do?"

"Then going to jail must be my fate, at your hands."

"You don't care if we put you in jail?"

"I would prefer to live in conditions that would allow me to learn more from your holy people. The situation of my life is such that I do not have a passport and have no money at this time to get a new one.

"If you really have no money, how do you live?"

"The same way any *sadhu* lives in your country. I live in temples, helping in whatever way I can, and people provide me with what I need.

"I can feel that you are a man of spiritual heart," I continued, for the first time feeling that perhaps *he* was the miracle I was praying for. "I trust that you will be guided to do the right thing by God."

"But Babaji, there is nothing I can do. You have broken our laws and I must put you in jail," he replied in a not-too-convincing tone. I knew that he did not want to do it but I wasn't sure if he could just let me go. It was obvious that he was the last in line and it would be his decision.

"Babaji," came his hesitant voice, after several minutes of silence, "how is a man such as I to live a life of dedication and service when my fate is to be in a job such as this?"

I was slightly shocked. He was asking for spiritual guidance. I felt myself in the familiar role of a *sadhu* being asked for help, not a criminal one step from life in prison. A greater presence came over me and I let my eyes gently close and waited for the answer.

"Do your duty, even if it be humble, rather than another's, even if it be great," I said, quoting from the *Gita* (3-35) that I knew so well by now.

"What you have been called to do as your work within society is your karma;

that which outlines the course of your life. What you choose to dedicate your actions to creates your destiny. Dedicate all your actions to the good of all the world and your soul shall know peace and you shall know God."

From the stillness of my inner world I could hear him translating what I had said for the others. There was some soft discussion before he asked, "Where does this wisdom come from, Babaji?"

"One may say that it comes from the sincerity of your question and the desire of the one before you to help you. Where there is love for God, there will be love of humanity. Out of love arises wisdom."

Only the whirling of the overhead fans pushing stale air about the stuffy room broke the serenity of the moment. I opened my eyes to see the chief staring intensely at me and the other officers leaning over his shoulder to get a better look. I smiled and bowed to them with my hands folded in front of me. I knew that the moment of truth had come. He was contemplating what to do with me.

He motioned with his hands for his subordinates to stand back then turned to talk with them in Hindi, while I listened to catch what I could. Then, pulling his chair closer and leaning toward me he said, "Babaji, you may go. But you must never tell anyone that you were brought to this office or that I let you go. I will lose my job if you do and I have a family to support.

"I will have to send you with two of my men to the US embassy to get a new passport. That is the only way I can justify my actions to the people in this office. Do not tell them what happened here today. Please forget what happen here today, Babaji."

"Thank you, sir," I calmly replied, while feeling like jumping for joy from within. "May God bless you for your wisdom this day."

"I feel that He has blessed me through our meeting this day."

As I left with two policemen, I felt as if I had been clutched from the frying pan only to be tossed into the fire and considered, for the second time that day, making a run for it. I knew it was a long shot trying to get a passport without any money but I was flying on faith as we approached an old English mansion with expansive lawns and gardens surrounded by a high brick wall and elaborate wrought iron gates. Suddenly, I was uncomfortably close to the long arm of Uncle Sam. On impulse, I bowed to my escort, as if to say, *you may go now*, and approached the front gate alone.

I told the guards at the front gate that I had lost my passport and, after surrendering my walking stick, was led to the appropriate desk where a secretary handed me the standard forms and asked me to fill them out. My *sadhu* attire of white robes and bare feet caused subdued chuckles from workers who shuffled by or poked their heads out of opened doors.

After completing my forms, I sat and observed the activities of this little piece of the USA tucked away in an upper-class suburb of New Delhi. The place was in crisis. The air conditioning was out and old ceiling fans pushed air about the room; ties were loosened, buttons undone, and suit coats discarded. I wanted to suggest that they adopt the national dress of loose fitting cotton clothing but just sat and chuckled to myself.

I was finally led into a large office with high ceilings, oriental carpets, and large windows thrown open this day to the heat and humidity of the world outside. Behind an oversized desk sat a chubby man, ringed in sweat and breathing heavily, who took my forms from the secretary without looking up at me.

Prayer was in my heart as he reviewed my papers while wiping his sweaty brow with a handkerchief.

"Everything seems to be in order, Mr. Heckel," he announced after a long wait. "There will be a fifty dollar charge. I don't see your money with the form, Mr. Hec...." He paused in mid-sentence as he looked at me for the first time since I had entered the office and tried to contain his shock.

I was down to one hundred pounds, draped in worn cotton cloth, with long curly hair hanging loose around my head and face. My eyes were those of a madman, peering out of sunken sockets without blinking or showing recognition. Barefoot and with a begging bowl in hand, he had his reasons.

He recovered his composure and asked if I had the money, to which I replied, "No".

"And just how long have you been in this country without a passport?"

I went blank. I didn't know how long. Suddenly I felt tricked by such an obvious question. I tried to concentrate but nothing came, so I said, "Don't know"

"Oh. I see," he muttered to himself while looking me over more carefully.

"You know, son, you're on American soil now," he said through a cocky grin. "I think we should just see what's up with you."

He pushed a button on the intercom but got no answer so he lifted his bulky frame up and walked slowly toward the door.

"You just sit tight, son. I'll be right back," he snickered as he stepped into the hallway.

My first thought was, *it's all over,* but my second thought was, *not just yet.*

Inspired by the instinct of survival, I took one step toward the desk, snatched the forms with my free hand and with my next movement was on the windowsill preparing to jump. I landed in soft dirt and began to run along the perimeters of the building keeping to the cover of the flowerbeds. I rounded the corner and was thinking of making a break across the open lawn toward the high brick wall when I spied an old Indian gardener sleeping under a shrub in front of me.

Take the gardener's coat and put it on! commanded a voice from within me. And my awareness shifted.

I tiptoed to where he was sleeping, picked up his official green jacket and put it on. I quickly wrapped my spare cloth about my head as a turban and moved to where he had left his wheelbarrow at the edge of the open lawn.

I picked it up and began to move quickly across the open space towards the back of the compound.

Slow down! demanded my inner being. *You are an old man. You are tired. Slump your shoulders. Your right leg hurts. Walk with a limp.*

I slowed, hunched over and started to limp along, pushing the wheelbarrow ahead of me. By this time, everything was happening in slow motion and every step was an eternity. But I could see a vision of my escape unfolding through the veil of time as my awareness leapt minutes ahead of the present moment. I could see myself, through this warp in time, going over the back wall to freedom.

There was shouting at the far end of the compound but I never looked back. I could intuitively sense that the guards had rounded the corner of the building and were looking at the old man limping across the lawn. I resisted the temptation to turn and see if they were coming after me and intensified my thoughts of, *I'm just an old man.* Step by slow step, I limped towards the back wall, now only 100 feet away and getting closer.

Fear and excitement had been suspended and I was deep in a spell when I reached the back wall. I calmly placed the gardener's coat on the wheelbarrow, picked out my blanket and begging bowl, and scrambled up the pile of garden debris that was almost to the top of the wall. There I caught hold of a lower limb of a tree and swung myself onto the wall. With freedom just 10 feet down, I lowered myself on the edge of the wall and dropped to the ground.

CHAPTER 30

DEBBIE

It was late afternoon by the time I entered the temple grounds and made my way to the main shrine to say a prayer of thanks. Feeling like a born-again *sadhu*, twice clutched from the gates of hell, I took hold of the cord and clanged the bell loudly three times, *"Bum bole Shivaji, yah ho!"* I shouted.

"Bum bole Shivaji," boomed the voices of friends and disciples gathered under the temple tree.

Soft chanting, accompanied by the *cling, cling* of finger cymbals and clouds of temple incense swirled forth from the entangled vines shrouding the ancient shrine beneath the sacred tree. I looked about me to see the garden filled with people sitting in small groups finishing their feast to the goddess Lakshmi. Prem Lal and the boys greeted me enthusiastically, wanting to hear my story. I told them everything was in order and not to worry, I was not leaving. I decided I would not leave the temple yet and my return was a signal to the *pundit* that I belonged here.

After taking some water at the pump and receiving a large banana leaf full of milk rice and *puries*, I walked to my *dhunie*. My hut was untouched but sitting in the shade of my palm-branched roof were two *sadhus*. They had left my seat at the head of the *dhunie* unoccupied, a sign that they accepted my position as the resident *sadhu* of this temple.

"Om Namo Narayana," I greeted them, laying out my blanket and assuming my position at the head of the *dhunie*. They both enthusiastically returned my greeting, as if they had been waiting for me. One of them was very old with long white hair and beard that outlined his nearly black face and accentuated his sparkling gray eyes. I had noticed him several times sitting in the temple grounds observing me from a distance, although we had never spoken to each

other. The other was younger (if one could ever really tell the ages of any of these mysterious holy men) and he wore the orange cloth of a renunciate, with matted dread locks dangling to his mid back. His thin, chocolate brown body was streaked in orange paint and his sparkling brown eyes shone like those of a young boy. His general appearance was that of a person with a healthy sense of humor.

We sat in silence while I ate my meal. They exchanged a few comments about my mannerisms, which never failed to amaze the older sadhus, before the white haired one, sitting ramrod straight and stroking his long feathery beard, motioned for Prem Lal and his crew to come join us. They talked among themselves while I finished my meal and rinsed my hands from my *comundle*.

"Babaji," said Prem Lal, taking a seat on the raised platform with the other *sadhus*, "these holy men would like to talk with you. This is Baba Vishnu Diva," he said, pointing to the older sadhu dressed in spotless white cloth sitting to my right. "And his friend Baba Prem Dass." We greeted each other with palms joined together and bowing our heads slightly, saying nothing.

"They would like to know, why you have come to live here in this temple?" he asked, looking to the others, who nodded in approval.

I had thought about that myself during my walk back to the temple. I didn't know exactly how to say it but trusted that these men could understand.

"Spirit has guided me to be here." I began, pointing to my heart for emphasis. "I have been connected to this temple for thousands of years and I must have something to finish here in this lifetime."

They both smiled in obvious approval as Prem Lal translated my message. Some discussion followed between them before Vishnu Baba turned and talked directly to me. Prem Lal translated his message as meaning that both of these men had recognized me as a reincarnation of an ancient Baba, who sat on this spot before, and had come to pay their respects to me. They knew that I had come to return this temple to the people by challenging the *pundit*.

"Be careful Babaji," Vishnu Baba concluded. "The pundit has fought with many *sadhus* and he has been violent before. He will not let you stay here."

"That may not be important." I replied, feeling even more strongly that our clash was necessary within the destiny of our souls. "I may achieve my purpose by just provoking him to violence."

The situation had become much more than just a karmic cleanup of the garden and I began to experience many visions and dreams of my former involvement with the pundit and our struggle within this temple in ancient times. I now knew that, as a wandering *sadhu* over a thousand years ago, I had sat at this temple and taught many people of the wonders of God and their duties within the emerging society. The *pundit* had also been a wandering holy man and we had disagreed on who had the right to sit at the head of this *dhunie* and how much access a low-caste person should have to the knowledge of the sacred scriptures. We were both living a lifetime of a thousand years ago within the time-space reference of the twentieth century.

During the next weeks, things began to change. Food and milk were brought to me everyday by some of the women devotees. More people came in the evenings to talk with me about spiritual philosophy and seek guidance in personal matters. Students in greater numbers appeared in the observatory, all reminding me that final exams were coming soon and not to forget them. My two new *sadhu* friends came often to sit with me and told me there was a movement on to have the *pundit* recognize me and to send notice to the government of Rajastan that I was living there.

The *pundit* had made only one appearance during the week. Although visibly surprised and frustrated at my latest defiance of his will, he made no new attempts to throw me out.

I had just finished carrying water in a leaky bucket to the rose bushes lining the far wall and was preparing to take a bath when Prem Lal and two other independent tourist agents entered the garden escorting a young western woman clutching tightly an oversized black leather purse under one arm.

"*Om Namo Narayana,*" we greeted each other.

"This is our Baba," Prem Lal said, by way of introduction. "He can answer your questions."

"I'm Debbie." she began, nervously looking about at my small hut. "These men tell me you are a great yogi."

I laughed a bit while glancing at my benefactors, who had retreated slightly and were talking among themselves. "No one really knows what a great yogi is these days," I said, wanting to put her at ease, "so, for them, I'm a great yogi. I would say I'm a student of the science of yoga. Perhaps some day I will deserve the title of 'great yogi', but today, that is not important."

"What are you doing here?" she asked, glancing inquisitively at my hut once again.

"I live here."

"This is your..." She couldn't come up with a polite word to describe the place, so continued saying, "How long have you been here, living like this?"

"I've been in India over a year and a half, but in this temple only three months," remembering now what had eluded me at the embassy.

"What do you do here?" she asked, clutching her shoulder bag and looking around at my gang, who were nearby discussing something.

"It's alright," I said, feeling her anxiety. "They won't harm you. Where did you meet them, anyway?"

She relaxed and recounted the events of the morning. She was from New York, here to buy clothes for her shop. She had been trying to cash traveler's checks and had met Prem Lal near the American Express office. When she told them that she did not trust them, they began talking about their American guru, and she asked if they would bring her to meet me.

I assured her that my boys could be trusted, up to a certain point, and that I would help her if she wanted. I called Prem Lal, who told me in Hindi that he did not have all the cash and wanted her to give him the checks, signed, and he would take them and get cash. He explained that if he had to bring her to the head of the black market, he would loose most of his profit. I arranged for them to take her checks, half at a time, while she waited with me. While we waited she talked of her business and how she wanted to have a guru or study yoga (something like that) but she was so occupied with making money that, right now, there wasn't time for anything else. Within an hour the transaction was completed and Prem Lal returned with the last of the money and a full bottle of milk in appreciation for my help. She was pleased and even offered to take me to a restaurant, but I insisted that I preferred to eat here in the temple.

"But what do you eat here?" she asked, preparing to leave.

"I eat whatever the people bring me," I replied, which caused her eyes to open even further.

"You're really into this thing," she said, shaking her head in disbelief.

"'This *thing* is my life. You're really into making money, aren't you?"

"But that's normal! I'm earning a living and I get many personal benefits," she replied, clutching her bag tightly again. "What do you get from living here and taking care of this group of thieves?"

"Life can also be based on what we give to others, not only on what we receive."

"Can I come visit you again Babaji?" she asked after a long silence, during which our gaze remained fixed on each other. "I will be here for a few weeks and I would like to talk to you, if it's all right."

"I'm here every day. Come anytime."

We became good friends as the tension-filled events of the next two weeks slowly unfolded. With final exams less than a month away, large groups of students came every evening to talk with me, hanging out in the temple more than studying. I tried to tell them that I was not going to help them unless they made some effort, using my father's tactics when I had asked him for help writing my papers. *Pundits* and *sadhus* from other temples began to visit and, with the help of Prem Lal, who by now was spending more time in the temple grounds than on the streets, we discussed the favorite theme of Hindu priests and holy people — the manifest and un-manifest aspects of God.

"You're worshipping God in your heart; a God you say has no form but only a presence of energy and light." One of them commented to me. "Is it wrong for us to continue to worship God through our various forms?"

"In matters of God, one must do that which he believes in, not what others do. Human evolution may be perceived as a process of developing a relationship with God, which is the direct experience of the total unity within all existence. What you choose to believe will determine your particular form of worship. In matters of God, there is neither right nor wrong.

"At first, there is only belief or no belief in Its existence," I said, remembering my own process. "When one believes, the form of worship grows out of those beliefs. It is never a fixed form but constantly changing according to one's continuing experiences of God."

"Then where are we heading in our evolution if there are so many different ideas of God?"

"The next phase of human evolution is that God shall become a unifying experience, not a faith, belief, or form of worship."

"How can you answer their questions with such authority when you have been here for such a short time and say you knew nothing of God before you came?" asked Debbie that night after the others had left.

We paused in our stroll around the garden and I waited for the correct answer to come.

"There is one experience after which all else is known," I heard myself saying.

"I guess that makes you some kind of know-it-all. How can you be so pretentious to say you know everything?"

"It's not that I know everything. I have experienced that there is a place where all is known. For some reason, I have limited access to that place through the questions of others.

"Look, Debbie, I don't understand what's happening to me. I have these way-out mystical voyages that leave me, in some strange way, connected to all life. I call it God because people seem to accept that God might exist and, at least here in this country, they respect one for dedicating life to such a possibility."

"Then you plan to live the rest of your life here in this temple?" she asked.

"I can't say what I'll do for the rest of my life. Right now, I'm trying to live one day at a time. Who knows, we may run into each other on the streets of New York some day."

"No!" she said, grabbing me by the arm to get my attention. "Don't ever go back. You're crazy, you know that?

"I mean, they'll think you're crazy," she went on, trying not to offend me with her conclusions about my mental health. "Look, you're walking about half-naked, with that emaciated body and those sunken, half-gone eyes, looking like some starving orphan. And, on top of it all, you talk about seeing God and knowing everything. What else are they going to think?

"I think you're a special person. I see how you try to help those who come to you and how you ask for nothing except a little milk in return. But you can't live like this back in New York.

"Don't go back!" she insisted. "They'll lock you up in a minute."

CHAPTER 31

OUSTED

During the next ten days, a frenzy of student activity settled over the temple grounds as final exams were approaching and what had started out to be a little game of the Patron Saint of Exams became a full-time occupation. Mothers came with their sons to ask for special favors, insisting their future welfare depended on my help. Every night the observatory was filled with mumbling students, anxiously memorizing useless facts, and I was besieged during my evening walks with pleas for help and promises of even my own cow if I would pray for them. The faith of the Indian people astounded me and my heart melted in response. To help them relax and expect the best I promised, if they studied hard, I would do something special for them.

The day before exams, I gathered the students closest to me and told them I would perform a special ceremony for all the students who had been studying here for the last months. I lit my dhunie with firewood scrounged in the streets that morning and we all chanted a simple mantra, *Sri Ram Jai Ram Jai Jai Ram Om*. I poured ghee, donated by one of the mothers, over the flames while silently blessing each one of them in their efforts that week. We went on for over an hour chanting enthusiastically and, in the end, there were over fifty students gathered around beating on their books and clapping their hands. This was the first time in my life I had done such an impromptu ritual and I prayed hard that the real patron saint of students was listening and would come to the aid of these young men in their need.

"Go now and have faith in yourselves. You will pass," I declared, after the *ghee* had finished and the fire was dying down. "*Bole Sri Sat Guru, Shivaji Qi Jai!*" we all shouted together before they filed out to the park to resume their studies.

"Here Babaji," said Pretan my original student disciple, who had been sitting next to me during the ceremony and stayed after the others left. He took a bottle of milk from his bag and handed it to me saying, "Don't forget me, Babaji. My first test is in the morning."

"Then don't you think you should study?" I asked, knowing that he was a student like myself, hardly ever studying, happy to just get by.

"No, Babaji. I know that you will fix it all for me. I will come for the bottle tomorrow," he concluded, hustling off in the direction of the main gate.

"How can you deceive them like that?" scolded Debbie, who had been observing our ceremony. "You're filling them with false hope. You don't really believe that you can help them?"

I thought for a minute while she was taking a seat at the *dhunie*.

"I guess that's my problem." I replied, with a twinkle of mischief in my eyes. "I do believe that what we just did will help them. And if we all believe together, the better the chances. I don't know how or why. This is a new experience for me."

"What if it doesn't work? What if they all fail?" she exhorted red-faced, insisting that I see the world her way.

"Then we'll have to try something else next time," I replied with a smile. "I didn't tell them I could help them. They came to me believing I could and that might be all that is necessary in the end. Stranger things in life have been proven to be true, why not this?"

She sat quietly while I cleaned up around the *dhunie* and prepared to heat the milk in my *comundle* over the smoldering fire. There was a nervous frustration about her this night. We had talked a lot over the last three weeks and I enjoyed her company, even through our world views were strikingly different.

"Why do you keep coming here and arguing over the way I live?" I asked, picking up a handful of freshly fallen mulberries and offering them to her. "Why don't you go hang out with the hippies in the park or spend some of your money in a restaurant?"

"Oh, stop it!" she snapped back at me, tossing the berries into the air. "You're the craziest goddamn guy I've ever met. I don't know. Something about you has caused me to question everything in my life. Now I don't really know what I want.

"When I first came to India, I only wanted to buy goods and make a lot of money," she continued, stumbling over her words. "I thought that would make me happy, make me feel secure. Then I meet you, who has nothing and looks like he's starving to death, and you seem peaceful and content with your life." She fumbled with her bag before slapping her hands hard on her knees saying, "Do I have to live like this in order to be happy?"

"Relax, Debbie." I replied. "Nothing in your outside world has to change for you to be happy. Not even earning more money. Happiness is a choice, not an attainment.

"This is my way. It doesn't have to be yours. We all must choose how, where, and with whom we want to live. Everything necessary to learn, grow, and be happy can be found within whatever you choose to do in life, in every situation and circumstance.

"Happiness doesn't come from what you do but rather from why you do it, how you do it, and for whom you do it. Don't earn money to be happy but be happy earning money."

"You mean that someone can find peace in their heart earning money? I don't have to give up everything?"

"To renounce all material desires is only one of the possibilities we have in life and not one well-suited for many. Dedicate your work to the happiness and well-being of all people and enjoy life as it unfolds day-by-day."

"Thank you," she said wiping away tears with her sleeve. "You've helped me feel better. I've been struggling with trying to give up everything since we first met, and I just can't do it. Now I feel that I don't have to. What a relief."

"No, Debbie, you don't have to give up anything you don't want to. Life is an opportunity. Live it that way. It's not as serious as you think."

The next week passed in a cloud of prayer and positive expectations. I dedicated all of my work in the garden to the success of my students. I chanted and prayed for them while carrying water, sweeping the pathways with a broom that I'd fashioned from palm branches, and pulling the new crop of weeds from the rose bushes. Day after day, exuberant students would come by bringing milk and fruit and telling me how something magical had happened in their exams; they just knew every thing. At the end of the week, we all celebrated with a big feast, cooked by their mothers in appreciation of my help. I gave special thanks to whatever gods might have helped and could not shake the feeling that I had learned a valuable lesson in the process.

The *pundit* walked in during our party and did a double take when he saw all the students and mothers gathered about my dhunie. He lost his cool when one of the mothers went to insist that he feed me as the resident *sadhu* of the temple.

"He can't stay!" he shouted, waving her out of his way. "He's not a *sadhu*. He's not even a Hindu. He doesn't belong here."

"You can't make him leave," someone argued back. "He has done more for this temple than you ever did. If you throw him out, we'll put an end to your tricks around here."

They continued shouting until he stomped out the gate, his aura glowing livid red. The women and students assured me that he would not have his way, but I sensed that a showdown was near. Since my return from the police, he had threatened to remove me several times, but Prem Lal and the boys had stood in my defense, even threatening him if he tried to touch me.

A few days later, I was just finishing my morning's work when Debbie came to say she was returning to New York the next day and wanted to say thanks for everything. We were sitting in my hut sharing some bananas and mangos she had brought when the pundit burst through the gate accompanied by three men carrying bamboo sticks. He walked towards us with frustrated determination and I knew his anger was about to be his undoing.

"What should we do, Babaji?" she asked, as they approached. "I'm scared they'll harm us." The same thought had flashed through my mind. I could feel he was set on action this time.

"Don't get angry at him," I replied, as calmly as I could with the goon squad bearing down upon us. "He must do what he's about to do. It is his karma and, I feel, my mission completed. I'm going to just sit here and let them do whatever they are set on doing. You can do whatever you wish."

"I will stay too, Babaji."

"You must leave now, Babaji!" shouted the *pundit*, turning vivid red and panting heavily. His burly assistants began slapping their clubs into their free hands, revving up their adrenalin to charge.

"This is your last chance!" he shouted, turning his half-crazed eyes on me for the first time. "Are you leaving, or do we have to throw you out?"

I closed my eyes in response to his demands. Seconds later they attacked. I could hear the crashing of palm branches and feel the ground shaking beneath me as his goons released their destructive pleasures upon my hut and its surroundings. I could feel dirt flying and hear bricks falling to the ground but not one hand was laid on me directly. In five minutes, it was all over and he screamed, "Now get out!"

I became absorbed in meditation, praying to forgive them in their ignorance and resisting old reactions of anger. When I opened my eyes some time later, the remains of my hut lay in a shattered heap before me and every inch of ground had been torn up except where I was sitting. I could tell by the undisturbed ground next to me that Debbie had held firm during the onslaught and must have left afterwards. I moved to release the pressure on my knees and a piece of paper tumbled from my lap onto the ground. I picked it up and opened it to find fifty dollars and a note.

Thank you, Babaji. I have been afraid all my life and always needed someone to protect me. Now I know I have found a source of courage within myself. I hope we never meet in New York.

Love, Debbie

A voice, which seemed to come from all around me, gently commanded, *Pick up your blanket and go to the train station. Your work is finished here for now. You will be leaving.*

PART FIVE

THE RETREAT

AT TIMES, THE JOURNEY ALONG THE RAZOR'S EDGE
REQUIRES SOLITUDE TO GAIN PERSPECTIVE ON THE MISSION
THAT LIES AHEAD

CHAPTER 32

ALMORA

When I left the temple in New Delhi I was not sure where I was going but, like so many of the divinely orchestrated events of the past two years, a destination was not necessary. While riding the train the next day, a man came up to me and said that if I got off at the next station and took the secondary line, I could walk into the foothills of the Himalayas. I do not know what prompted him to suggest this, but I took his advice. Within a few days, I was walking along narrow foot-trails and climbing through wind-swept pine forest.

There were few people, a real treat in India, the country of eternal crowds and no concept of privacy. The features of the peasants were more Nepalese and Tibetan than the plains people of India-round, smooth faces with high, protruding cheek bones and stocky bodies, slightly bent at the waist from carrying heavy loads on steep hills. They were friendly, offering me food and shelter at night, but reserved and obviously unaccustomed to seeing a westerner dressed in *sadhu* robes wandering about the mountains barefoot and carrying a begging bowl.

After two weeks of wandering, I came to the remote hill station of Almora and was introduced to Mary Oplinger, an American woman who had been in India for twenty years. After listening to the high points of my mystical odyssey, she suggested I wait for the return of Lama Govinda, a Bolivian-born, Tibetan monk who lived near by.

My first night with Mary, over curried creamed spinach, yogurt and cucumber salad, and hot *chapattis* covered in *ghee*, she talked of the mystical traditions of India and Tibet and told of her visits with the great saints of India. Mary had been a friend and student of Edgar Casey in the United States and Rudolf Steiner in Europe (neither of whom I had ever heard of at that time).

198

She had been with many of the great yogis of India: Ramana Maharishi, Swami Muktananda, Sai Baba, Ananda Mai Ma, Swami Ram Dass, and Mahatma Gandhi, all of who were held in the highest esteem and revered as examples of enlightenment by the Indian people. That evening would prove to be the first of a memorable series of gourmet vegetarian meals, prepared by her cook and gardener, Prem Singh, during which we enriched our minds and spirits through conversations and reflections on metaphysical and mystical realities. In her grandmotherly way, she guided me to a deeper understanding of my mystical quest and helped me to glimpse its potential.

Mary was a humorously mysterious person. She would walk about her garden talking to the plants and spirits and flip in and out of different dimensions throughout the day, giving the appearance of a doddering old lady. At dinner she would often pause in mid-sentence, her fork poised rigidly in her hand, for ten minutes or more as she sat silently with her spirit adrift in other realities. When I ventured to ask her of these sudden journeys she would only mumble, half-coherently, "Oh, they have called me again, have they?"

"Who has called you, Mary?" I asked, some nights later hoping she would tell me more.

Eyeing me suspiciously before making a casual gesture to dismiss the entire thing, she nonchalantly replied, "Oh, it's really nothing."

When I insisted further she said, "They say you know, so why should we talk of it." Adding with mischievous certainty, "we all exist on many planes of consciousness, don't we now? Surely you are aware of parallel realities?"

"Well, I have glimpsed such things," I answered, checking out her reaction to my confession. " I'm beginning to realize that *I* am many beings evolving simultaneously within parallel realities. What can you tell me about such things?"

"Oh me, dear, dear, I guess all I could tell you with certainty is that you are evolving within a sea of consciousness on many distinct levels of awareness and other *yous* and other *worlds* do exists. As we become less attached to our own self-importance in this time-space dimension, our parallel identities make themselves known in diverse ways," she concluded, scrutinizing me over the top of her reading glasses.

Later, when our friendship had deepened in trust and acceptance, she told me of her relationship with spirit guides and masters she was in contact with and how they worked through her. I could relate to the fact that we all existed simultaneously on many dimensions of reality and that we were guided from these levels, but the concept of entities 'working through her' baffled me. She said that her master would visit her in his etheric body, but it was much later in our relationship that she referred to him as The Babaji, ascended master of the Himalayas.

After a month at Mary's and no sign of Lama Govinda, she introduced me to an old Danish *sadhu*, Sunya Baba, 'the sage of silence,' who lived in a garden retreat up the ridge. After hearing my tale and with a little gentle insistence from Mary, he offered me one of his spare cabins on Kali Mat ridge until Lama Govinda returned.

In his youth, Sunya Baba, now in his seventies, had been a renowned botanist in charge of the royal gardens of the Danish monarchy. He now lived in a magnificently overgrown garden of about two acres filled with flowering shrubs and trees. Discreetly tucked in among the dense tangled foliage, which formed tunnel-like pathways winding at random through this half-tamed jungle, were a series of mud huts and stone cabins, all of which he had built with his own hands and occupied at one time during the twenty-five years of living in his retreat. He first gave me a hut overgrown in vines, which was a pack rats' nest of debris and neglect saying, "Here I insist on absolute silence. You may stay for a short time, but please, I'm not a man of many words and do require my privacy."

When he came by a week later, he was pleasantly shocked that I had cut the hut free from the encroaching jungle, repaired the door and windows, which could now be opened and shut with only the minimum of struggle, and resurfaced the mud floor and walls with a fresh layer of cow dung and straw. Seeing my industrious nature and the striking improvements to his once dilapidated shelter, he offered me another slightly larger stone cabin, nestled in a more secluded part of the garden. It stood in a similar state of disrepair and was equipped with an old straw mattress, a small table and a rickety chair that I soon restored to sturdiness. It had a tiny fireplace in one corner with a few well-worn cooking pots. This was to become my next home as I plunged deeper into meditation in search of inner peace and enlightenment.

From the teachings and suggestions of Yogiji, Jungle Baba, and what I had gleaned from the *Gita*, I pieced together a basic understanding of the Hindu system of meditation: sit with your back straight and concentrate on any specific point, such as the point between the eyes, the ebbing-and-flowing of breath, or an inner prayer or sound; keep returning your concentration to that point every time the monkey-like mind steals away with your attention. Over a year of disciplined practice had conditioned my body to sit crossed-legged without great pain or discomfort. My honed concentration and sharp discernment of mind and spirit allowed me more frequent opportunities to slip through the space between two thoughts, into worlds of peace and splendor. These energy-filled moments of bliss were the incentive that kept me returning day after day, month after month to probe the mysteries of my mind, searching for the keys that opened doors to worlds of pure spirit.

The tide of thoughts rising from within the restless mind would break in upon this peaceful place and carry me away to concerns of every worldly thing. Catching its cunning tricks and remembering the world of peace within, I would return repeatedly to the eye of wisdom and peer through the etheric veil toward other dimensions, until my concentration could not hold to a thought-less world.

Rising, I worked around the garden for an hour or so, fulfilling an unspoken agreement with Sunyaji to help him restore his creation to its former glory. In joyful silence, I cleared the pathways, removed piles of organic debris from the overgrown flowerbeds, and restacked sections of the collapsed walls that terraced the steep, rocky hillside. Morning walks to the spring half a mile away, to fetch water and have a splashing bath, and long afternoon jaunts in the forest, gleaning small twigs, pine cones, and prized fallen branches, filled the spaces between sitting meditations and punctuated my day's structured routine.

Mary fed me a select diet of metaphysical books from Edgar Casey to the I Ching, with a lot of Ramana Maharshi, Baba Muktananda and Lama Govinda to spice it up. I delved into these great volumes of wisdom hoping that they contained some truth to open the doors further to the spirit. But, all that was revealed was information of a rational nature, not the feeling I was seeking. My spirit soared within this expanding environment of love and acceptance flowing from Mary and Sunya Baba. My content heart and peaceful mind fantasized living out the rest of my life on the pine ridge of Kali Mat.

The silence of Sunya's cabin offered the perfect place to explore the mysteries of my mind, except for one thing–mice. Having been abandoned so long, the cabin was the playground for hundreds of little creatures that came out to play whenever I sat to meditate. At first, I took it as one more distraction to over-come through concentration, but soon I was spending more time controlling my anger toward them than observing my breath. One night, after the sound of one of them drowning in my bucket of fresh water terminated my meditation and I was sitting in front of the fire preparing *chapattis*, an idea occurred to me: *communicate with them.*

I stopped what I was doing, took a few deep breaths and concentrated hard on the thought, *What can I do that will make you keep quiet during my medita-tions?*

Food! I heard clearly within the stillness of the room.

OK, I'll leave some food for you each night, if you'll be quiet.

The next night, before sitting for my evening meditation, I put a broken-up *chapatti* on a shelf by the door. Miracle of miracles, it was silent during the entire hour of my meditation and for the rest of the night. Things continued the same for a week and I was praising myself for the brilliant solution to the problem until one night they began to kick up a ruckus again.

*I thought we had a deal,*I thought to them. *What happened?*

Where's tonight's food? I heard within my mind.

Sure enough, I had forgotten the food that night. I got up and put some pieces of *chapatti* on the shelf and returned to the silence of my meditation.

That was the last night I forgot my part of the bargain. From then on, with a few exceptions, we lived in harmony with each other.

With the onset of the cold, winter months, my disciplined routine of long hours of sitting meditation, interspersed with the basic necessities of hermit life, led me deeper into the mysterious inner world of mind and spirit. The more I probed these dimensions, the more I could detect a series of interconnected relationships between breath and thought and mind. Mind was defined by the flow of my thoughts, not the flow of my thoughts by mind. Mind revealed itself to be a process that, without the presence of thought, did not exist; a process created to allow me to relate, as an individual, to the external world. But thought was not a simple expression of mind and the more I concentrated, the more its multidimensional nature revealed itself.

It was clear now that the patterns of my thoughts were related to the rhythm of my breathing: *Mind followed thought while thought followed breath*. Most thoughts derived their reality from the concept of my individuality in relationship to the material world about me and appeared to be waves of identity arising, primarily, out of desire or fear. When all my awareness could be concentrated on the movement of my breath, the presence of thought and the process of mind loosened their grip on my supposed identity and previously hidden dimensions of peace and unity opened up.

I relentlessly probed the deeper mysteries of my being using focused concentration on the great mantra of Ramana Maharshi: Who am I? Repeating it with concentration and feeling, I reined in the straying mind and coaxed it back to the point between my eyes and my quest for blissful enlightenment. I devised several ways to reverse the flow of the wayward mind by catching it with focused awareness and breathing it into retreat, while I followed its retreat though a progression of thoughts, arriving at last to the shadowy light between my eyes from whence it had strayed. Frustrated at times and often filled with nagging doubt about the results of such efforts, I clung to words of Jungle Baba: "In matters of meditation, progress is not measured by outer things, but by the inner peace it brings, not in weeks or years, but in lifetimes lived beyond the reach of doubt and fear."

Even with the senses reined in and focused attention fixed on one point, other mind-related thought processes such as inspiration, creativity, imagination, intuition and premonition, could surface from within the depths of my consciousness, perplexing my efforts. These levels not only created a specific identity within the individual self and the material world but also contained within them a certain type of non-sensual pleasure — a self-gratification and pride — which created more subtle levels of attachment. But they also gave glimpses of other realities and more universal expressions of self. This inspired me to believe they could be powerful allies along the path to self-realization, like bridges leading to the land of pure spirit.

More than thought, the subtle domain of awareness itself became the seed of hope and the guiding light in my quest to know the true self. The endless stream of thoughts could be slowed and even cease to exist in the present moment through the regulation of the breath and one-pointed concentration. Even then, awareness of inner light, spiritual guidance, visions, energy manifestations and an elusive sense of universal self would continue in their absence. At times, due to a unique alignment of positive intention, focused concentration, and total surrender, all sense of self in relationship to individuality and the material world would vanish, and *I* would become one with the All. In these moments, the rhythm of my breathing would merge with the rhythm of the universe and it would appear that whatever was breathing me was the source of all movement within creation. This suggested that awareness, both individual and universal, was rooted in the breath. The breath was a mirror image of a greater universal process and, if not the source of consciousness, was at least our connection to it.

I worked consistently on breath awareness using the many breathing exercises from my jungle training to slowly penetrate the level of awareness that was breathing me. I learned to both observe and regulate my breathing. Counting my breaths in certain rhythms of inhalation, retention, and exhalation, alternate-nostril breathing focusing on channels of light circulating throughout my body, and countless hours of observing the rising and falling of my breath while sitting in meditation, walking in the mountains, and working in the garden, helped me see that the flow of thought, and my very existence, was related to this movement. I began to realize that a deeper philosophical truth might be: *I breathe, therefore I am.*

Beyond thought and breath, exciting new horizons of energy and light loomed as signposts along the path to self-realization. In moments of clear perception arising out of focused attention on my breathing, I could perceive that the flow of breath was related to an equal and opposite movement of energy and light, as if my breathing process was acting as a generator, or dynamo of life force. As I took air down into my lungs, an opposite flow of energy moved up my spine and, as I exhaled, this current arched around and flowed down the front of my body forming a continuous circuit. Although connected to the breathing process, this energy seemed to sustain every cell of my being. By focusing my awareness in certain centers along my spine and breathing deliberately into these areas, I could accumulate and store energy there. Coordinating this energy-generating technique with Yogi Baba's system of the three locking gates along the spine and directing the energy with my imagination to rise up my spine, I could circulate light and energy throughout my body. All of my mystical journeys had one thing in common: They were filled with light and energy and left me feeling at one with all life. I was slowly integrating into this source of light and oneness.

What started as a necessary impulse to seek solitude in the cool morning mists along the river in Katmandu and watch my thoughts float by in puzzling disarray was now a dedicated act of love and devotion and my most viable means of probing the great mystery of God. I could now see these attitudes of reverence and devotion, more than my disciplined determination and perseverance to continue long hours of meditation, was opening the world of spirit to me. While it had been my quest for enlightenment that had caused me to plunge headlong into disciplines of diet, breathing, and meditation, my attitudes of devotion and surrender to a greater organizing intelligence were proving to be the most effective means of bringing peace to my mind and opening my heart to life.

As the winter rains passed and the first buds of springtime appeared, I resumed my working routine in the garden and repaired the moss-chinked slate roof and rotting wooden gutters of my cabin. The sun, still low in the horizon and lacking its summer intensity, brought warmth to the cloudless days, inviting me to wander the hillsides for firewood and exercise. I was working off winter's sluggishness by gathering twigs and small branches high on the pine-studded ridge one afternoon, my burlap sack nearly full, when I paused on a steep, rocky ledge to rest. Before me loomed the etheric-capped peaks of the mighty Himalayas and beyond them the frontiers of Tibet, where sheer physical isolation had kept the mystical tradition alive.

As I gazed at the mountains of eternal snow, I felt that special energies were there guiding humanity through the darkness of material existence. I felt so inspired living at the gateway of these great monuments to nature and imagined beings from some other realities watching and guiding me as I groped for understanding within the ignorance and limitations of the human condition. A resounding voice filled my mind and I heard:

In the regions of the eternal snows abide the etheric Masters of Light who wait to teach and guide those who love's call has thus prepared their hearts. Many minds and hearts must be turned to them so that all who choose to help may know their presence and message. Seeded upon the Earth are souls whose memories are only slightly clouded by identification with their individuality, who will awaken to the light and open new doors of wisdom and love when the time is right. The Masters of Light require those of Earthly form, who are now guided by the shadow of ignorance, to throw off their cloak of self-importance; clothe themselves not in material addictions but bathe themselves in the incoming light of wisdom that seeks to unite all life-forms into one. They care not to change your world but rather the way in which you all relate to it and to each other. They are here, not to save you, but to offer you the wisdom to save yourselves.

The spring weather continued over the next week and I walked to Almora, two hours down the mountain, to replenish supplies. I was down to my last seven dollars of Debbie's gift but had simplified my expenses to two dollars a month, including treats. After much experimenting, my diet had settled in at brown rice and lentils cooked together with only salt for seasoning once a day and whole-wheat *chapattis*, toasted in the embers of my fireplace, with morning and evening tea. Monthly trips to town always brought prized goodies such as fresh fruit, green vegetables, peanuts, and sweet milk cakes, in addition to rice, lentils, whole-wheat flour, tea, and raw brown sugar paste.

Carrying my supplies in a great bundle on my head, I concentrated on my breathing and counted four steps on the inhalation and exhalation while repeating OM rhythmically to myself during the long gradual assent into the foothills. Walking became a kind of stimulating challenge of both concentration and physical stamina, taking me into trance-like states, and I often regained awareness of the physical world as I entered the grounds of the 'garden of silence'.

One evening, I arrived home in my walking trance as splashes of crimson clouds drenched the snow-blanketed eastern peaks, signaling the end of another day. After hanging everything in bags from the rafters to protect it from mice and splashing myself in a token bath, I sat to meditate before lighting the fire to cook my *chapattis*. Wrapping my legs one on top of the other in the full lotus position, I did Yogi Baba's stretching and vibrating exercises, rocking back and forth and dropping my tailbone gently onto my rolled up scarf. These exercises were only to be done in this yoga posture and he encouraged me to develop and use it. With my legs in this position, the energy channels at the base of my spine would be open and my body would have maximum stability and firmness. Since coming to Kali Mat, I had been slowly stretching the ligaments and tendons in my pelvis, knees, and ankles to be able to sit like this for an hour or more before the pain became too great a distraction to my concentration.

I finished the counting of my breaths and had fixed my inner gaze on the third eye, steadying my concentration by repeating, *Who am I*, when **Bang!!** In an instant measured only by a shift of awareness, an explosion of bliss and light, like a cosmic atom bomb, went off in my lower spine and attachments and identities began to evaporate. This force of shocking magnitude ripped up my spine, tearing away at all traces of self and threatening me with instant annihilation in the wake of its surge. In a flash it was at my heart flushing out the last traces of attachment to people, places, and things and dissolving them in its all-consuming flame.

Images of my father and mother appeared in its ravaging thrust and I started to form the thought of, *Oh, no, not them*, when heaven and hell collided within me. The force, once halted in its upward expansion by my moment of hesitation, began to rock me violently, burning up the energy channels of my body in its ferocious attempt to get free. My body began to shake ever more violently and it began to hop about the room, locked rigidly in the lotus position, as jolting waves of energy threatened to consume me from within.

The thought of, *I'm dying*, flashed before me and I looked down see my physical form jumping and slithering with frantic contractions below me. I alternated between feeling intense heat and energy destroying my physical being, demanding surrender unto my own death, and floating above it, engulfed in a hazy calm. I let go of life as the heavens of my soul parted and shadowy worlds of translucent reality beckoned me from beyond. I was being sucked through the veil between two worlds and lost all will to cling to any identity when I heard a commanding voice shout out: "BREATHE!!"

It shocked me and called back my human identity in a split second. I was surprised to discover that, even in that state of panicked disorientation, I could still perceive an energy pattern that I knew to be my breath. It was trapped in a series of spastic contractions, as if the will to breathe had been knocked out of me. I was groping for re-identification with it as if, at any second, it would merge into a greater rhythm and cease to sustain my life form.

For what seemed like hours (and turned out to be so in the end), I clung to this faint, halting expression, coaxing it along with my weakened will to resume its customary flow of expansion and contraction, until slowly life once again stabilized. At some point I remembered feeling the density of my physical form, drenched in a cold sweat and pressed limply against the wooden floor, legs still locked one upon the other, and the first thought returned to my ravaged mind: *Who am I?*

CHAPTER 33

HIROSHIMA OF MY SOUL

Spastic twitching continued to ripple through my fear-shattered being for over an hour. My breathing was stunted and shallow but it had finally regained some of its natural rhythm and I could now turn my attention to my physical surroundings. The room was soaked in darkness but, by the light of the slice of moon peering through the small window, I could detect that I was laying on my back near the door, ten feet from my blanket, with my knees protruding before me. Excruciating pain in my lower back and legs urged me to wakefulness. I found the will to move my right arm and groped at my twisted legs in a feeble attempt to free them from the lotus position. After several tries, I managed to unhook them and they fell, throbbing in pain, to the wooden floor. I curled into a fetal position, still coaxing my breath to stay with me. Thought would not come in its usual persistent flood but, in keeping with the hesitant rhythm of my heart and lungs, presented itself in spurts of recall, impressing upon me the magnitude and destructive potential of the force I had just encountered.

A whisper calling from the depths of my being, as if to soothe my battered soul, was saying: *You will never be where breath is not.* The image of Shiva Baba from the Monkey Temple in Katmandu, with his soft, penetrating eyes and inquisitive smile, vaguely impressed itself upon my recovering awareness. He bowed and I gave thanks — to what or to whom I could not imagine. My benevolent image of God, master of love and light, had been blown away. Yet I prayed with greater necessity than before.

Then the image began to distort and the face became that of Jungle Baba, then Yogi Baba and Light Baba. They each smiled upon me as if to say: *You made it.*

Did it have to be so hard? was the only thought I could formulate in my shattered mind. I would later remember this image and try to probe the deeper mysteries of these four faces and why they all appeared to be monitoring my quest from within my soul. There were times when I was sure they were part of a karmic conspiracy to transform my identity — to what, I was not sure. But after such a near annihilation of all I knew to be my identity, that question began to burn within my mind.

When I regained consciousness again, pinpoints of starlight filtered through the dusty panes of glass and for a split-second I thought the experience had gone the other way and I was floating somewhere in heaven. The lifeless hulk of my physical body cloaked about me and a pulsating pain in my head drew my attention to the reality that I had not ascended but was still curled up on the warped floor boards near the door, cold and bathed in the secretions of fear. With considerable effort, I pulled my depleted self across the floor to the flattened mattress and, without rising, wrapped my blanket and woolen shawl around me and lay shivering in the still blackness of the room. I could not allow thoughts of this mystical blowout into to my consciousness because a burning sensation would arise at the base of my spine and spurts of energy jolt upwards from just the thought of it. I tried my mantra but my exhausted mind could not be brought to a point of concentration. At one point I tried to sit up but the shaking intensified and my breath halted in spastic contractions, so I abandoned that idea and lay panting and praying, waiting for daybreak.

When the first gray shadows of the overhanging trees came into focus, I pulled myself up and leaned against the stonewall, still uncertain of the exact state of my body or mind. Among shuddering fear and emotional prayers of thankfulness, I allowed the events of the previous night to reenter my aware-ness, checking from time to see if I could move all my parts and that my vision and hearing were functioning. My first attempt at standing brought the weird sensation of rubbery arms and legs that would only half-respond to my will to move them. My physical body did not feel solid any more. Commanding it, I managed to stumble out into the garden, now alive with bird song and the rustling of leaves in the low canopy of vegetation, to take a piss and splash icy water on my face and neck. I tried to walk but a drugged detachment from my physical body and the sensation, like I was alive but still was not living, allowed me only a few strained steps before plopping to the ground in anxious frustration. I wanted to cry but even that expression of self-pity was beyond my present level of detachment. I pulled my knees to my chest and, resting my dazed head, watched the swirling patterns of violet-pink clouds take form in the pale gray sky above.

What was that? I puzzled to myself as I dared to allow the images of my anni-hilation by bliss to replay within my shaken consciousness. This was not the first time that spirit had awakened within me and transformed me into a floating sphere of light and bliss; but this time something was different, as if the source of all energy within the entire universe had exploded within me. All my other mystical experiences had presented themselves with energy, light and bliss, but within reason of what I was capable of surrendering to in that moment. This, however, had been a force so overwhelming, bliss so intense, that it was painful. I could not imagine how it was possible to be residing within this frail body of flesh and blood without consuming it and the entire world about it.

This was the outstanding aspect of this manifestation — it was coming from within me, not from some cosmic source out there in the universe somewhere. When it was released at the base of my spine, for a split second I was the source of all life itself. Within me was the force of all creative potential of the universe exploding in blissful undulations to the limits of eternity. Its light, bright beyond the most intense white, was a liquid luminescence pulsating, swirling and surging forth into manifestation. How could I contain something so powerful without it consuming me?

I was thankful to be alive but I was not sure why. The mystical horror of the previous night had shattered my illusions of peacefully drifting off in enlightened bliss, leaving the material world behind me. My quest, which up until that moment had been one of disciplined training of mind and body to slip between the veil of time and form and be assimilated into the dimension of enlightenment, became a moment-by-moment confrontation with fear and death.

For months I could not meditate or do any strenuous breathing exercises. As soon as I sat down, crossed my legs and began to concentrate, this force would explode from the base of my spine, rocking and shaking my body and bringing within its waves of bliss an all-consuming fear of personal annihilation that no rational attempts at surrender could overcome. My disciplined routine of meditation, work, eating and sleeping, gave way to sleepless nights filled with shocking blasts of heat and energy racing throughout my body while I lay shaking and shivering beneath my blanket, separated by drowsy, aimless days of anxious anticipation of yet another explosion or even death. I would alternate between moments of great bliss and exhilaration, when I would feel alive and energetic, working some in the garden and walking to the distant well for water, and times of frightening frailty and disorientation, when I would sit and stare off into space, hardly noticing or caring where I was or what needed to be done. Days might go by without eating and then I would eat ravenously for two or three days, sleeping long hours in the day and pacing about the garden in the shadows of the moonlight most of the night.

During this time I never went to visit Mary or Sunya Baba. My only regular activity was long walks in the mountains to collect firewood or fetch water and build up my physical strength. Walking brought a certain security and helped ground me when there seemed to be no established pattern to life. Several times during these outings, jolts of energy overcame me as I was sitting in some isolated place looking out over the majestic Himalayan range. My body would hop and shake in the wake of waves of bliss while I clung to the rhythm of my breathing in a distraught attempt to remain alive. The duality of bliss and fear presented a contrasting background for these experiences, neither allowing me to turn away nor fully surrender. Through it all, I remained determined to not give up in my quest for the ever-elusive goal of enlightenment. I forced myself, against all fear, to sit and meditate and struggled to restructure my life in some disciplined way.

About two months after the Hiroshima of my soul I was sitting in the early morning rays of sun filtering through the stands of tall flowers, having just finished reading Arjuna's frightening vision of the all powerful Godhead:

> Like a fire at the end of time which burns all in the last day,
> I see thy vast mouths and terrible teeth. Where am I?
> Where is my shelter? Have mercy on me, God of gods,
> Refuge Supreme of all the worlds. (*Gita*: 11- 25)

By this time the energy attacks had mellowed. The channels in my physical body, as I was later to understand, had expanded to accept these potent manifestations. They were now confined to the evening and nighttime hours, allowing me to resume my daytime routine of working, cooking and meditating. Strength and solidity had returned to my physical body. Most important, the all-prevailing apprehension that had racked my being with doubt and fear over the past two months was giving way to a healthy curiosity as to how to surrender more fully to these assaults of power and bliss.

I had resumed my weekly visits to Mary's, making vague excuses of illness for my absence. Our Monday night chats over gourmet delights filled both stomach and soul with fuel for greater peace and happiness. One morning, I bounded down the steep, windy pathway and entered the picket gate of Mary's garden. Mary appeared from within the house and exclaimed, "Lama Govinda has arrived! Next week he will be starting his Thursday afternoon sessions so we can go and chat with him.

"He will be most interested to meet you, I'm sure," she added, taking her seat on the veranda.

"When did he arrive?" I asked, taking a seat in my favorite armchair.

"A few weeks ago, I think, but we just received word yesterday saying he would be open to receive visitors next week. Must be awfully tired. He's coming from California, I believe."

I visited with Mary and we made plans for her to come by my cabin on her way to Lama Govinda's next week since he lived not too far from Sunya's garden. She seemed a little anxious as I was leaving and I chanced to ask if anything was wrong.

"Funny you should ask," she began deliberately, half-peering over her reading glasses with an expression that told me she wanted to talk. "It's you that

I'm concerned about, OM Baba. You don't look particularly... let's say healthy. Perhaps I should say healthy in a psychic way."

I moved uneasily in my wicker armchair and lowered my eyes to stare at the irregular pattern of the brick terrace. "Now I'm not one to pry, mind you," she continued, removing her glasses and folding her hands softly in her lap, "but something has happened to you over the last two months that has... let us say, altered your energy, perhaps in not-so-healthy a way.

"Was the *illness* you said was keeping you away by any chance a mystical one?" she asked, catching me up in a stern look of concern.

"You might say it was something like that," I replied sheepishly, avoiding her eyes.

"Then it was as I expected!" she interrupted, wagging her finger at me. "The Goddess has called you and you were unprepared. Many don't live to tell about it, you know. I knew when I saw you two weeks ago. You had that look behind your eyes that said that some part of you had died and I could feel a fresh anxiety about you. Would you tell an old woman such as myself what it was like?"

After invoking the pity of an old woman there was little I could do but come clean and tell her about the nightmare of my soul I had lived over the last two months. She listened attentively, waving her paper fan in the still heat of midday and shaking her head from time to time, saying only, "Hum..." I finished on a positive note, saying that my strength had returned and *Shakti's* energetic thrusts had become milder of late. Mary stared at me in deep silence for a long time, making no attempt to hide the fact that she was surveying my energy channels with her 'special vision,' as she had called it on many occasions.

"I have known others who have lived such devastating experiences," she commented at last, breaking a heavy silence that had settled over the veranda like stagnant air. "But there are not many who can tell it like that. The kiss of the serpent, although a blissful and a much-sought-after experience, can be the kiss of death. Silence, I would say, is a healthy reaction at this time."

I tried to get more information from her but she would only say, "Fools readily speak about that which they know nothing, while the wise are given to silence, even when they know."

CHAPTER 34

Star-Lab Arain II

Returning from Mary's, I entered through the wooden gate of the Garden of Silence and made my way along the narrow path to my cabin nestled in the tangled foliage. A fresh breeze was just beginning to stir as I took a seat on a wooden bench behind the cabin and watched the patches of fluffy pink clouds flirting with the slice of silver moon hanging in the graying sky. The last burst of song rang forth from the chorus of birds bidding farewell to another journey of the sun. A great peace settled within my heart.

Closing my eyes, I concentrated on the sounds of the birds and the shushing of the wind dancing among the pine boughs. I found that my awareness could float on sound and, with relaxed concentration and giving the rein to my imagination, I could become the wind and be whisked away on its ethereal flight. Like a catnap in the back of the classroom, I drifted off on the wings of my imagination that night, surrendering my personal identity to *Shakti's* mellow jolts and drifting within a dream-like reality.

After some time soaring on my imagination, I found myself in a specific time-space coordinate. A hazy, violet fog, which permitted infinite expansion in all direction yet outlined a defined space of imperceptible scope, defined its perimeters. It was filled with crystalline light-forms of different colors and intensities. An orb of sparkling light, like an ethereal life-form of luminescent consistency, was moving through the space at a right angle to where I was located, stopping at various light centers in its path.

"You are of an unsteady consistency to hold to the frequencies of this dimension," I sensed a communication within my awareness. *"You must have been projected here from another reality for emotional adjustments but I don't find any accompanying equations specifying the adjustments required. There are*

strong identification patterns with a material dimension within your consistency. But that would be impossible. Such relationships don't permit entrance into this station, unless… all identity was temporally suspended, and there have not been any such occurrences in…… Let me see, when was it?"

I focused my thoughts towards this undetected presence. *Please tell me just where I am, whoever you are.* I was not having a vision or a dream but was in the vision itself. Everything about me, although not solid as I was accustomed to seeing it, was consistent and identifiable to whatever mechanisms of perception were functioning at that time.

"Earth!" I felt the thought pattern arise in an area close to my heart. *"I've placed your vibrations now! Let me come into greater consistency. This is an event! An Earth person here in Star Lab Arain II."*

A pinpoint of hot light appeared and transparent fibers of various shades and intensities began to swirl in oscillating patterns about this light until a wispy outline of an oval shape took form in the space before me. It had no features of head or arms but could only be described as a globe of energetic vapor with an energy field of defined consistency.

"Best I can do, I'm afraid. I haven't been assigned to your frequencies in many revolutions. One gets out of shape, you know."

Where am I? I questioned within myself. *What are these colored light patterns? And who are you?*

"Always wanting to know. I remember when I was last on assignment in your frequencies we were working on a solution to that rationality crisis. Ah, but these things take time. When creating perfection, it's the intention that counts.

"You're on the level of creative impulse, my young earthling, and I can't imagine how you got here. Had some accident, left your physical body somewhere and drifted by, did you? We'll see. These, what you called 'light patterns'—interesting metaphor, that is—are the life-sensing monitors of Arain II, an advanced scanning station within the creative impulse dimension. We're monitoring life development processes throughout all of creation and forwarding suggestions for certain adjustments to impulse-relay stations, located inter-spirally in relationship to hot spots of life development, so they may implement the necessary rebalancing required to heal the energy disturbance."

Somehow I understood everything it was broadcasting but I was perplexed as to why I was in such a place. It did not seem to have any direct relationship to enlightenment.

"Oh that. Don't give it too much awareness. It was just a concept we had to introduce many revolutions ago to repair a missing feeling in your evolutionary pattern.

"Here, let's bring the Earth scanners into relationship and see if they can splice the inconsistencies in your memories."

The light patterns shifted in relationship to my awareness until a new display appeared close to me and I could distinguish, for the first time, that these fields were made up of infinite tiny grains of light, not fixed in relationship to each other, but constantly moving within the whole. The effect was that of an extremely slow-moving kaleidoscope suspended on a backdrop of white mist.

"There we have it: The Earth Archives. Let's skip the early stuff about its formation out of rotating hot gases and star dust." Without disappearing, the images rapidly rearranged intensities and appeared different. *"And the phases of biological development taking place in the stabilized environment, and we come to life-forms sustained in the biosphere."* The puzzle blinked to a pause and trillions of pinpoints of light began to dance to a waltz of varying intensities and colors.

"This register here shows present status of life-entities in your station of material frequency. Oh, it looks good! The star people are returning, though slowly, and the group of souls held over from the last adjustment have completed half a revolution and are beginning to have access to their ancestral memories of spirit origin."

"What are those clear dots that seem to have a more intense radiance?" I impulsively asked.

"The clearest, most intense are life-forms who have, through one form of development or another, realigned their awareness with their light origin. A few may have material bodies, but most would be forming a light network about the planet, sustaining their ethereal presence in pockets of undisturbed energy that would be uninhabitable to the fragile physical body.

"The patches of faded light interspersed among the darker shades are souls and groups of souls who are assimilating the light frequencies of their cosmic origin at this moment and soon will be ready for the next adjustment."

I could now distinguish the subtle differences in the shades of white light, dancing among the tapestry of darker shades, forming constantly shifting patterns in the grains of life.

"Not much light for all the darkness," I said. "I always suspected we were destroying the planet."

"The planet, destroyed? No! No! It is a high frequency, life-sustaining biosphere established many millions of your years ago. It can serve for many more revolutions, with periodic adjustments, of course.

"I can detect by this sensitivity layout that there will be enough light beings aware of their divine potential to pass through the veil of transformation by the time the adjustment occurs. You see, the light is beginning to return in great waves of consciousness. Those lights you see are only the advanced potential creating new identity patterns within the malignant thought realms of fear and disbelief of your planet. The main influx of light consciousness will expand off of those patterns as the opposing forces of destruction create voids into which they may

flow. It is set up so the dark will yield to the light through its own aggression and destructive identification.

"Let's bring up a biosphere status perspective. We'll give it a probability factor of plus-or-minus a generation, which should be clear enough for our purpose."

A new rearrangement of the intensity in the configuration of light patterns was instantly before me in holographic reality comprised of seven energy bands of oscillating frequencies rotating in opposite directions to each other about a central point of brilliant white light.

"All the varieties of human species that presently exist within the Earth biosphere have been introduced or grafted onto its frequency to allow for the development of higher conceptual attitudes such as oneness, gratitude, joy, cooperation and compassion. Some varieties are doing better than others due to awareness expansion into non-material realities. Even so, the harvest of clear thought-fields this round shall be one of the best since free will became available to the mind process."

"'Harvest of clear thought-fields'? What do you mean by that?" I puzzled in the flow of my understanding.

"Yes, you're accustomed to it having more importance than that on your level of identity. It is amazing that you drifted in here, but we will continue. We must be getting closer to the reason you're here.

"Those seven energy fields represent major patterns of spin and rotation within constantly expanding and contracting frequencies that maintain certain consistent relationships of movement. They sustain the consistencies of gravitation and electromagnetic fields, chemical bonding relationships and life-balancing cycles, thought-fields and awareness frequencies. They are responsible for maintaining the fixed relationships of the Earth sphere to its sun and other mother stars.

"You can see broken, unclear areas in some of the outer bands, especially in the ones stabilizing thought frequencies. They indicate that the technological stress of removing minerals from the crust of the planet, destruction of biological harmony, industrial leaching of the energy grid through the over-generation of electricity, poisoning of the gaseous spheres, and the destruction of chemical stability is coming close to creating new fixed relationships. They also tell us that thought patterns of destruction and violence, created by identification with material individuality, are slowly approaching the critical level necessary for the adjustment.

"The natural tendency of a life-support system such as your Earth is to stabilize into new life-sustaining relationships, as long as the central core is sufficiently stable to absorb the initial chaotic reverberations of the frequency shift. By the time the adjustment is coordinated, the core pressure will have been reduced to new levels through volcanic eruption and land mass shifts, so that the new relationships can be created.

"Then we could reintroduce life-forms with clear thought-fields and the proper genetic memories of life's purpose and its spiritual origin into the stabilizing

biosphere. They will have been molecularly altered through the experience, as will the life-forms that pass through the transmutation within the hollows of the Earth, and ready to start the process of identification with their light bodies. They will then construct another civilization in different gravitational and magnetic frequencies that will allow for the necessary influences of light to enter into the awareness process.

"We could be seeing our first light-bodies in common use within the next three to five generations. Less if we can introduce a powerful unifying influence on the belief systems around which the core souls will be arranged."

The subtly shifting intensities of the light module before me, which was somehow responding to this explanation and reinforcing my comprehension through a knowing feeling, mesmerized me. The wisdom was entering through the channel of my imagination, like shooting a mystic video of feelings and intuitive sensations with no rational censoring imposed upon the process.

"Belief systems of the core souls? What does that have to do with the environmental disaster facing the planet Earth?" I asked aloud.

"Well, that is a rather technical point but it may have something to do with your visit here. Let's see.

"The essence of life is movement of light. We are sure you can understand that or you could not be sustaining this dimension as you are. The life-forms, who will be sufficiently prepared to participate in the transmutation process we call the adjustment, are grouping together around certain belief systems about God and reality, which allow sufficient light to penetrate the density of their material forms. Although inadequate to allow full integration into levels of spirit, these belief systems do serve to distract the awareness from attachment to individuality, the greatest limitation that has arisen since free will was allowed to run the course of its natural development.

"Belief about anything creates a fixed set of relationships within the awareness process and influences the consciousness of the life-form. Your species lost contact with its light origin when free will was given rein within the field of personal expression. Fixed mental relationships or beliefs began to accumulate about your fields of consciousness, and light, your link with spiritual origin, began to be cut off. You then became dependent upon the limiting conceptual process of language, which cut off your awareness from the subtle realms of feeling, imagination, and intuition, bridges to your divine origin.

"It was decided to take advantage of this occurrence by introducing specific belief systems about your origin, purpose, destiny, and relationship to Divinity that would allow light to infiltrate the darkness. They have served well over the last ten to twenty thousand years of your conscious development to keep the channel open but they are inadequate for the next phase of development — your identity with oneness.

"Because alterations inflicted upon the biosphere, electromagnetic sphere, and

gravitational sphere by your developing civilization have accelerated the conditions necessary for the transmutation of the physical, mental, and emotional frequencies, there may not be time to introduce sufficient influences into the process to unite all these belief systems into a harmoniously functioning whole before conditions are just right for the adjustment. It appears that the process itself will have to be the catalyst for such a unification."

"But why did you introduce this *free will* if it was destined to create such problems? Or did some screw-up happen along the way?" I felt the need to know.

"Oh no. We do not introduce anything from this level. Just monitor and make suggestions to certain star stations that have a specific impulse relationship with the life-forms in development there. Their technicians will implement the proper adjustments of the seven bands of life-sustaining frequencies when the timing is just right.

"Life is based upon the principle of movement and flow, out of which emerges inter-dependence, co-existence, inter-penetration and cooperation — the constituents of unity and oneness. Choice is an essential aspect of consciousness, out of which movement is sustained on all levels of creation. Even a star explodes with an expression of its free will. Choice is vital for the cycle of creation to be completed, for awareness of cosmic unity to be sustained. Without it, there could be no movement.

"We knew it was going to be a critical phase of your life-development process but the relationship between ingenuity and ignorance in the human species has surprised us at times!"

I felt a strange sensation of doom and gloom and the lights before me began the react to my feelings by pulsating and swirling about in chaotic patterns. An eerie feeling of hopelessness flooded over me.

"Calm down! Your rational attachment is going to cause us to blow a gyro-circuit!

"Life cannot be destroyed! When placed under the stress of annihilation it will always readjust to another frequency relationship. The form may be altered but not the direction of its movement or its relationship to The Light. We are not trying to save the life-forms on your planet from destruction, nor the planet itself, but rather influence their identities and relationships to light, so as to prepare them for the new frequency modulations that will sustain the life-forms of the Earth plane during the next revolution.

"Besides, there are other planets, galaxies, and universes for that matter. Calm down! Attachment is the ultimate expression of human ignorance."

"Then why is this adjustment, which you so elusively refer to, necessary? Why can't life just go on the way it is?"

"We have hinted to you that your species has been genetically grafted onto the consciousness frequencies of the Earth's biosphere through a long and tedious *process of affinity and attraction. The purpose of creating such a relationship is the development of light vehicles that will allow for the next phase of conscious-ness expansion within the process of perfection creating itself. Until certain levels of awareness have been integrated into the human consciousness and vibrational frequencies of light can be sustained within the denser substance of material form, an incompatibility will exist between the developing life-form and its life-support system.*

"When the consciousness of unity, which I believe you refer to as compassion within your developing conceptual frame work, has been assimilated into your fields of awareness, then the harmonious coexistence of your life-form and its supportive environment will be possible. You are really trying to unite as one being with the Earth herself.

"Unity is not a concept but a reality upon which life is based. Alterations of your life-support system due to the lack of awareness of this unity can only create changes that will bring greater awareness of unity in the end. That is why out of random, chaotic development, unity will always arise."

A sense of calm and reassurance came over me as I felt that everything was in perfect divine order, although that order appeared to be spiraling out of control.

"There need be no control," came the thoughts of my illusive guide. *"That which arose out of perfection needs no controlling factors. Superior intelligence, higher guidance, and God for that matter are but shallow concepts arising out of belief in, not experience of, a greater cosmic unity. These beliefs will certainly influence the process of human awareness, but never control it.*

"You now cling to concepts of God and higher intelligence as controlling factors because your identification is still separated from the whole. Although incomplete from a universal perceptive, these are precisely the belief systems that are allowing light to penetrate the density of your awareness. You are living a process, not a truth. A process requires that truth be relative to the present awareness of light and unity. It requires flexible belief systems that can guide the development of awareness, but not limit it to a fixed relationship, as greater wisdom is assimilated into human consciousness.

Part of me was exhausted. The light patterns lost their intensity and the foggy perimeters of this new world began to close in upon me. There was nothing to want, ask or remember which would hold me there. I felt great compassion surround me and waves of white light engulf me as a voice called out, *"Perfec-tion exists in every moment of eternity. Live it!"*

CHAPTER 35

LAMA GOVINDA

About a week later, I heard voices at my gate one afternoon. I left my task of straightening up a rose garden trampled by monkeys the night before and threaded my way through the thick foliage to see who it was. Standing in the archway formed by a climbing rose bush was Mary, who announced that she had come to get me to visit Lama Govinda. While she went to get Sunya in the garden above, I splashed some cold water on my work-stained body, wrapped a fresh white cloth about me, grabbed my woolen shawl and blanket, and arrived back at the gate just as Mary, and Sunyaji were coming back down the hill.

Our party proceeded slowly along the dusty road with Mary diligently picking up the smallest of twigs and sticks and tucking them in her little net bag, while carrying on a running conversation about Lama Govinda. The sun was still high in the sky when we turned off the main road and climbed a steep embankment. We followed a faint path passing into a dense enclave of native oaks and rhododendrons, choked with giant ferns and thick, broad-leafed vines alive with gleaming yellow flowers.

This microhabitat was the estate of a Buddhist foundation. Before Lama Govinda, the venerable scholar and mystic Evans-Wentz had been the resident Buddhist monk here. It was on this very estate that he translated the Tibetan Book of the Dead, the hippie Bible for the 'tune in, turn on, and drop out' generation. The British had plundered all the native hardwoods to fuel their First World War efforts, but this sanctuary had been preserved. The clarity and purity of its vibrations reflected a balanced coexistence between humanity and nature.

We all fell silent as Sunya Baba guided us up the mossy steps that led to a flat, grassy area terraced steeply on three sides. Nestled in an arch of gnarled oak limbs stood a stone house covered in ivy and surrounded by flowering shrubs. This was the highest peak of the Kali Mat ridge and commanded a panoramic view of the frosted peaks of northern India and Tibet. We waited silently, drinking in the energy of this power spot. I felt the importance of the moment jump in my heart as a servant opened the glass doors that led into a sunlit room.

Mary and Sunyaji led the way as we took seats on reed mats in front of a cozy corner of leather-bound books stacked on low shelves. A delicate, angular-faced man with a pointed gray beard and wispy white eye brows, dressed in red monastic robes, was seated in front of a low wooden desk with his legs tucked underneath him. Seated crossed-legged to his right was a stout, jovial woman with short dark hair, who had already engaged Mary in conversation about her recent trip to the United States. Mary had spoken of Lee Gotami, Lama Govinda's artist wife, who shared life with him as a monk and fellow seeker along the path.

Mary broke away from her conversation to introduce me to Lama Govinda and his wife and a pleasant round of formalities followed. Sunya Baba then engaged the Lama in a lengthy discussion on certain technical points about sound and mantra from his book on Tibetan Mysticism, which they both seemed to enjoy immensely. I watched intensely as Lama Govinda listened with great concentration to the questions and slowly formulated his answers, quoting from many Buddhist and Hindu texts and using several examples from his own life to emphasize his point. It was clear from his way of expressing himself that he was not trying to impress us with his knowledge. He was a soft-spoken, humble person who seemed to thrive on this personal exchange and was truly interested in imparting his understanding to us all.

Somehow the conversation turned to the concept of time and my interest picked up. Mary was trying to find out in what form time existed on other levels of reality and Lama Govinda was replying that time was nothing more than a means of measuring human experience. Beyond this level, the limitation of time was not necessary because experiences were not analyzed, but felt and lived in the moment.

"Might time be considered a process of the rational mind; that which measures space?" I asked, finding this concept interesting.

He turned to look at me, stroking his feathery beard before replying, "It is really the principal structure of the rational mind, that which gives it form and allows it to function and interact with the material world. Some Hindu scholars believe that *maya*, the web of illusion, is woven out of the cords of time. Albert Einstein deduced that time is not fixed but relative to the speed of light," he concluded with a sparkle in his eyes.

Sunya Baba asked a question about Einstein's relationship to Hindu and Buddhist philosophy and Lamaji stated emphatically that Einstein and many other noted scientists had been greatly influenced by eastern thought, but used it as a background to their own theories rather than trying to incorporate it directly.

"In the Tibetan system," he said, "science and religion have not been separated as they have been in the west. That western science has turned its back on intuitive knowing and denied the place of mystical insights within their disciplines, I see as a great limitation.

"Buddhists see life as a multi-dimensional process whose interconnectedness and interdependence is the essence of the process. Life cannot be understood from a purely rational, material perspective such as reducing it to its smallest part. The seen and the unseen are constantly exchanging energies through vibrational frequencies that interpenetrate the two realities."

I then dared to ask, "Is consciousness one of those frequencies?"

He stared hard in my direction again and started several times to answer, cutting himself off each time, as if unsatisfied with what he was about to say. Finally he clearly replied in his heavy Germanic accent, "I would say that consciousness supports those frequencies and is the means of their interpenetration."

We exchanged smiles and he went on to answer more questions about the Tibetan system of meditation. Lee talked some more about their travels to Tibet and the United States. We never reentered the mystical realm that day, but for the next four weeks I was a regular attendee of the Thursday afternoon gatherings, whose numbers increased as people from the lower ridge heard of them and made the two hour walk to listen to Lama Govinda give his simple and clear explanations of the world of mysticism. His intellectual understanding was not what really interested me, but his presence, which radiated an inner calm and tranquility of mind, truly impressed me.

One day in early June, I arrived at his house a little late for his talk and, entering quietly, took a seat to one side of the room. To my surprise, there were only two other people there that day, neither of whom I recognized from the other gatherings. Lamaji paused in his explanation of the Buddhist concept of the void, or emptiness, to bow in my direction and motion for me to move closer to him. We had had many lively and interesting conversations by then and we both enjoyed each other's company.

An older, gray-haired man, who was sitting with a younger blond woman in western dress, asked a question about whether the emptiness was the shadow of or other side of the all?

Pausing as he did when a question was sufficiently deep to require thought, he stroked his wispy beard before answering. "Emptiness does not mean that there is nothing there. Everything is there but only in an undifferentiated state. It would be better to call it a state of awareness beyond individual distinction of things.

"When you look up, you say, 'I'm looking at the sky', not oxygen, carbon dioxide, and water vapor, because you're not aware of these things. You're capable of perceiving it only as the sky. In the same way, from within the void, one is not capable of distinguishing differentiation of separate things because they are as yet..." he paused with a twinkle in his eye, his slender finger held skyward, "un manifest. They are only potential."

"Are you talking about some state of universal oneness where all things are united together in some common vibrational unity?" I asked, remembering my mystical feelings of total unity.

"The true distinction of this state is that of awareness, not of the unity but of a void," he replied, after some thought. "Awareness of the unity might be the first distinction, where consciousness takes on form or definition."

"Does consciousness unite all things into nothingness?" I asked.

He turned slightly, took off his spectacles and smiled. Then he asked in return, "Where does such a question come from, my young *sadhu*? And do you know the answer?"

I felt a little uneasy, not really knowing why I asked this question. He smiled again and with an almost imperceptible nod of his head prompted me to answer.

I cleared my throat and said, "I have had experiences where everything exists in a state of perfect unity, a balance and harmony of action and interaction that in no way alters the whole. I can't be sure it is the same state you are calling nothingness and perhaps we stumble over words cluttering a wordless path. Language becomes severely inadequate when defining the un-manifest, yet we try, mostly for our own pride." We smiled to each other and held our gaze silently for several seconds before I continued.

"There is something in this state of total awareness that acts to hold it all together, or might even arise out of its togetherness, and supports communication and interaction among all of its various parts. The best I can define it is a frequency out of which all other frequencies arise or which contains all other vibrations. I call it consciousness, but it could also be related to as nothingness, I suppose."

We smiled into each other's eyes for another moment until he asked with a smile, "where does consciousness arise from my young mystic?"

"Out of movement," I answered spontaneously. "Creation is based upon a movement, like expansion and contraction, which in turn gives rise to spin and rotation, attraction and repulsion, division, multiplication, structure, form, and other energetic configurations of matter.

"Consciousness is the result of the interactions of all these original movements of creation energized by the tide of expansion and contraction. Awareness and thought, the basic expressions of mind, may be related to as activities of consciousness."

"Good!" he commented, clutching his beard, as if wringing it for his next question. "And why did the first movement take place?" he asked with a sly twinkle in his eye, as if we had arrived at both the first and the last question.

I closed my eyes, sensing the magic of the moment, and waited for the answer to arise from the place of all-knowingness within me.

"Perfection has but one need: To express itself. Out of this inspiration arises the initial impulse to move toward the manifestation of its perfection. All life springs forth from this initial inspiration and breathes itself into existence.

"Beyond consciousness there is nothingness, yet when there is no more nothingness, there is only consciousness."

A breathless stillness absorbed the room and I savored the moment by keeping my eyes shut and listening to the soft chirping of birds in the shrubs outside the window. The image of Richard from Katmandu flashed before my inner eye. I remembered having felt that answer before, but now it was mine, not theirs, whoever they might be.

"Thank you," came the voice of my friend and I opened my eyes to see a hint of mist in his eyes and an expression of deep appreciation on his face.

"Is there anything you would like to ask me, my young *sadhu*? A voice within prompts me to ask you this."

The meetings were usually filled with many people, all asking questions about Buddhist philosophy, that I did not feel comfortable being so personal. I had been hoping for sometime to ask about the energy attacks consuming me for many months. They had settled into acceptable threats to my annihilation, confining themselves mostly to the evenings or when I was tired, but I still could not sleep for more than a few hours at a time and the mixture of hot and cold, energy and exhaustion, fear and bliss, was a lot to keep together, to say the least. I was not sure just what to ask but I opened my mouth in faith and told him the story of the last four months, ending with, "What is it and why is it happening to me?"

During my explanation his face had passed through a wide range of expressions, from interest to surprise and amazement when I confessed my ignorance about the whole thing. He shifted his position, unfolding and folding his legs, something he rarely did during these two-hour talks, and he was now staring at me in bewilderment. I did not know what to expect.

"I am a scholar," he began with a sincere expression on his gentle face, after a pronounced time of silence, "and from my studies I have heard of such manifestations of energy, but I have learned more today by observing your face and listening to the emotion in your voice than any book could convey. My master once told me that a book may give you knowledge but only experience may grant you wisdom. I can see that your experience has granted such wisdom. May my knowledge be that which helps you to accept it as such," he continued, in a tone of genuine humility.

"What I can say to you is that this experience is not achieved through long and hard disciplines but is granted according to your evolution, which would include your intentions, motivations, dedications, all the memories you bring with you into this lifetime, and how you choose to live your present reality.

"If it is happening to you it is because it is supposed to be happening!

"You must choose to live it how you can. No one can guide you in this better than your own self. Who could tell you how to create the delicate alignment of will and intention that this experience demands of you?

"I have not experienced such a thing but I have heard of such happenings during my many years of searching. I would say that the key at this point is the fear. Ask yourself 'why am I afraid?' Why not identify with the bliss?

"If Shakti comes and asks for your surrender, it is because destiny has called her to you. This experience, from what I know of it, is a blessing and asks of you only surrender in return. Don't get caught up in trying to understand it. Accept it and give thanks. Gratitude might be the missing attitude in your mystical quest."

My heart was expanding with joy as I joined my hands softly together and bowed my most respectful and sincere bow since coming to India. He had answered the question I had been asking all the gurus and holy men and women of India for over two years. 'He didn't know, but if it was happening, it was meant to be. Why fight it?' All of a sudden, fear floated away and peace flooded into my heart. I was healed at last.

Our little exchange took over an hour while the others sat transfixed by our conversation. By rising to her feet, Lee signaled to us that the session was ending but Lamaji and I stayed locked in a visual embrace, clinging to this special moment. We bowed again, rose to our feet and followed the others out in silence. The far peaks of the mighty Himalayas were shrouded in violet clouds and the crystal blue sky was fading to an orange gray. We stared in silence at the parting of the sun and the silver slice of moon hanging on the horizon. I felt the power and wisdom of this sacred place and gave thanks to the couple who now kept it alive.

CHAPTER 36

KALI TEMPLE

During the next month my spirits soared as I reentered the realms of deep meditation with greater enthusiasm than before, encouraged by the wisdom of my new friend and teacher, Lama Govinda. The goddess Kundalini tickled me with her presence at times, but, with all fear gone, the tumultuous explosions of power and bliss that had rocked my being into shadowy realms of doubt and fright were welcomed by me as the means to open the doors to new levels of self. I found, from examining my fear, that I was still clinging to the world of desire and pleasure and that this attachment was the source of my unwillingness to surrender my total identity to the world of the unknown. The disturbance in the energy channels of my physical body was due to this duality of renunciation and clinging fighting a war within my being. With firm resolve I moved forward into the uncharted depths of my being, guided by the light and bliss of my soul which now flashed before me regularly as I sat in dedicated absorption, seeking the self residing beyond attachment and fear.

The intense heat of the summer was passing, although the winter rains were still months away. My life had once again settled into an addictive routine of more than eight hours of sitting meditation interspersed with gardening, cooking, collecting firewood, and carrying water from the distant well. One afternoon I was walking up the steep footpath leading from the well with a bucket of water perched upon my head when I heard the cry, "*OM Namo Narayana*" from the far embankment. I stopped and cautiously turned to see an old *sadhu* sitting in the soft rays of the afternoon sun, motioning for me to join him on his blanket. I picked my way over to where he was sitting, set down my bucket, and squatted beside him. He was slim, his hair and beard were slightly gray and he was wrapped in various faded orange cloths. He sat on a thick wool blanket, used mainly by *sadhus* who live deep in the mountains, and next to him was his brass *comundle* and a simple one-stringed instrument fashioned from a hollowed-out gourd and curved stick.

He talked slowly in Hindi, wanting to be understood, while I gazed into his half-closed eyes and sensed a friend. He wanted me to go to the top of the nearby mountain with him and spend the night at the Kali temple. I knew the temple from my afternoon walks and paused only a moment to feel his request within my heart. I bowed, indicating with a few words and simple gestures that I would return soon, and headed off towards my cabin still puzzling over this strange invitation. Within half an hour, I returned with my *comundle*, woolen shawl and blanket and we started up the winding trail. His feet danced up the path, stirring up no dust, as if he was barely touching the earth. Within minutes he was way ahead of me and I labored to keep him in sight.

Trring, trring, echoed the sound of his one-string gourd in the stillness of a late summer afternoon.

Trring trring, and I knew he was calling me.

I caught the rhythm of his strumming in my breathing and stepped surely as the trail became steeper. Step for step, with the twang of the string, I climbed, being pulled up the slope by the tone itself. Minutes later I knew I had entered into an altered state of consciousness as he increased the pace of his strumming and I just floated up on its energy, feeling no strain on my physical body.

When we reached the ridge he was only a few yards ahead of me on the path, holding the instrument high in his right hand and beginning to strum faster. We flew along the ridge winding in and about wind-twisted pine trees while climbing steadily all the way. I was seeing nothing of the landscape as color and form had faded in intensity. All my perception had been drawn into the *trring* of his instrument. Some energy created out of this special state of awareness was carrying me along the path. I was touching the earth and I was not, because my awareness was in the ringing *trring* of the string, not in my feet or even my breathing. I could not feel my feet touch the ground, yet a part of me accepted that this was happening.

The trail began to climb steeply again but his cadence maintained its rapid pace as each step sprang from the one before, energized by the sound hypnotically pulling me higher and higher. I knew that if ever the thought, 'I can't do this', flashed within my now-stilled mind, I would fall to the ground exhausted. Yet, beyond all thought I floated on up the mountain. My vision was totally blurred by the altered awareness. The steep, rocky hillside and wind-swept trees blended into a kaleidoscope of shapes and forms dancing on a fluid landscape of vibrating colors. A high-pitched frequency buzzed loudly in my ears and an orb of radiant light surrounded my body. Up, up and on up the mountain we climbed carried along in an enchanted spell.

Trring, Trring, Trring, and we stopped. I was hardly breathing. It was more like

I was asleep or lying down, not racing up a mountain trail. The familiar celestial ringing in my ears that always accompanied heightened states of awareness was still audible. The face of my guide was distinguishable only as a pink glow of radiance against the dull gray of the stone hillside. I was suspended in a bubble of soft energy with my breath still detached from material reality.

Trring! And bang, my breath drew in suddenly and my vision cleared. I was standing in front of the Kali Temple perched on jagged cliffs at the far end of the ridge. Standing between two arched pine trees that formed a natural gateway to the temple was Light Baba, palms joined over his heart in silent greeting. His hair and beard were the same but the astonishing glow radiating from his white robes was more brilliant than at Sidh Kuti. His eyes still shone with knowingness and a deep peace radiated from his ageless face.

I started to cry out in great pleasure and surprise but his raised finger shot to his lips, signaling me to silence. He bowed to my guide, who saluted in turn with a, *trring*, as he turned and scurried further up the hill to the Shiva temple, hopping and gliding like a gazelle with invisible wings.

I expected Light Baba to talk to me within my mind but no thought communications came. I felt a surge of love pour out to him and he smiled a gleaming, radiant smile that made no other communication necessary. He seemed to be looking into my soul and noting every experience that had transpired since our parting, leafing quickly through my memories, pausing momentarily in memorable experiences such as the gift of my cloth in the train, my adventure in the temple in New Delhi, and the *Kundalini* release last winter. His expression never changed but I felt a certain approval from his heart.

He motioned for me to follow as he started along a non-discernable trail across the rocky outcropping and down a path into a gully so steep it was like a hole, open only on one side to the thick forest wall. We reached a place in the mossy path where steps were cut into the stone embankment leading to a shallow pool of water. We made our way down using the jagged rocks as handholds until we were standing on a worn, flat stone about six feet across and two feet wide. Large ferns formed a lacy canopy over the crystalline pool in front of the rocks and tiny droplets of water trickled down the velvety moss covering the rocky walls on three sides. In the wall nearest Babaji was carved a small, concave altar containing only three round stones of faded orange, yellow, and black colors and a crude stone incense holder.

The special feeling of ancient sacredness that surrounded this place brought peace to my heart and my mind yielded in an attitude of total surrender to the moment. Light Baba signaled for me to set my blanket on the embankment and take off my cloth while he did the same. He first poured water over his head while chanting in an undertone to the Goddess Kali or perhaps to a goddess even more ancient than her. Increasing the force of his prayer he repeatedly scooped *comundles* of cold, clear water and poured them over my head until, with a loud, *"Bum Bum Boli"*, he fell silent. I hardly felt the water. My awareness was in the feeling that something magical, beyond the actions or the elements, was being brought into alignment. Some preparation was taking place.

We returned by a trail on the opposite side of the gully, picking up several fallen branches along the way. By the time we reached the temple, a pale pink glow filled the eastern sky and grayness gripped the surrounding pine forest. He pointed to a flat, smooth stone and signaled for me to meditate while he went to the temple and made an offering. I heard him breaking up firewood off in the distance. I was already in an altered state of awareness and needed only a little guidance of my breath to reach a deep state of meditation.

When I reentered identification with my physical body and opened my eyes, darkness had come. In the hazy light of the nearly full moon I could make out the figure of Light Baba standing near the Kali temple staring in at the figure of the terrifying goddess. I joined him but he seemed to be in some other state of consciousness and did not in any way acknowledge my presence.

Make an offering from your heart to the Goddess Kali, and then follow me, I heard within my mind.

I stepped into the small shrine and stood before the image of the bloodthirsty goddess of destruction with a garland of human skulls draped about her neck and wielding in her many arms weapons of destruction. An uncomfortable feeling came over me, interrupting my certainty and causing my breath to constrict in my chest.

She is fierce yet wise in her ways, he was saying in my head. *Ask that her vision may guide you this night; that the wisdom of destruction may also be known within your heart."*

"I am your servant, Oh Great Spirit. I call upon your fearful, destructive form to be my guide this night!" I prayed aloud, pouring spring water from my *comundle* at the feet of the image.

I stood transfixed, not knowing weather I would be struck dead on the spot or if the heavens would open up and legions of demons descend upon me.

"Follow me now," I heard after a marked silence.

He led me out the gate and down the slope to a hidden cave formed by a giant slab of rock jutting out of a sloping crevice burrowed into the mountain. A fire danced in the center of the ledge that formed the floor of the cave and Light Baba's blanket was placed before it. He took his place and I spread my blanket to his right and sat down. No communication came and we both stared into the leaping flames in silence.

I must have shut my eyes and drifted off because when I noticed him again he was selecting glowing coals from the fire and placing them in a small clay saucer. He then selected various dried herbs from a cloth spread before him and placed them on the glowing coals while blowing to create a small cloud of smoke. The echo of his mumbled chant softly reverberated within the cave for a long time as rising plumes of smoke swirled about my head.

Then, without standing up, he shuffled to the back of the cave on his haunches, indicating for me to follow.

"There," he said, pointing to an opening about three feet in diameter secreted away in the back of the cave. "The womb of the Goddess. She will come to you there."

He showed me how to crawl up the low wall and into the inner space. My mind resisted the idea of entering into a dark, confined space in a smoky cave, but anticipation conquered reason and I crawled in. The darkness consumed me. I squirmed around until I found a position with my back against a contoured recess in the stonewall and pulled my knees up to my chest. The air was surprisingly fresh and cool so I began to concentrate on my breath and waited. I realized that I was entering some form of altered reality when tiny pinpoints of light appeared, floating in the total darkness, and a high-pitched, celestial ringing began filling the entire space with a sea of pulsating sound.

The smoke from the fire and the burning herbs did not enter this chamber at first but, after several minutes, a strong fragrance reached my senses. At first just whiffs that seemed to awaken me but suddenly a burst of smoke rushed in and I clutched my cloth up around my eyes and nose and might have passed out if I had not found a pocket of fresh air between my legs. A second cloud of smoke drifted in and I began to desperately struggle with the feeling of confinement and suffocation, sensing death clutching at my parched throat. I wanted to cry out for help and escape this hole but as soon as I felt this urge, I was no longer capable of doing so. I no longer was within my physical body.

I was looking at the star-studded sky, which seemed to be moving toward me at great speed. There was no moonlight, no Kali Temple and no ground below me. I was calm and still as if watching a movie screen waiting for the show to begin.

Off in the distance I could perceive a flash of energy charging at me while spinning around madly. Then she appeared before me, dancing wildly and flinging her deadly weapons in all directions. Her eyes were pools of fire and her wide-open mouth was filled with long, pointed teeth dripping in blood. Everywhere about her were human skulls floating in the wake of her terrible destruction. Suddenly she raced at me spitting fire and blood in all directions and I braced to meet my death.

Then, in an instant, she was no more and only the heavens, a glow with fire and smoke, stood before me. Out of the sky came huge fiery balls colliding with one another and sending showers of liquid fire plunging to the Earth. The planet rocked and shook and great clouds of smoke rose up creating a crimson inferno in the sky.

There was a moment of calm when the very planet seemed to wobble and shake in fear of what was to come. Then it appeared through the haze — a gigantic ball, exploding in fire like the sun, streaking through the atmosphere, heading directly toward the Earth.

"John Brown!" I screamed to myself. "Oh no!" *The Lord will send fire and brimstone to rid the planet of all non-believers'!* He knew what the rest of us never dared to imagine. The adjustment had come.

Looking down I could see the planet ablaze with fire and smoke. Turning to the sky, I could see the 'death star' whirling and spitting destruction in all directions as it hurled toward the Earth. Beings of light appeared in the fiery sky. People, gathered in hopeful prayer, perceived these angelic messengers and looked up in faith to the heavens. Within this apocalyptical vision, rays of light began to appear from beyond the Earth and descend like tunnels through the blazing inferno to touch the surface of the planet. A flow, like golden drops of water, began to move within these light beams ascending to the heavens. Great orbs of light suspended just beyond the atmosphere of the Earth began sucking human light-forms through translucent tunnels into the safety of their energy fields. I knew within my being that people were being lifted off the Earth to avoid the full thrust of human annihilation, just minutes away.

Then, with explosions of great magnitude, the planet collapsed under the tremendous impact of the 'death star'. Volcanoes exploded, mountains crumbled and fire and smoke rose up as the great mass of the planet wobbled and shook, threatening to fall out of the heavens. The last thing I witnessed was it slowly listing to one side, like a great sinking ship. Then the sky filled with a billowing cloud of smoke and giant plumes of gas and water vapor, obscuring my vision.

Radiant orbs still formed a network about the mass of clouds and smoke but the shafts of light had been withdrawn. Concentrating upon them, I was drawn into their presence and found myself in a spacious chamber of translucent amber with panels of white light around the perimeter. The room was filled with thousands of human forms encased in cocoons of energy and light, varying in intensity and tone but all of golden light. They were alive but not living. No breath or thought activity could be perceived but movements of energy within their light-fields told me they were somehow alive.

A thought message filled the conscious space:

"Destruction has taken place so that life may continue. Your spirits are marked forever with the resonance of this sacred transmutation.

"When the Earth's liquid core has stabilized and new magnetic frequencies can be established, you will be reintroduced to your biosphere, which will have passed through its own dramatic transformation. The actual space-time relationships and electromagnetic frequencies of the planet will have been altered due to the new rate of spin and no previous technology will exist in any form. It will be sometime before even the first hazy rays of sun will brighten up the blackened sky and much longer before you will look upon the stars at night again.

"Wise people have been chosen to guide you in the first generations of your new root race, for there are many lessons yet to learn. You were all chosen, not because you believe and think the same, but because, in the moment of truth, you turned to a presence greater than yourself and you cared as much for the lives of everyone who shared the experience with you as you did for your own.

"You will build the next civilization on that same feeling that enabled you to be transported to this station—unity consciousness. All other beliefs have now been shattered through the direct experience that your essence is love.

"You must learn to live this feeling and pass it to the generations who grow from your beginning in stories, legend, and myths, so that none will forget and begin to kill another soul for a little bit of Earth again.

"We suggest that you practice joy and gratitude among yourselves and reestablish reverence and respect for the living Mother Earth. It is she with whom you will be required to make the first peace, by asking her forgiveness and entering into a new relationship of coexistence. That which your predecessors rejected as primitive and superstitious will be recalled from banishment and form the link to worlds once outside your ordinary range of perception. From these places you all will learn to live in total unity and grow in light and love."

I sailed out beyond that space in time to view the Earth jewel as an emerging emerald with pockets of civilizations dotted about her greening surface, each unaware of the others' existence. I saw communities that had survived below the surface of the ancient Earth and those whose prayer and faith had protected them in sacred valleys beyond the reach of Kali's destructive wrath. Adventurers set out to re-map the surface of the planet and search for traces of humanity. When they came upon another human being, they asked not 'where do you come from?' but rather 'how did you survive?' For it was this that marked the spirit of those who still lived and breathed upon the planet Earth.

Then everything went black and the web of Kali released me from her vision of worlds to come. I knew for certain what she tried to say: Destruction is the shadow of creation.

I jerked back into my physical body and gasped for breath in the dark, cool womb. It was such a relief to be back that even the suffocating confinement was reassuring. My body ached from more than sitting, as if I had lived the fears of all humanity in one instant.

I prayed with tears flooding down my cheeks. I prayed with a heart filled with gratitude, not questioning God's existence or love. I prayed and cried.

When I returned to myself again, I was lying on my blanket in front of the fire in the cave of the Goddess. Light Baba was sitting next to me gently rocking and staring off into the blackened forest, lost in silent communication with some form of God. A radiant glow surrounded him more brilliant than ever before. He turned to look into my eyes and I saw who I knew he was all along. His face became transfigured before me into an ageless figure of divine pres-

CHAPTER 37

THE CAVE

Slowly, step-by-step, I placed one foot in front of the other, breathing heavily and laboring under the heavy load of rice, lentils and flour as I made my way up the far mountain to my cave. It was now late afternoon of my second day of walking and my body was tired, but I was filled with hope and expectation for the next experience awaiting me around the bend in the road.

It had been difficult to explain to everyone just why I was doing this. Since my vision of the adjustment, nothing in the material world attracted me to want it, need it, or possess it. I felt more detached from everything and just did not care enough about anything to form the customary attachments and fears so essential to live a *normal* life.

Several weeks after my vision in the Kali temple, I had a dream in which I saw myself entering a cave atop a distant mountain. With the certainty that I was supposed to find that cave and live in it, I searched the far mountain and found it hidden in a cliff face near a small Shiva temple, just as it had appeared in my dream.

In the cave, away from outside influences of any kind, the restless thoughts of the impetuous mind would yield into perfect peace and God's light would be forever with me. This was my plan and the source of strength that now carried me on when my physical body and rational mind would have stopped me a long time ago.

My closer friends, aware of my mystical process, gave me great encouragement and accepted, without questioning, my decision to make this final retreat. Both Mary and Lama Govinda said that most people who go through this type of mystical opening must retreat completely from the world for a time or even until the end of their lives. Mary cautioned me to be wise and take care of my physical body, "It is your vehicle to perfection. The universe is your limit, but the Earth is your ground. Don't you forget that!"

Lama Govinda had talked to me for several hours one afternoon about the manifestation of the Kundalini and its mystical meaning in terms of death and resurrection.

"It is a death. A death of ignorance you might say. You will no longer see the shadow of the world and be fooled into believing it is real. But what will be left? That is the unanswered question. What will be left of your identity and your relationship to the world?

"I would like you to remember that the end of the quest is here," he said warmly, pointing to his heart. "All mystics discover that the arisen energy must descend from the head to the heart. The Spirit must enter the flesh. This up here," he emphasized by placing his delicate hands around his head and looking intensely into my eyes, "is wisdom — a deceptive mistress that can fool you into believing that *you* are the one who knows.

"When the power rises up the spine to awaken this wisdom, a seductive love affair begins. But they must descend together to be united in love in the heart. Then one has brought the Spirit into the material world. Power, wisdom, and love can then function in perfect harmony with one another."

Mary, after drilling me in her humorous way about why I wanted to do anything so ridiculous as live in a cave where there was sure to be scorpions and mountain lions, gave me an extra blanket and loaded me down with tea, raw sugar, and other goodies.

"I see it in your eyes! You have had a terrific vision!" she concluded on our last night together. "It now possesses you and gives you no other choice than to chase it to the end of the rainbow, or into a musty cave. Remember, the vision might *not* be the quest. Don't get hung up on it!"

I also saw it as my only choice and, having made it, my entire perspective of life again shattered and rearranged into yet another challenge of detachment and surrender. I was not sure I had reached the point where I could live in a musty cave, but I kept these nagging doubts at bay by chanting OM softly to myself and placing one foot deliberately in front of the other. And, step by slow step, I was on my way to the top of the mountain, tired but excited by it all.

The sun had already set and a cool breeze met me as I rounded the last bend leading to the Shiva temple. I fell exhausted into a lean-to along side of the temple and, after starting a fire to brew a cup of mint tea and munching on some dried puffed rice, curled up by the fire and slept a deep, regenerating sleep.

In the morning, after a stimulating bath in the icy creek and a long meditation followed by a warm cup of tea, I went to see the cave. It was a ten-minute walk along a narrow rock ledge that opened out onto a flat stone about twenty feet in diameter. Below the stone was a flat area of rock and lose stones maybe twice the size of the flat rock. Tucked in the near corner of that ledge was the cave.

I hopped off the large stone and looked over the edge at the steep slope running down the narrowing gorge. Dotted about the gully were stunted trees clinging to rock outcroppings, whose twisted and knurled trunks leaned skyward in search of light, forming silhouettes against the mossy cliff face. There was a penetrating stillness surrounding the area and an isolated silence, punctuated only by the occasional birdcall and the faint babbling of the creek far below.

I went inside to a narrow long space some six feet wide and fifteen feet long with a smooth stone floor and rough stonewalls. At the far end of the cave was a large fire pit set into the natural formation of the rock with a mud and stone flue designed to carry the smoke out a convenient opening. It smelled like a damp forest floor. A mosaic of spider webs, bird's nests, and dried leaves filled every corner. It was most definitely a cave adapted for a person to live in and, most definitely, no one had lived in it for a long time.

I set to work cleaning out the cave and the surrounding ledge with a rough broom I fashioned out of green twigs and gathered firewood to start the *dhunie*. When I finished, I noted to myself that it was not exactly what my father had in mind when he sent me to university, but it did have plenty of seclusion.

In the afternoon, I carried hot coals from the temple fire kept smoldering from the previous night and placed them in the center of the cave. While chanting the OM Shiva mantra, I tossed some branches from an evergreen shrub onto the coals to create a cloud of smoke that completely engulfed the musty, dank cave. Then I sat on the big rock outside while the smoke purified my new home. I chanted OM in a low reverberating tone to the majestic trees, mossy rocks, and the multitude of birds and unseen critters who were my neighbors and co-inhabitants of this magical corner of the world. Just before sunset, I lit the sacred fire, following the procedure Jungle Baba had taught me for a hearth you intend to keep going for a long time. I moved in my food supplies and the small pot and the thin metal plate used to cook *chapattis*, which, along with my *comundle* and cup, pocket knife and small metal tongs, made up my kitchen. From the lean-to I brought a hand-hewn board, two feet wide and six feet long, and placed it on two flattened sticks to form a seat a few inches off the ground. I placed my blanket on top of this and wrapped up in my woolen shawl to meditate.

At first, the silence was overpowering and I could not get out beyond my thoughts because my senses were exploring their new environment at night; feeling the energy of the closed-in cave and the life in the rocks and trees all about me. I shook with the expectation of being absorbed in Spirit as I closed the gates of the senses on the world of time and form.

This feeling stayed with me for the first three months as I plunged deeper into meditation and the quest for enlightenment. Following the suggestion of Lama

Govinda, I began to bring my point of awareness down from the third eye spot and center it in my heart. This was difficult at first as old habits of breathing and concentration resisted any changes but I found that by consciously holding my breath after the exhalation and imagining light expanding in my heart center during my pre-meditation exercises, my awareness would settle into the heart. After some time, the truth of the words of the *Gita* — "Keeps the mind in the heart and places in the head the breath of life." (*Gita*: 8; 12) — revealed itself to me in the form of a new, profound level of meditation.

I was not *out there* in the mystical dimensions of pure wisdom where I had been searching for it these past years but *I* was somewhere deep within the heart. I felt closer than ever before to some exciting new identity and intensified my efforts to be in a peaceful state of no-thought.

The rains had been late in coming and the spectacular autumn show of color grew more splendid with each passing day as ancient rhododendrons, ablaze with bright red flowers, dotted the thick green canopy below the ledge of the cave. I had settled into a routine of filling in the time between meditation with cooking, cleaning, carrying water, and gathering firewood in the gully directly below the ledge. At a certain time in the morning, direct sunlight warmed the large flat rock outside the entrance of the cave and I could sit and read my *Gita* while soaking in its healing rays.

I tried to keep up my physical strength by exercising in the morning sun and taking long walks in the afternoons. I ate one small meal a day, mainly of rice, lentils and stinging nettles, which, on Mary's advice, had become a staple of my diet. I had tea in the mornings and afternoons, sometimes with a *chapatti*.

The fire became my constant companion. I sang songs of worship to it at sunrise and sunset and passed long hours at night floating in its hypnotic spell. From the first night I never let it go out and the energy of the hearth and the presence of the fire spirit grew stronger within the cave each day. I practiced special empowerment exercises of drawing the fire spirit into my heart, using a specific breathing technique of Yogi Baba, calling on its energy to transform any remaining attraction to the material world into surrender unto God. And lighter and lighter I became each day.

It was this close relationship with the fire that allowed me to enter into one of the disciplines that Jungle Baba had given me well over a year ago. Jungle Baba, Navarnji, and Yogi Baba never slept more than two hours at a time and were always up sitting in front of the fire and meditating at all hours of the night. He cited a passage in the *Gita* that said:

In the dark night of all beings awakes to light the tranquil man.
But what is day to other beings is night to the sage who sees.
(*Gita*: 2-69)

He insisted that a real yogi was aware of his relationship to God and Spirit even when he was asleep. He suggested that I could gain mastery over my dreams if I would follow the practice of awakening between 2 and 4 pm and saying awake for an hour or two watching my thoughts and breath. He said that during these early hours of the day I would encounter the least interference from the fear-inspired thought forms of civilized humanity. I had tried time and again during the last year but, except for my time alone in the hut in the jungle, my strong addiction to sleep would only allow me to pull myself up to a sitting position and pass a few drowsy moments before crashing back into the dullness of sleep.

Here in my cave, this practice came alive with greater ease. Each night I would rise, go outside to relieve myself and then sit in front of the fire meditating, chanting, or drifting in the peace of my breath. Everything about cave life was peaceful but these moments in the night had a special quality of clarity and intuitive perception. The thoughts of the material world, even those concerned with the simple tasks of gathering firewood and hauling water, had to be constantly kept at bay during the day with will-power and determination, but these special moments of watchfulness in the night were all for the spirit.

It was during one of these quiet moments in the middle of the night that I was brought to new levels of detachment. The fire had died down and I was drifting in thoughtlessness when a faint clicking noise somewhere over my head kept disturbing me. I took a burning stick to investigate the sound. I moved a sack of flour I had suspended from the wall on a short cord and I saw her. A small, silver-gray scorpion tucked in a recess in the stonewall with her tail cocked to strike. The tales of deadly scorpions in the caves of the Himalayas were the main deterrents from anyone living in them and more than one yogi had been found dead in his cave from a sting.

My first instinct was not to kill it. The possibility of scorpions in the cave had been in the back of my mind but, now that I was face-to-face with one, I did not feel fear or concern for my life. I knew I had reached some bizarre level of personal detachment when I just said, "I'm a peaceful being. We can share this cave together. Is there anything I can do for you, my friend?"

Would you sprinkle a bit of your flour on this ledge for bait? I heard within my mind.

I took a bit of flour from the sack and sprinkled it near her, put the sack back in its place and sat down. It was more than a symbolic surrender of my very life. From that point on, I was living a moment-to-moment confrontation with death.

During another one of my nighttime vigils I was attacked by something even more deadly — my mind. I was sitting in front of the fire, half-meditating and half-dreaming, when holographic images accompanied by loud music filled the cave.

Ajax, the foaming cleanser, boom, boom, boom.

Wipes the dirt, right down the drain.

TV commercials assaulted me in animated reality, echoing within the cave and driving me to near desperation. I had not seen a television in over two years, yet these memories were tucked away in secluded recess of my mind.

See the U.S.A. in your Chevrolet.

They kept coming for over an hour, pounding my awareness with a barrage of garbage injected into my mind years ago. I felt as if someone had pulled a plug within my mind and all the accumulated programming of civilization was spilling out into the cave. How many more useless impressions were left within me? Did I have to purge them all before finding peace?

It was not as easy as simply waiting for all this useless junk to spill out and be done with it. This electronic garbage distributor was more powerful and persistent than I could have ever imagined. Its message, stupid and violent, had been driven deep within my subconscious; a part of my being had been violated by an unscrupulous force more clever than I had given it credit for, greedier than I had ever imagined. Not only did the commercials not fade away into unconsciousness but, for over a month The Lone Ranger, The Three Stooges, talking horses, flying cars, ghosts, goblins, and Superman flooded my awareness, followed by the multitude of deaths, murders, and massacres I had unknowingly allowed to be transfused into my delicate consciousness while sitting in front of the omnipresent TV screen. Driven to near desperation, I fought back with focused concentration on mantras and prayers to all forms of God until slowly the childhood terrors were purged from my mind and peace returned.

CHAPTER 38

GOING WILD

One of the noticeable effects of this new lifestyle was the propensity of *going wild*. I now had a keen sense of the forest and could feel the presence of animals and had some kind of communication with them, even if it was only in my imagination. I smeared my body in ashes to keep the bugs away and let my hair mat into tangled curls. I walked naked in the forest, except for a piece of cloth wrapped around my testicles, often covered in mud and grime while getting water or firewood.

All fear of death or injury were gone and I scurried up and down the steep banks of the ravine, sinking ankle deep into a carpet of rotting twigs and leaves, jumping from moss-covered rock to fallen tree trunk, gripping to them with my bare toes like an animal of precise balance and keen instincts. I used a certain low guttural hoot as my voice in the forest and birds and squirrels would come up next to me while I was sitting in the sun on the big rock. I felt like an integral part of the surrounding forest community of birds, bats, butterflies, squirrels, mice, scorpions, and mountain lions. The trees-sacred monuments of biological life-oozed energy and their mystical presence soothed my soul.

The gully became my playground as I explored its untracked beauty, following the creek-bed steeply down the mountain, climbing over huge fallen trees from another era. One morning, I left my bundle of dried branches on a mammoth trunk and penetrated farther to where the gully leveled out into a hollow before dropping off sharply into a rugged rock face. In the middle of the hollow stood a magnificent rhododendron tree with massive branches clawing at both sides of the steep gully. I crawled my way through the latticework of giant ferns and rotting debris until I was close to the main trunk, which stretched six feet across and was covered in moss and miniature ferns. I lay my naked body on the carpet of green moss at its base and gave thanks to be in the presence of an ancient being, a true reminder of the sacredness of all life.

The entire hollow had a magic feeling about it as I sat there listening to the soft buzzing of insects, the wind playing in high branches, and the trickling of the creek below. All about me, lacy ferns were joined by a filigree of delicate spider webs, showered in bright red flower petals released from the canopy above. I was sitting in the center of nature's masterpiece, smelling the sweet dampness of the Earth, feeling the sheer power of her stillness, and floating in an ocean of color, light, and sound. I closed my eyes and followed the ebbing and flowing of my breath until nature herself was breathing me, lifting me up and carrying me off upon her universal sacredness. Suddenly, I felt a surge of energy circulating about my body and filling me with joy and gratitude. I was feeling nature herself seeping out of this ancient tree, bubbling up all around me and filling me with the spirit essence of life. *This is the experience that gives life its true meaning,* I thought as I lay breathing in rhythm with the universe. In the heart of my imagination, the tree of life talked to me, saying, *We are the keepers of life's biological matrix. Live with us, not from us, and God's mystery shall continue on this Earth.*

As I lay there in silence for a long time, I became aware of a distant rustling as if I was not alone. I sat up on my haunches and listened for some time to a distinct movement in the forest. The sound was coming closer from an unexplored direction, which appeared to be covered with even thicker forest clinging to steeper rock faces. A few minutes later, I detected movement in the underbrush fifty yards away and saw a large, black-faced monkey covered with white fur moving deftly down the steep terrain. Three others, none of whom detected my presence, followed a short distance behind. I squatted motionless as an entire pack of monkeys passed, following the others down the mountain. It was not unusual to see monkeys in the forest although they had never come by my cave.

A playful spirit awakened within me and I decided to see how far I could follow behind them without being discovered. I moved ever so silently over the moss and twigs until I picked up their trail that went steeply down the rocky cliff face. I could hear them moving further on ahead of me as I was forced to slow down and concentrate on maneuvering the difficult descent by clinging to exposed roots and rocks to let myself down.

When I came out of the old-growth forest and into the lower-elevation pines, I could see them further up ahead. I hurried along until I was close behind them, stopping to rest for a minute. It was only then that I noticed how far we had come and realized we were approaching an isolated farm a hundred yards further down the mountain. Then I understood what this pack of monkeys was up to and why they had moved so quietly through the forest. They were on a raid of the farmer's garden.

I moved out from behind the tree that was sheltering me and onto a small rock to get a better view, but as I did so, I noticed a slight movement behind me. I turned quickly to see a large male monkey, as tall as me when standing on his hind legs and outweighing me by forty pounds at least. He was coming down from further up the mountain in the company of a female with a young monkey clinging to the underside of her chest. We seemed to recognize each at the same moment and held fixed to each other's gaze, waiting for the next move. I was sure he would call out to warn the others below, but he made no sound of any kind. He just stared at me, trying to figure out just what species I was and whose side I was on.

Seized by another moment of playfulness, I leapt from the rock and hopped on all fours down the mountain another twenty feet and came to a stop. I looked up, scratching my armpit in a classic monkey imitation, and motioned with my head for them to follow me. *Most people think I'm crazy*, I thought to them, scratching my head with my other hand, *so you can probably understand me just fine. Come on, let's get some food.*

I leapt from my perch and scampered down the mountain, scratching my armpit and making low guttural sounds as I went. They followed, wondering what this furless, mud-caked freak was up to. After a few minutes of this charade, I felt completely connected with this primitive expression, making strange sounds and even feeling my skin covered in a soft fur. I could sense a long, curved tail coming off the end of my spine, giving me a new dimension of balance and agility. I had gone too far in my role-playing. A monkey spirit possessed me.

I came to the edge of the forest, scampered onto a pointed rock and scratched my head naturally while watching the rest of my band sneaking through the low grass on their way to the garden. I was breathing hard and sweating profusely but the monkey spirit wanted to go on. I looked back and motioned for my escorts, now squatting a respectful distance up the hillside, to come down but they looked as if they were not coming any closer.

I watched as the advanced raiding party stalked closer to the garden fence and quickly hopped over, disappearing into the corn patch. Others were still approaching from different directions when dogs started to bark and mayhem broke lose. Black-faced monkeys, twenty or more of them, hopped over the fence into the corn patch or leapt onto the apple trees, grabbing what they could as the dogs circled the fence, barking wildly. Two men and a woman appeared from behind a shed beating on pots and pans and shouting loudly at my companions, who quickly stuffed what they could into their mouths and both hands and beat a hasty retreat back up the hillside.

I craned to get a better view just as the first of the younger monkeys scurried past, heading like lightning up the mountain. The rest of the pack soon followed with ears of corn and red apples dangling from hands and mouths. They moved with such incredible speed and agility, racing up the hill and disappearing into the forest above that, in a minute, I was all alone looking at five angry peasants running up the hill, tossing stones and shouting at the top of their voices.

I suddenly realized that I was the only member of the raiding party who had not escaped and the enraged farmers were fast coming upon me. I turned and scampered up the hillside as fast as my exhausted legs would carry me, as small stones whizzed over my head. I can not imagine what went through the mind of the irate farmers when they saw my bare ass sprinting up the mountain, but I did not stop to look, not wanting to have to explain myself as the monkey god, *Hanuman*, reincarnated in the body of a hippie freak. *And what if they believed me?* I thought playfully, while scampering up the hill and screeching like my monkey friends.

A hundred yards up the mountain I ducked into the cover of a small bush and listened carefully to see if I was still being followed. I could hear the farmers talking farther down the hill as if they had given up the chase. I sat still and waited.

When I could no longer hear voices and thought they had returned to their houses, I broke cover made my way slowly up the steep hillside. I had not gone more than a few yards when I heard a soft crying sound coming from under a bush. I pushed back the upper leaves and saw a tiny baby monkey curled up under the leaves shaking with fright. As I was deciding whether to pick it up, I heard shouting from below, but now much closer. The peasants had not returned but were lying in wait for the monkeys to return. Without turning to look, I picked up the baby monkey and took off up the hill with angry voices in hot pursuit.

I scampered up with amazing speed, zigzagging to stay under the pine canopy, until I came to the old forest, where I took cover in the dense undergrowth of the oaks and rhododendrons. I set the frightened monkey down, expecting it to run further into the forest, but it stayed where I had set it without moving. When I had rested sufficiently, I picked up my new friend and continued through the trees until I came to the rock-face that demanded considerable concentration to climb back up again. As I was planning my route up, I noticed the black furry faces of two monkeys perched on a ledge fifty feet above me. I could not see them completely but I knew it was the male and mother who, I figured, had lost her baby in the mad scramble to escape. I held the monkey in the air to show it to them and motioned for them to come down and get it. I could not figure out how I was going to climb up with it anyway.

There was no movement for a long time and I could sense that they were not sure if they could trust me. I set the frightened youngster down where they could see it, moved a bit down the hill and squatted to watch. The old male swung deftly down the cliff face, scooped the baby up and placed an ear of corn where it had been resting. Turning once more to look at me, I felt him saying, *thanks*, before bounding back up the rock face and disappearing into the underbrush.

I retrieved my reward and retraced my path, arriving hours later to the security of my cave and a good *chapatti* feast. I had made new friends that day and I could not remember having had so much fun since I was a boy.

About a week later, I was finishing one of my morning meditations when I heard crashing sounds outside on the ledge. I peered out the door to see three soldiers with rifles drawn, pointing at the cave. My first absurd fantasy was that the farmers below had told them about me and they had come to get me, and I shrunk back in horror. I took another cautious look to see them approaching the cave, as if they had come to get me. I was trapped.

The impulse to resist swelled up from within me and I sprung out the door and onto the big rock, moving like a cat in defense of her home. They jumped back and steadied their guns, but when they saw a naked freak smeared in ashes, perched on his haunches staring down at them, they halted. Their eyes opened wide in astonishment as they saluted me with their joined palms over their hearts, one of them even getting down on his knees.

They began to speak in their language but I understood everything even before they said it. My awareness was able to recognize their thoughts because I knew well what my thoughts were. They had been on a march to the top of the mountain and had snuck away from their platoon, planning to rejoin them in the afternoon. They apologized for interrupting and inquired if I needed anything.

I thought clearly, "*Yes, may I have a bidi?*"

"Would you like a cigarette, Babaji," one of them replied, holding out one for me to receive.

"*No, I prefer a bidi,*" I thought clearly back, without making the slightest sound with my voice.

I had been mystified by the way Light Baba could talk to me in my mind and, in this moment, I was living that reality. My personal thought patterns were so clear and the surrounding environment so peaceful that I could feel the thought field existing between us and, to some degree, communicate within it at will. My one fixed intention was to communicate with them without saying a word and, because of that, it became possible.

They produced a *bidi* and helped me to light it. They continued to ask questions in their language and I projected back my answers about what country I was from and how long I had been living in this cave. Slowly, first one of them and then the others realized that I was not talking but they were hearing me in their heads. They pointed to each other, then to their heads, like little children who had discovered something new. Finally, they sat on the ground in front of me and were quiet. I stopped thinking and merged with the peace of the surrounding forest. We sat in silence for over an hour before each of them touched their heads to my feet and slipped on out along the narrow trail.

The rains finally came, bringing with them the damp reality of cave life. The one thing that had kept me going during the first months in the cave was the routine. I had continued my disciplines of bathing twice a day in the creek, washing out my white cloths, taking long walks everyday and exercising in the sun whenever possible. This fragile form of material security was now fading fast as the weather made it difficult to walk in the mountains, take baths everyday or be outside the cave at all. The mind relentlessly assaulted my awareness, telling me I needed something or that a mountain lion would come in the cave at night. I resorted to chanting throughout the waking hours to keep from talking to myself or thinking about any part of life.

My main focus was meditation, but the necessities of cave life kept me in touch with the surrounding world, if only symbolically. I had no contact with other humans except a short conversation on one of my evening walks or to say thank you to the local peasants who had begun to bring me potatoes, onions, and apples every two or three days.

The once-dry walls of the cave became damp and there were several places where the seepage was considerably more than just condensation. I had to keep a good fire going all the time to ward off encroaching humidity. During the lulls in the rain, I would search the ravine for fallen limbs, drag them up to the ledge and stack what small amount I could in the unoccupied space of the cave. About the time that I was beginning to wonder if it was going to be possible to live there all winter, some woodcutters brought me several large trunks and a pile of thick oak limbs. With these as the base for my fire, I could find enough smaller branches to keep a fire smoldering day and night.

Then one night it snowed and my confinement became more severe. My struggle against the cold, damp conditions filled my material preoccupation. I melted snow for water, went to the bathroom just over the ledge and twice a day endured the icy challenge of scurrying down the ravine barefoot to drag up more firewood, which, by now, required drying before it would burn without filling the cave with blinding smoke.

Returning from one of these excursions late one afternoon, I was struggling up the hill with a big fat limb when I felt the presence of something on the cliff overhead. I stopped and the gully fell silent against the background of the babbling creek. I knew without seeing her that there was a mountain lion thirty feet directly above where I was standing.

I live with a scorpion so what is there to fear in a big house cat, I thought.

I'm just living here the same as you, I thought to her. *Only my life is a little more complicated than yours, that's all.* I pulled strongly on the limb to emphasize my point. There was no doubt that we were in perfect communication and, I felt, friends of the forest.

Yes, peaceful one, you may share the forest with us, I felt her saying back to me. She had acknowledged my right to be there. We had no conflict.

A storm hit that night with icy rains and snow driving the temperatures below freezing, even within the cave. I brought as much firewood inside as I could, fixed Mary's extra blanket over the opening and retreated to the sanctuary of my hearth. Wrapped in my frayed white cloth and warm woolen shawl, I sat in front of the fire chanting and meditating, cooking and sleeping, losing track of night and day, full moon and dark moon, lost in the cave of my heart. Sleep, prayer, and meditation blended into one awareness, separated only by some vague film of personal identity.

Meditation proved to be the fortification of my soul during these times of complete withdrawal from all material contact. The study of my breath, its ebb and flow, its regulation and direction had given me a certain mastery over my material body. I could, with only the slightest effort, enter into the space between two thoughts by directing my breath to slow down and bringing my awareness into my heart. Worlds of light and sound would burst upon my consciousness, carrying me off beyond the limits of my physical reality. There I would stay, beyond the cold dampness of the cave, absorbed in other worlds; the universe itself was now my playground.

The alternative realities beyond the physical dimension were all sustained within a frequency of expansion and contraction and my breathing was my link to these worlds. There was only relative time and space according to what frequency I was capable of holding my identity within at any one moment. More and more I was not living only on the material plane. My life and all my experiences of reality were taking place on many different levels at the same time and slowly the material world lost its importance for me.

Hope and expectation surrounded each meditation that it might be the last effort that would forever dispel the illusion. Among the outward horrors of my inhospitable reality, I felt closer than ever before to that elusive state of enlightenment.

The physical world fought back, unwilling to let me dissolve it through concentration and detachment. Dysentery, my constant mentor during the last two years, struck with a new fury. Yellowish liquid poured down the ledge and gripping cramps doubled me over in pain. With no way to get sufficient exercise, my body weakened and I entered into a constant struggle with my health. Whenever the weather cleared for a while, I tried to resume my walks but each time I had less strength and could go but a short distance. Thanks to the few peasants living in the area I had sufficient food, mostly rice, lentils, potatoes and onions. I tried to eat more but the dysentery would not let up.

The weather cleared two months later but I still could not get my strength back. Night and day blended into one another and I would often come out of a meditation thinking it was daytime, only to find the cave cold and chilly night air seeping in around the blanket draped over the opening. It was during one of these middle of the night disorientations, staring into the mellow flames of my hearth, that a distinct stillness suddenly came over the gully. Intuitively I knew the mountain lion was nearby. Within minutes I detected soft paw movements on the ledge above the cave and I knew I had a visitor.

I asked in the silence of my mind, *What is it that you want?*

Only the warmth of your fire, my friend, I felt within my mind. *I will protect you, not harm you.*

Suddenly, my mind was a rage with doubts and fears. Did I trust what I felt she was saying? Or was she really waiting to sneak into the cave while I was asleep and attack me? Was I about to die?

I struggled with the uncertainty of my frazzled mind until I could not take the fear and anxiety any longer. *If I really trusted God, myself or the mountain lion I would just walk out of the cave and turn and greet her. But could I really do that?* I thought, intrigued by the idea. *Go ahead, do it. It's only your life.*

I stood up slowly and walked to the entrance where I paused for a long time in a haze of doubt and fear, until I gave up the struggle and walked out into the filtered moonlight. With legs shaking and heart waning, I looked up to the ledge above the cave and saw two piercing eyes looking down at me. My vision blurred with terror as she rose to a crouching position and leapt straight at me. I stood there in suspended fright, not reacting in any way, as she flew at me, then passed right on through me, like the fantasy of my fear-shattered mind that she was. I was bathed in a cold sweat and my rubbery legs were about to give in underneath me as I looked to the ledge again. The two pinpoints of reflected light were still staring down at me.

"This is absurd," I mumbled to myself. "What's happening? What is real anymore?

"Don't fear me, friend, I will protect you," I heard within the stillness of the moment.

I stumbled to the entrance to the cave and looked up again and said, "Thanks, I think I need your help."

With scorpions inside and mountain lions on the roof, I was living with death all around me, but I saw no reason to protect myself in any way.

CHAPTER 39

EMBRACE LIFE

After seeing the glowing eyes of the lioness suspended in the moonlight, all form, consistency, and meaning of my life shattered. Until the moment that the phantom lion leapt at me, I was really only playing with the idea that I was not afraid of death. That experience made it an inner reality. In that moment of suspended time as she flew through the air, claws extended and mouth wide open, a million images of hundreds of lifetimes flashed before my mind's eye. Yet, more frightening than my imminent death, nothing mattered.

I felt my way back into the dark interior of my sanctuary, wrapped up in my shawl and closed my eyes to meditate. From that moment on, meditation, dreaming, sleep, and wakefulness were all the same hazy blur of reality. I hardly ever went outside the cave except to get water and firewood; I did not have the physical strength to think of moving from the cave. I was not scared or distressed, but rather, I felt more connected to a universal presence that accompanied my every breath.

At first, my body hung heavy about its bony frame, encaging my soul. Then slowly with the passing of days, as if from within the core of my bones, I felt an energetic connection with an etheric mist absorbing me into its presence. I felt no hunger or cold even though the nighttime temperatures hovered around freezing. I ate out of a sacred routine, preparing each pot of boiled potatoes and onions as an offering to the gods of Heaven and Earth. I was now, more than ever before, living within my etheric being and relating to life as an energetic capsule supported in this soft glow of life force.

My imagination was the principal stage upon which my life was being played; yet it was no longer a child's toy of hope and joy but the creator of all reality. I journeyed on its wings to worlds of wisdom where I talked to radiant beings about the dream-like nature of all reality and the illusion of anything permanent existing within the fields of constant change. Life was a dream I was dreaming each day, renewing its mystery constantly by *believing* in its form and consistency.

As material consistency became a vague background against which emerging realties danced and played, I became aware of new aspects of creation, which amazed and confused me. Sitting one night in front of my hearth, softly chanting my Sri Ram mantra, I was lifted up by the force of this etheric mist into a frequency matrix of pulsating sound and light that put me on yet another unknown level of reality. I was not observing this vibration but was an integral part of its ebb and flow. Then I realized where I was. This matrix of sound and light was the created reality of my mantra itself. The intention of the sacred sounds had been projected out into the creative dimensions of the universe and an actual form of energetic consistency had been created, not only by me, but also by hundreds of thousands of people using the same mantra throughout many ages. I realized that I was floating in the combined intentions of many beings to be united with God through this very mantra.

After that realization I became aware of thousands of similar matrixes of reality, some filled with light and bliss while others were arranged out of fear and darkness. The creative realms became a complex labyrinth of multidimensional projections out of which people were constantly assembling their realities. By fine-tuning my imagination through intention, I journeyed to other dimensions where there were similar patterns of creative potential without desires for God or fears of being without but only a clear formation of the unity of all life and the presence of an all-pervading spirit. These etheric dimensions had no need of material things to constitute their reality because there was no fear of loss or deprivation.

We *are* the creators of our own reality, I realized. Yet our ignorance of this fact causes us to constantly create and recreate, out of our own fears, a negative scenario instead of harnessing this potential for our peace and liberation. Thoughts and sounds were indeed vibratory frequencies arranging etheric substance into intentional patterns, which were to become the seeds of future manifestations.

I somehow knew that my access to these realities was the result of my extreme detachment from the physical dimension, as if I was on the cusp of personal identification. *But why? Who am I?*

My outer, physical world was also in a new state of vibrational relationship, as I seemed to have slipped back into the perceptions of total bliss that I remembered from my experiences in Varanarse and at the Monkey Temple outside of Katmandu. When I ventured out of my sanctuary, the forest was not a fixed, solid world of recognizable form and structure but a pulsating, swirling collage of color, sound, and light dancing before my virgin senses. I laughed and shouted for joy as spirits of the forest floated before me in the etheric mist, which united us all into oneness. Every tree and every flower were surrounded by spirit energy, which was their life force. All life had its spirit origin long before its material form appeared and this spirit energy was holding the material form together.

I was no longer disconnected from anything. The etheric mist, into which I had been absorbed, now joined me to all other living things and I could, with only the slightest focused intention, become a tree, a flower or a bird. One day, as I sat at the entrance way to the cave watching the energetic waves of nature swirl about the giant trees before me, the honking sounds of migrating birds high in the sky overhead caught my awareness. In an instant I was there, flying along in their flock, flapping my wings and softly honking. The cold wind pierced my warm feathers as I followed the calls of my flock soaring about me. We were in perfect communication, keeping our formation through sound relationship as the winds drifted us about. The formation offered us the perfect combined wind resistance and drafting possibilities, making our flight a group effort, not an individual challenge.

Our positions shifted within this formation as the lead birds became tired and fell back in the flock and others moved forward until I was at the apex of the wedge, straining against the head-winds and guiding the flock southward. The winds were mild but unsteady and sudden gusts would carry my feathery body up and drift it from side to side as I adjusted my drift with a slight arching of my wings and flaring the tips of my feathers. It was not unlike balancing on one leg by moving one's outstretched arms up and down, except that here I was balanced on an invisible cushion of air, honking to my family to keep our formation as we moved southward. After a short time as flock leader, my wings grew tired and the cries of the others pressed in until I could not hold the lead any longer. Arching my wings and catching more wind, I floated back into the flock until the cries of the other birds drifted away and I found myself sitting at the entrance to the cave thanking my friends for the marvelous flight!

Had I really been in flight with a flock of birds? I mused to myself while tripping out on the kaleidoscope forest before me. *Of course I had. But the body never moved. Who am I anyway?* Short dialogues like this were common as my rational mind kept trying to convince me that it was the controller of my life and that I should not pay too much attention to my imagination. It was too late, however, because the realms of my imagination had, by now, become fertile ground for the exploration of my true identity.

With all fear of insanity long gone, the arrow of time no longer kept me moving toward the supposed future and I was free to explore the present moment through tangents of mystical flight. Total surrender to my imagination had broken the web of my personal illusion and, at times, even my identity as a human being could be suspended. With each passing fantasy, from monkey's tails to bird's wings, I began to realize that the present moment was the doorway to all other dimensions and was the only moment when the illusion of time no longer blinded me to the infinite potential of my true being.

But all these mystical wonders had one detrimental aspect, my physical health. Mary had warned me not to forget my physical body, as if she had seen my entire trip in the cave and knew the real dangers were not the scorpions and mountain lions but my own self-neglect. I now felt no pain and often observed intestinal cramping and liquid shit with a certain bizarre detachment, as if it was not happening to me or was of no consequence. I continued to go through the motions of physical existence but, with each passing day, life was becoming a universal experience and who I was within it all became the tantalizing mystery that gave it some vague purpose.

One night the cave filled with bright, white light and the presence of an unknown spirit invaded my sanctum. My heart quickened and I felt an over-whelming wave of compassion surrounding me. I wanted only to surrender completely.

"*Tomorrow will be your day,*" I heard a resounding voice.

"My enlightenment!" I called aloud.

"*No, it will be the day of your physical death,*" I heard clearly in reply.

"But I'm here to find my enlightenment!" I insisted. "If I must die that's all right but don't let me come back to this world of pain and suffering. I have given everything to reach enlightenment. Why can't I have that?"

"*My young ascetic, that too is part of the supreme illusion. There is no such thing as your enlightenment, because there is no such thing as a personal self. Enlightenment is a universal awareness, a unity with all.*

"*As you disperse the appearance of the personal self, all concepts of reincarnation, enlightenment and any personal attainment for that matter disappear. Your identity becomes a relationship with cosmic unity.*"

"And what of this idea of the *real self?*" I asked. "Is that also an illusion?"

"*If you believe that the* real self *is a personal self, then it, too, is part of the great illusion. The real self is really the realization of the no self. You do not exist apart from the whole. You never have and never will. You, all of you on the planet Earth, are really one being!*"

"I don't get it," I said, feeling frustrated. "Who am I?"

"*Who you are is an experience and the purpose of life is your choice.*"

"Are you from the Masters of Light?" I asked, humbled by the truth I was feeling from this presence.

"*No. They are working with awakened people who want to help the world go through its transformation of consciousness, not those who want to leave the Earth behind.*

"*Life as you now live it is nothing more than a big self-deception. You look at what is wrong with the world, what you don't like and can't agree with, then hide within the concept of a perfect self waiting somewhere beyond responsibility and involvement. You have confused the un-manifest as being real and the manifest as being the illusion. They are both one and the same. Can you see that to live without acknowledging the manifest is the same as to live without awareness of the un-manifest?*

To exist within the reality of them both, in harmony and humility, might be closer to what you are seeking as enlightenment."

"There is where you're wrong," I argued back. "I'm living in both worlds. I do see their inter-relatedness."

"Look down there," it suggested softly. *"Tell me what you see."*

The request seemed ridiculous because I did not know how I could look down at anything from inside my cave. Then I received a shock. Below me was a dark, shadowy reality in the middle of which was a small bundle of dirty rags. At first I did not see any importance to the vision. But then I realized that the shadowy reality was the cave and the heap of rags was my body curled up on the tiny board, essentially dead to the world. *How long had it been since I was there? Had I eaten or was I just living in the memory of the last time I ate? Was the body still alive?*

Until that moment, I was sure I was sitting up near the fire talking to some spirit that had entered the cave. One reality had merged with another and I did not know which one I existed within any more. A note of seriousness rang out within my consciousness. I was concerned. For what, I was not really sure.

"It's me, isn't it?" I asked, with a greater respect than before.

"Yes, that's what is left of your present physical body. It is still alive, although extreme selfishness has consumed most of it. You did have a good idea at first."

"I don't get it. What went wrong?"

"You were always doing it for yourself. Your entire quest was an escape from something you judged as being wrong, something you did not want to live with. So you killed the world you didn't want to live in, that's all. No big deal!

"True spiritual consciousness begins with care and concern for the peace and happiness of others, not trying to find an escape for yourself. If you had entered that cave hoping to open the doors to an alternative reality so that others may follow or so that your light may guide someone else through the darkness, then things might be different. Your enlightenment was a selfish quest and your spiri- tuality an escape!"

"But all those experiences... The messages? The wisdom from the Masters of Light? What was the meaning of all that?"

"A gift is a gift. What you choose to do with it is another matter. Although you avoided the trap of thinking you were the next prophet to confuse the world with half-truths, you still failed to see the universal meaning behind it all. You failed to see your common unity with all other beings and act from that vision.

"The masters and all the messages will one day be experienced as parts of your

own higher-self and you will laugh that you could have been so far removed from your true potential to have related to it as anything other than yourself. At this time in human development, these levels of higher self can best be accessed through relating to them as some other being, because detachment from individuality is yet incomplete.

"Your intentions are powerful thought amplifiers. They determine your reality. As your intentions become formulated around sharing enlightenment with others, your own individuality is released and your universal self can think and act through you. Spiritual masters, guiding the process of Earth-plane beings, monitor their level of intention; a level in which there is no deception because from there arises the impulse for all thought and actions."

"So there was no truth in any of the visions either? It was all self-deception?"

"Truth is not found in the vision but in how you relate to it; how it guides you to greater unity rather than individuality.

"If you see the end of the world and decide to get out before things get worse, that is your truth but it might not set you free, as you're finding out right now.

"The spiritual cancer of your civilization is self-righteousness. You think everyone, including God, is wrong. If you see a little light you try to own it by explaining its relationship to yourself.

"True spirituality sees the perfection in all that is and does not let one's limited vision of right and wrong lessen the work of God. Yes, the blind are leading the blind in economics, politics and science, but nowhere is this truer than in the area of spirituality. Even science looks forward, beyond its past misconceptions, to new horizons of reality. Yet spiritually continues to look backward, hoping that misinterpretations of past visions will somehow prove to be true in the future. To know thyself is not to chase fictitious goals of the blind who have gone before you, but to explore, in faith and love, the uncharted regions of your soul," said my guide.

"But my vision of the universe?" I protested. "The frequencies, the dimensions, the breathing? I still don't get it. Is this all some conspiracy of the mind?"

"That has become your reality because you believe it is so. For any being identified with their individuality, reality will always be the rational interpretation of their perception, not the actual perception itself. As you believe the universe to be, so it becomes for you. And if others believe along with you, it becomes their world also. Thought molds reality by conditioning perception to see the universe the way you believe it to be. Beliefs are but islands in the sea of consciousness.

"Until you can experience the universe not as being outside of you but within you, it will always remain a perception; an idea or concept. When the deeper unity is known, anything one might say about it is true and at the same time not true, because all rational concepts then become relative to the belief systems out of which perception arises.

"*Can you share your universe with the universe of others?*" the guide asked.

"What are you saying?" I replied, beginning to feel that death was much simpler than all this double talk.

"*Yes, that is the true value of all your visions. By sharing them with others and trying to achieve a common vision, you will be cooperating with all of human evolution. What you could learn about human unity through sharing your vision with others will fill in the missing pieces of your metaphysical puzzle.*

"*You are not on this planet alone and your evolution is not taking place in a human vacuum. The essential unity of all creation is your true self. Out of that you have come and unto that you will return. To know yourself is really to see yourself in the heart of all other beings.*"

I was overwhelmed by it all. How could one be so close yet so far at the same time? I wanted to be upset or worried but these emotions would not flow at this time.

"Who are you, may I ask, and why did you come here tonight? Why didn't you come six months ago and tell me all this when I was just entering into this ordeal?"

"*I am the part of you that does not want to die in that cave, that wants to make this human journey of value.*"

"You are a part of me? Now I'm more confused. What relationship to me do you play?"

"*Who do you think told you that you were not going to die in that bus accident and to breathe when the serpent kissed you?*

"*I am, let us say, your potential. That part of your consciousness that is not limited to the identity and conditioning of either Tom or OM Baba. When you stop identifying with who you think you are or what you believe your great mission to be, you will discover that there is more. Your potential is to identify with the divinity within yourself and, through that experience, relate to the divinity within all.*

"*You are alive in a historic context as well as an absolute perspective. In the near future, a transmutation of human awareness will begin on the planet Earth and your divine self would like to play a part in that process. Your soul was created out of starlight and stardust spiraling out into the infinite sea of potential to fulfill the very destiny of creation itself. Star-born you are and a member of a yet unknown family of light. Why don't you try to live that reality?*"

"I don't get it," I puzzled. "If the planet is going to be struck by a fiery asteroid, what could be so positive about the future?"

"*Your vision of the probable future has arisen out of your pessimistic attitudes and beliefs about the future of the planet Earth and her evolving species. That is your truth but not The Truth. The future is never fixed but grows out of an infinite sea of potential. And you are constantly creating that future through your beliefs. Why not join others who want to create a positive future for the planet and change your attitudes and vision through the process?*

"The missing link to your understanding is really the assistance planet Earth and its evolving species can receive from etheric masters of wisdom and compassion who are monitoring the changes in your beliefs and attitudes from an inter-related dimension of consciousness. They have a plan and their adjustment is to alter the magnetic grid around your planet and influence the consciousness of humanity to identify with the light and unity of their true potential so that the fiery messenger will not destroy but transform your planet and its inhabitants. But this plan cannot be implemented until there are sufficient souls attuned to these new frequencies of love and light to stabilize this new grid when it is activated.

"Yes, your natural environment and the entire Earth biosphere will be under great strain but it was created as an experimental grounds for human evolution in the first place and has certain built-in programming that will prevent it from being completely destroyed. The Earth is your school and she will, in the end, teach you through her sacrifice. As human ignorance brings her closer to collapse, spirit wisdom will awaken those souls who have learned from the errors of previous civilizations. Their new consciousness shall be sufficient to hold the new frequencies of unity and light while the world and its consciousness completes its transformation.

"These new frequencies of light are drawing near to your world already and within the next twenty five years of Earth growth many people will begin to communicate with other dimensions of reality co-existing within their own time-space coordinates. These first communications will help to crystallize the inter-dimensional channels, paving the way with new spiritual paradigms arising out of group belief systems that will aid in the process of transformation. This will be due, in part, to the conscious changes in attitudes and intentions developing within human thought patterns, but also, to the new alignments with beneficial cosmic influences and, later on, with actual shifts in the electromagnetic field of the planet.

"The seeds for this transformation have already been sown within your consciousness but they have fallen on your barren self-righteousness. You are only paying attention to what is happening in your own narrow field of individual self and cannot yet perceive the group enlightenment process that is taking place around you.

"You cannot yet see that everything that happens to you concerns the lives of all other beings sharing this planet with you. You are not separate from them unless you choose to be so. And if you do choose to ignore your common unity, you cannot participate in the human awakening that is set to take place on your planet.

"What the originators of the concept of enlightenment failed to realize is that things are the way they are for certain reasons. They were looking at the pure

potential and believed it was the self. The consciousness of humanity is limited in its perception of its true identity, not only for the obvious reasons of Earth-plane conditioning and powerful thought fields that envelope most areas of the world, but also because of fixed relationships operating within the planetary sphere. These relationships create vibrational fields that you call gravitational and electromagnetic fields, which act, not only as supporters, but also as limitations on human consciousness. These fixed relationships are approaching a critical point of imbalance, due to the destructive tendencies of your present civilization and new cosmic alignments of your solar system within the universe, and will seek new harmonious relationships in the future, giving birth to a new potential for human perception."

"Are you now telling me that life is not definitely over for that withered body lying down there? "

"That depends on whether you can feel that there is a greater purpose to life and decide that you want to participate in the process of human evolution. It really depends on whether you want to live or not."

"I'm not sure. In that world I become helpless before the desires and fears that everywhere surround me. My biggest fear is that I will forget this feeling of oneness with the Great Spirit I find so easily here in the forest. I fear that the source of wisdom and light will dry up inside of me."

"Separation from The Spirit is the source of all human fear. Whether you forget or not is your own responsibility.

"Take time to feel this unity each day. See all other beings as perfect and you shall learn to live your own perfection. Work in harmony with the divine plan to create a new world, not destroy the old one. Offer yourself in service to this divine plan. At all times, it is your first responsibility to identify with positive belief structures and expect the best. Work to bring peace not violence, harmony not destruction, acceptance not rejection, hope not despair and love not fear to your planet and its peoples.

"At the same time, the test of true intentions is really to know that people who see life differently from yourself and even those who identify strongly with negativity are not wrong. They are living in the way they must in order to learn their lessons, to know their own light. If you criticize or reject them, you will be identifying with their beliefs and their darkness."

"Thank you," I said with sincere gratitude. "If I do live, what is to say I will not fall into the darkness of my own selfishness again and forget God?"

"Nothing can ensure that you will not forget but there are ways to stay in contact. Do one thing every day that you believe will maintain contact with your own divinity. Dedicate your existence to the peace of all beings. Live as if you have a purpose that concerns the well-being of all fellow travelers along the path of human evolution. See light in others and become light yourself. Realize that every ray of light and love you share with the world is your enlightenment.

"Certain crucial attitudes, such as gratitude, acceptance, devotion, reverence, and service unto a cosmic unity, divine intelligence, or even a sacred unknown, will help you remain in relationship to the spiritual dimensions you now fell, even when the distractions of earthly life push in upon you. Joy to be alive and the celebration of your relationship to other beings will become the elixir of your soul."

"But what should I do if I return? I can't see anything of value down there."

"The essence of life is choice. One lives in the flow of opportunity created out of one's choices. You will do what you are drawn to do to share yourself with others. The best place to start is to share with others who you are right now — your fear and sadness, insecurity and doubts — and grow from that experience. Learn to love and accept yourself and others more. Try to see life as an opportunity, not as a punishment for something you have done wrong. Learn to love and accept life and others as they are. That is the work to be done by every human being.

"Forget the concept of an absolute perfection and try to live your own relative perfection each day. Perfection is the acceptance of what is! **Until your last breath, life is an opportunity to realize your unity with every living thing.**"

I realized in that moment I was in the cave because I was scared of the world and the people who live in it. I was desperately afraid that I would forget and become blind to the light within me. That is why I chose the cave: To force myself to remember God each day and not become distracted by material desires and fears. I was running away, not from the world, but from my own weakness in the face of it.

I wanted to cry but even that emotion of self-pity was not possible now. The most difficult of all: I was not even sure I had a choice in the matter.

"Please tell me, is it over? Or am I to make some decision at this time? What is it that I'm supposed to decide?"

"That is not an easy question. Let's say that you are trying to decide that life, as you now reject it, might have greater value than you had previously considered. And I could give you a little hint: The value is in what you have to share with others, not what you hope to achieve for yourself."

"I tried to leave that cave many times but didn't have the strength to walk more than a few yards to get water. That body down there is closer to death than to life. What would I do if I decided to live? That cave is half-a-day's walk from the nearest help. Am I to return just to die with awareness instead of an illusion?"

"Only a small percentage of life is rational. The rest is a sacred mystery where everything is possible. It must remain a sacred mystery and your developing human consciousness must accept It that way and learn to relate to It from that perspective.

"Don't ask the mystery to reveal itself in order for you to choose yes or no. You decide and let the mystery work out the details."

"Please, could you answer one more question?" I requested within the uncertainty of the moment. "Is there really a God?"

"There is really only God. And God is the spirit that unites all things into ONENESS!"

The light burst into a thousand stars and the heavens opened to reveal a dark void calling me. The universal polarities of nothingness and everything pulsated all about a tiny orb of light that was my soul. I was suspended in a timeless eternity as beings of light encircled me, filling my soul with love.

And I knew that life had a greater purpose.

Epilogue

First came the awareness of sound, a high-pitched, celestial ringing echoing everywhere. Then faint pinpoints of dancing light that slowly expanded to fill my awareness. Within this collage of sound and light a faint movement penetrated my perception and ever so slowly an identity was reborn.

The breath! This movement is my breath! I realized. Some degree of life still existed in the forgotten shell of my physical being but it was ever so far away, ever so vague, and, as yet, ever so unreal.

For what seemed like the passing of a great deal of time, I observed this movement; first with a certain detachment, as one would watch images on a movie screen, then with greater determination to identify with it, to feel it, long for it, and become one with it again. When this fragile identity had been reestablished through my growing desire to live, my sleeping senses began to awaken. I first felt the weight of my physical body pressing against the rough board and the sensation of the coarse woolen blanket against my skin. These were, however, faint stimulations against the ever-expanding background of the expansion and contraction of my breath.

Then, as if someone had thrown a switch called *will*, electric currents raced through my shattered nervous system and thought began to flood in upon my awareness. The last six months raced before my mind's eye until the entire encounter with the *spirit of my potential* replayed itself in painfully slow motion, making it all too clear where I was and the new challenge I now faced.

I sat up with a strange sensation, as if some other force was lending me the energy. My eyes opened into gray dampness and I began to perceive an unusual irradiation, like an electrified mist engulfing me. I looked for my breath, the only point of reference I could now hold to, and it was still there, coaxing me on to further awareness.

My first conscious act was to pray. Whether automatic or truly inspired, out of fear or thankfulness, I cannot really say. Breath and prayer were my only recognizable identities, real or illusionary.

After some time of breathing and praying, a flood of inspiration arrived and I knew I had to move. My first thought was the fire and I turned to focus my awakening eyes on the hearth within the semi-darkness of my tomb-like shelter. Without any difficulty or pain, I leaned over and felt the ashes. They were cold. My sacred fire was dead. Refusing to accept this reality, I dug my hand down into the ashes in search of some warmth, some sign of life. I felt it; just a faint glimmer of hope that there was still one coal with some life left in it.

I quickly brushed away the top layers of powdery ashes, leaned over, and gently blew on the sensation of warmth I had perceived. Two, three, four concentrated breaths and I saw a faint glow appear, as if my heart had started to beat once again. I began to chant a mantra to the fire-god *Agni*, as I had done thousands of times before, until I had three coals glowing red. To this I added some dry leaves and twigs and, before long, smoke turned to licking flames and sacred life was returned to me, if only symbolically.

I found one thin branch in the far corner and, with surprising strength, broke it into small pieces and fed them slowly to the budding flames while chanting in a soft voice to all sacred forces in the universe. Time passed while I squatted on my haunches in front of the gentle leaping flames until I heard clearly within my head, *Life is now your choice once again!*

I said a prayer to the sacred fire, sprinkled some ash-stained water from my *comundle* on the mellowing flames, and prepared to leave my sanctuary for good. By the diffuse sunlight filtering into the small opening of the cave, I gathered my blanket, woolen shawl, arm bag, and *comundle* and stepped out into the light of a new day. The forest was teeming with smells, colors, and sounds as if my senses perceived life for the first time. I turned, looking for the last time at the tiny cave, and gave thanks to all the spirits of this sacred place tucked away in this quiet corner of the planet, then headed out along the narrow ledge that led to the Shiva temple and the world beyond.

I stopped for only a short prayer at the main shrine, then walked up to the dirt road and headed down the mountain. Light seemed to surround me and the physical strength that now propelled my emaciated body forward was definitely coming from outside myself. I chanted OM softly to myself out of habit, for there were no clear thought patterns within my mind to subdue, nor was I in the process of consciously planning my next destination. The entire transition was a miracle. Some other force was in charge and I had neither the strength nor the will to take control.

Down, down, down the mountain I went, concentrating only on the next step and the next breath while nature danced in iridescent splendor before my awakening perception. All sensual stimulation seemed to be filtered through an ethereal haze of partial detachment, as if I was only half-alive, half-awake, half in control of my own destiny.

Turn here, came a clear inner voice and I moved right and headed for a narrow foot trail leading away from the main road and up a steep hill. Amazingly, it required no more effort to climb than it had to come down the mountain. Soon the path led out into a large open area, cultivated in terraced fields.

Over there, I heard within and turned to see a well constructed house set among giant pines. Moving now with determination, I entered the main gate, walked to the front door and stopped.

Knock on the door, came the insistent voice of my unseen guide. I did and waited calmly, thinking of nothing to say or ask if anyone should open the door.

A short time later, the door slowly opened and the figure of a beautiful woman in a green and gold sari with a bright yellow dot in the middle of her forehead stood before me. I felt a radiant glow appear around me. In slow motion I felt life drain out of me; my knees buckled, my arms and head fell limp, and I collapsed in a heap on the stone terrace.

It would be weeks before I regained the physical strength even to sit up, months before I could walk in the mountains, and years more of mystical adventures before India would release me from her enchanting spell.

ISBN 141207290-5

Printed in the United States
By Bookmasters